Tigers by the Tale

GREAT GAMES AT MICHIGAN & TRUMBULL

Edited by Scott Ferkovich
Associate Editors: Bill Nowlin and Len Levin
Contributing Editor: David W. Anderson

SABR

Society for American Baseball Research, Inc.
Phoenix, AZ

Tigers by the Tale: Great Games at Michigan & Trumbull
Edited by Scott Ferkovich
Associate Editors: Bill Nowlin and Len Levin
Contributing Editor: David W. Anderson

ISBN 978-1-943816-21-7
Ebook ISBN 978-1-943816-20-0

Cover and book design: Gilly Rosenthol

Image credits:
Public domain: pages 7, 10, 19, 22, 28, 37
Baseball Hall of Fame: pages 49, 56, 65, 74, 84, 90, 93, 100, 111, 117, 123, 132, 135, 141, cover

Society for American Baseball Research
Cronkite School at ASU
555 N. Central Ave. #416
Phoenix, AZ 85004
Phone: (602) 496-1460
Web: www.sabr.org
Facebook: Society for American Baseball Research
Twitter: @SABR

TABLE OF CONTENTS

1. Acknowledgments...1

2. Introduction..2
   Scott Ferkovich

3. Preface...4
   Basil M. "Mickey" Briggs

4. **April 28, 1896:** There Used to Be a Haymarket Right Here........................6
   Marcus W. Dickson

5. **April 25, 1901:** Welcome to the Big Leagues, Detroit 9
   Richard Riis

6. **July 16, 1909:** "I Never Saw Anything Like It"..12
   Phil Williams

7. **August 24, 1909:** An Honest Slide, or a Case of Malicious Intent...................15
   Jeff Samoray

8. **October 14, 1909:** "The Most Exciting World Series Game Ever" 18
   Mitch Lutzke

9. **April 20, 1912:** Frank Navin's Field of Dreams 21
   Jim Wohlenhaus

10. **July 4, 1912:** George Mullin Tosses First Tiger No-Hitter..........................24
    Mitch Lutzke

11. **September 20, 1912:** Smoky Joe Seeks a 17th Straight Win................................27
    Rich Bogovich

12. **August 4, 1918:** Cobb Single in 18th Defeats Big Train.......................................30
    Richard Riis

13. **April 30, 1922:** Charlie Robertson's Perfect Game 33
    David L. Fleitz

14. **June 13, 1924:** The Day All Hell Broke Loose...36
    Mike Lynch

15. **June 2, 1925:** "...Wild as Bedlam"..39
    Gregory H. Wolf

16. **May 10, 1927:** "I'm Glad to Be Back Here..." 42
    Richard Riis

17. **October 2, 1927:** Heilmann Takes Title on Season-Ending Spree 45
    Chip Mundy

18. **July 14, 1934:** The G-Men Pull Off the Miracle on Michigan............................48
    Jeffrey Koslowski

19. **September 10, 1934:** "Happy New Year, Hank!"..51
    Matt Keelean

20. **October 4, 1934:** Rowe Takes the Cardinals to School 54
    Gregory H. Wolf

21. **October 9, 1934:** "This is a Case For Judge Landis" 57
    Brent Heutmaker

22. **October 7, 1935**: Goose Goslin, Money Player 60
Scott Ferkovich

23. **October 3, 1937**: "Whistling Jake" One-Hits Tribe;
Stops Johnny Allen's 15-Game Win Streak.. 62
Terry W. Sloope

24. **May 4, 1939**: Who is That Kid?! 64
Bill Nowlin

25. **October 6, 1940**: Newsome's Performance Marked with Extraordinary Emotion 67
William M. Anderson

26. **July 8, 1941**: "Listen, You Lug..." 70
Marc Lancaster

27. **July 1, 1945**: "We Want Greenberg!" 73
Richard Riis

28. **July 18, 1947**: Hutchinson Ends Yanks' 19-Game Win Streak................................76
Mike Whiteman

29. **July 20, 1947**: 58,369 Fans Most Ever at The Corner.......................................78
Ruth Sadler

30. **June 15, 1948**: "Look at Your Wonderful Lights Here..." 81
Scott Dominiak

31. **June 23, 1950**: "A Fellow Doesn't Have a Night Like That Very Often" 83
Chip Mundy

32. **July 10, 1951**: "We're the Big Guys Now..." 86
Marc Lancaster

33. **May 15, 1952**: "I've Got to Get Married More Often"...89
Gregory H. Wolf

34. **June 17, 1961**: The Tiger Outslug the Yankees and Take First Place...................................92
Steve J. Weiss

35. **June 24, 1962**: "It Was a Long, Long, Long Ballgame".. 95
John Milner

36. **June 15, 1965**: "I Had Pretty Good Stuff" 97
Steven Kuehl

37. **September 14, 1968**: "It Was VJ Day All Over Again" 99
Scott Ferkovich

38. **September 17, 1968**: An Unlucky Hero Wins the Pennant 102
Jeff Samoray

39. **October 7, 1968**: Jose Feliciano Lights Tigers' Fire..105
Scott Ferkovich

40. **July 13, 1971**: "He Crushed It" 108
Scott Ferkovich

41. **October 2, 1972**: Lolich Fans 15 as Tigers Take Over First Place 110
Doug Lehman

42. **October 11, 1972**: Northrup's Wallop Wins It.. 113
Raymond Buzenski

43. **July 15, 1973**: Ryan Tosses No-Hitter; Cash Wields Table Leg 116
Gregory H. Wolf

44. **May 7, 1974**: LaGrow Knuckles Under to Wood in Classic Pitchers' Duel 119
   Will Bennett

45**. June 28, 1976**: The Bird is the Word 122
   Scott Ferkovich

46. **June 4, 1984**: The Bergman Game 125
   Maxwell Kates

47. **October 5, 1984**: Slurves, Yackadoos, and an American League Pennant 128
   Susan A. Lantz

48. **October 14, 1984**: Gibby Cooks the Goose 131
   Susan A. Lantz

49**. October 4, 1987**: Tanana Beats Toronto to Clinch Division Title 134
   David Raglin

50. **October 10, 1987**: Local Kid Sheridan Makes Good with Homer 137
   Jeff Samoray

51. **May 28, 1995**: "It's an Outright Crime to Lose That Game" 140
   Jerry Nechal

52. **September 14, 1998**: 18 Pitchers Used; 3 Records Set 143
   Steven Kuehl

53. **September 27, 1999**: Tears and Cheers: The Final Game at Michigan and Trumbull 146
   Gregory H. Wolf

54. Contributors 149

ACKNOWLEDGMENTS

PUTTING THIS BOOK TOGETHER WAS A rare privilege. And it could not have been done without the wonderful contributions of so many excellent writers and editors. A whole-hearted thanks goes out to each and every one of them.

This is the second book project I've worked on with my associate editors, Bill Nowlin and Len Levin. Once again, their expertise and professionalism made it all possible.

Allow me also to extend a very special thank-you to Mickey Briggs for the kind words, and for his agreeing to write such a fantastic preface.

I would be remiss if I did not thank Bill Dow, whose fine work was indispensable.

Thanks to the Society for American Baseball Research for all the great things they do in making projects like this a reality.

Thanks, Vinnie, for the great tasting subs.

Thanks, Rosie, for always making coffee.

And thanks, Maurice, for knowing that the answer to the trivia question was Rusty Kuntz.

INTRODUCTION

By Scott Ferkovich

WHETHER AT BENNETT PARK, NAVIN Field, Briggs Stadium, or Tiger Stadium, there have been many great games at the corner of Michigan and Trumbull. It was no easy task choosing the 50 that made the final cut for this book. I'm sure there are some notable ones that I did not include (like the game where the White Sox' Steve "Psycho" Lyons unwittingly pulled down his pants at first base). But that doesn't mean they weren't fun to watch or to be a part of. And in the final analysis, I'm confident that the 50 games I chose are worthy of remembrance.

For the record, I should point out that these are 50 great *baseball* games at Michigan and Trumbull. The Detroit Lions played some thrilling (and nauseating) football in the many decades they played there. But since this is a book about baseball games, published by the Society for American Baseball Research, well … you get what I'm saying.

A quick perusal will also show you that I actually have some Tiger *losses* peppered between these pages. "But Scott," you may ask, "how can you include Tiger *losses* in a book about great games at Michigan and Trumbull?" I actually asked myself this very question at the beginning, when I was putting the list together. But then I figured, if I restrict myself to only Tiger *victories,* that eliminates a lot of great baseball. And anyway, like the song says, if they don't win it's a shame. Maybe it *is* a shame, but it was still a great game.

When I told friends, family, and complete strangers that I was putting together a book on great games at Michigan and Trumbull, I sometimes got this reaction: "That place? What a dump!" A more common response was from people who grew up going to games at Tiger Stadium, or at Briggs Stadium, and missed it a lot, and wished they could visit it one more time.

Some of the more knowledgeable Tiger fans asked me, "Are you including the Greenberg game, the one where he hit the grand slam in the ninth inning on the final day of the 1945 season to win the pennant?!" You'd

be surprised how often this happened. It was almost as if they had an image in their mind of old, grainy, black-and-white newsreel footage with Hank hitting the home run while wearing the Old English "D" on a sunny day at Briggs Stadium. In fact, Greenberg was really wearing a Detroit road jersey when he hit it, because it was a rainy day in St. Louis. Thus, I couldn't include it in this book. It just goes to show that you can't always trust what your mind's eye is telling you. I can assure you that that is not the case with this book. Every effort has been made to "re-create" these games for you in a historically accurate way.

And it is not just a rehashing of the box scores. These stories are meant to be more than a dry recitation of the play-by-play. ("Incaviglia struck out. Tettleton struck out. Deer struck out to end the inning.") The game accounts you are about to read are meant to tell the "who, what, when, where, and why" (or "why not"), and describe the finer nuances and convey the drama that was sweeping through the ballpark. The accounts of these games tell the whole story of what took place at Michigan and Trumbull on a particular day. They are meant to be authoritative and accurate. We hope they are entertaining as well.

So what exactly constitutes a "great" game, anyway? To be sure, there are ones that almost by necessity needed to be included, such as the first game ever at Michigan and Trumbull way back in 1896, when it was called Bennett Park. (I was not at that game, but nobody will argue if I call it "great.") I included the All-Star Games, and some of the best postseason contests. Of the regular-season games, I employed a very scientific test: I looked at the events on the field, and if it seemed as if, at the end of the game, the fans shuffled out of the ballpark saying, "Wow, that was a great game," then I probably included it.

I saw my first game at Tiger Stadium in 1977, when I was just a kid. As some readers may recall, that was a time when the interior color scheme was a sea of green. The green seats perfectly complemented the bright green grass. Every square inch of wall, support beam, and guard rail was painted green. That was how Tigers owner Walter O. Briggs envisioned it when he expanded the place in the late 1930s. My earliest memories of the park are of that wonderful deep green everywhere you looked. Then, in the late 1970s, the management ripped out those green seats of rotting wood, and replaced them with plastic ones in clashing colors of Ty-D-Bol blue and candy-corn orange. Blue paint covered all the green everywhere, except for the grass. Adding insult to injury, they slapped garish white aluminum siding on the exterior, and generally made the park look like a giant Winnebago during Mardi Gras.

To generations of Tiger fans, the old ballpark at Michigan and Trumbull always meant green seats, the crack of the bat, the smell of a cigar, and the cry of the beer man. Unlike Ebbets Field, Fenway Park, or Wrigley Field, there was never anything romantic about Tiger Stadium. It wasn't charming or quaint. There weren't any writers from *The New Yorker* or the *East Coast Daily Flatulence* who waxed poetic about it.

But that is OK, because Tiger Stadium didn't lend itself to pretentiousness. It was utilitarian. It was a little bit industrial, a little bit pastoral. It was perfectly in tune with the gritty city it called home. When Al Kaline first laid eyes on it from the outside, he thought it looked like "a big battleship." Mr. Tiger nailed it, just like a throw from the right-field corner.

For all its lack of frills and creature comforts, it was a great place to watch a ballgame. So come with us now as we follow the red brick road back in time to the big battleship on the corner. Park your Buick in someone's front yard and pay the kid a dollar to keep an eye on it. Score a bag of peanuts from the guy on the street. Get an obstructed-view seat, a dog with mustard, and a flat beer, and enjoy yourself for a couple of hours.

Hopefully it is a great game.

PREFACE

By Basil M. "Mickey" Briggs

WHEN SCOTT FERKOVICH ASKED ME TO write the preface to this wonderful book that recounts the greatest games played at the corner of Michigan and Trumbull, I couldn't help but think immediately of my grandfather Walter O. Briggs and my father, "Spike," who took great pride in owning the Tigers and ensuring that the beautiful green ballpark that carried our family's name for 23 seasons (1938-1960) was the best venue in baseball.

Ted Williams once told me that Briggs Stadium was his favorite ballpark for hitting. Not because of the famous right-field upper deck overhang that sometimes turned lazy fly balls into home runs, but because of the outstanding "batter's eye" provided by the dark background between the upper and lower decks that framed the baseball perfectly.

I wish I could have been at the stadium on July 8, 1941, when Williams won the All-Star Game at Briggs Stadium in the bottom of the ninth by hitting a ball off the facing of the third deck. He told me it was his greatest thrill in baseball.

Just two years earlier, when he was a skinny rookie, he became the first player to clear the roof at Briggs Stadium after my grandfather completed the renovation that fully enclosed the ballpark by 1938. The home-run ball that bounced against the Checker Cab building on Trumbull was hit on May 4, 1939, just two days after a very ill Lou Gehrig took himself out of the lineup in Detroit to end his famous consecutive games streak.

Having watched several hundred ballgames there from the 1940s to the last game at Tiger Stadium on September 27, 1999, I was privileged to have seen some of the national pastime's most exciting contests and the numerous of Hall of Famers who graced that famous diamond that has been so wonderfully maintained by a group of volunteers called the Navin Field Grounds Crew.

I was at Game Five of the '68 World Series when Willie Horton famously threw out Lou Brock at home plate before Al Kaline came through with the greatest hit of his career, slapping a single to right-center field to give the Tigers the lead in that pivotal comeback game.

Sitting with my father near the Tiger dugout, I'll never forget that when the game ended, Cardinals owner Augie Busch, who was sitting in front of us, told my father, "That's okay, Spike, I would rather win the World Series at home anyway."

Of course we beat the Cardinals in Games Six and Seven in St. Louis to win the world championship. And poor Mr. Busch had to eat crow, washed down, I'm sure, with a bottle of Budweiser.

Three years later I was able to see the 1971 All-Star Game in Detroit. It has to be considered one of the greatest midsummer classics in baseball history.

Twenty-one future Hall of Famers were on those rosters and that is something I don't think you will ever see again. Six of them, Johnny Bench, Hank Aaron, Reggie Jackson, Frank Robinson, Harmon Killebrew, and Roberto Clemente, hit homers that evening. (Twenty years earlier the 1951 All-Star Game at Briggs Stadium had also featured six home runs.)

Talk about your field of dreams.

But the biggest blast I think anyone could have witnessed in all those years at the ballpark was when Reggie Jackson rocketed the ball into the light transformer on the roof in right-center. I can still hear the sound of the crack of his bat and see the ball rising. One can only wonder how far that ball would have traveled if my father had not installed those light towers in the summer of '48.

Although I missed Ted Williams's famous All-Star Game home run, I was very lucky to have seen some of the most dramatic home runs ever hit at the ballpark.

None was better than Kirk Gibson's second homer of Game Five of the 1984 World Series that sealed the ballclub's fourth world championship.

With the Tigers holding a 5-4 lead in the eighth inning, with one out, runners on second and third, and first base open, everyone was surprised that San Diego's Goose Gossage persuaded his manager, Dick Williams, to let him pitch to Kirk Gibson, who in the bottom of the first hit a two-run homer.

On the second pitch, Gibson drilled Gossage's offering deep into the upper right-field stands. I have never heard such a roar from a crowd. The ballpark just shook with that three-run shot. I just wished my grandfather and dad could have witnessed that one.

A half-century earlier, they did see Detroit win our first world championship, and the only other title won at home, when Goose Goslin hit the walk-off single to score Mickey Cochrane, the man I was nicknamed after. (My mother was pregnant with me during the 1935 World Series, and my dad told Cochrane that if he won the World Series and he had a boy, he would be called Mickey.)

But believe it or not, my all-time favorite game was the home run derby that occurred between the Yankees and Tigers on the warm summer evening of June 23, 1950.

I was sitting with my family and Elliott Trumbull, my great friend, who has been like a brother to me.

There were 51,400 fans packed into Briggs Stadium to see the first-place Tigers face the second-place Yankees while holding on to a one-game lead.

The ballpark was absolutely electric.

It first looked very grim because those "Damn Yankees" took an early 6-0 lead on two homers hit by Hank Bauer and one each by Yogi Berra and Jerry Coleman.

Little did we know that the fireworks had just started.

By the bottom of the ninth the Tigers were trailing 9-8 in what had become a night of round-trippers. The Yankees had hit six home runs and Detroit had belted four.

With one out and Vic Wertz on second, Elliott's boyhood hero Walter "Hoot" Evers stepped to the plate as everyone rose to their feet yelling, as we always did, "HOOOT ……… HOOOT."

He did not disappoint.

Hoot hit a tremendous blast over Joe DiMaggio's head in deep right-center field as the ball caromed off the fence at the 415 marker. Joltin' Joe's relay throw to shortstop Phil Rizzuto was off the mark as I'm watching Wertz score to tie the game.

Then all of sudden there's Evers rounding second. I assumed he would stop at third but then here he comes rounding the base and then crosses the plate standing and all of a sudden, my God, the game's over and we win on his inside-the-park home run.

Despite seeing the '68 and '84 World Series, without question that game was the most thrilling I have ever seen. To this day Elliott Trumbull calls me every year on June 23 to say "happy anniversary."

I know that all who had the pleasure to see games at that wonderful old ballpark have their own special memories.

Perhaps, like me, you may have even seen one or more of the greatest games at the stadium that Scott has selected.

And even if you didn't, I know you will enjoy this book as Scott takes you back to a different time and some very thrilling contests at that legendary diamond once known as Bennett Park, Navin Field, Briggs Stadium, and Tiger Stadium.

THERE USED TO BE A HAY MARKET RIGHT HERE

April 28, 1896: Detroit Tigers 17, Columbus Senators 2 at Bennett Park

By Marcus W. Dickson

IT'S BEEN SAID THAT "BEAUTY IS IN the eye of the beholder," and to Detroit residents in April of 1896, the barely finished wood bleachers and uneven, soggy field of Bennett Park seemed beautiful. On Opening Day, when the Detroit franchise of the Western League (already informally called the Tigers, and already sporting an old English D on their blue-gray home uniforms[1]) beat the Columbus Senators 17-2, it seemed that Detroit baseball was on its way back.

Detroit had previously been a member of the National League, and as such had become used to being a "major-league city." When the Detroit Wolverines won the 1887 postseason championship series against the American Association's Browns of St. Louis, Detroiters were sure of their status in the baseball world.[2] But the Wolverines folded the following season, and Detroit became a minor-league town, left without any meaningful professional baseball in the early 1890s. George Van Derbeck started a new Western League franchise in Detroit in 1894, playing for two years at Boulevard Park, an undistinguished, rickety, hastily-built wooden structure similar to most of that era.[3]

Van Derbeck's club had succeeded in the last two years despite the skepticism of many, and by October of 1895, he had announced his intention to construct a new field in town for the Tigers.[4] A new site was obtained on the northwest corner of Michigan Avenue and Trumbull Street, on the site of the former hay market.[5] Van Derbeck boasted that the site was so close to downtown that he "couldn't do much better unless Mayor Pingree would close up Woodward avenue and give us Grand Circus park."[6] The site was oddly-shaped, and because of this, home plate (still diamond-shaped in 1896) was in the southeast corner of the site, and the left-center-field fence was quite deep. The wooden stadium had a covered grandstand running from beyond third base around to about first base, with uncovered stands down the left- and right-field lines. It was partly constructed from wood from trees cut down to clear the site, though for some reason, several trees were allowed to remain standing, and in play.[7]

Construction of the stadium was significantly hampered by the weather; more than four weeks of construction time were lost, and the field was not in playable condition just a few days before the scheduled exhibition opener. Even so, 600 people came out to the unfinished site the day before the first scheduled exhibition, just to see the team practice.[8] That first exhibition game—scheduled for April 12 against the team from the University of Michigan—had to be canceled because additional rain had turned the field into a swamp.[9] The park's informal opening thus occurred on April 13, with a game against the Athletics, a local club, in a game won by Detroit, 30-3. A few other exhibitions followed, as warm-ups to the season.

Detroit then went on a five-game road trip to start the Western League season. The Tigers returned to Detroit for their April 28 home opener carrying a record of 3-2. Just the previous day, Detroit and Columbus had played a very tight game, filled with drama throughout, with Detroit emerging the victor, 8-7.[10] Facing the same team for the home opener, the Detroit partisans were thus expecting an interesting game against a tough opponent to inaugurate the new park.

Bennett Park had an official stated capacity of 5,000, making it one of the smaller parks in the Western League,[11] but that capacity was certainly exceeded—perhaps by as much as 3,000—on Opening Day of 1896, when eager spectators filled the stands, and then began to move into the field of play. The players on the bench were pushed into service to keep the spectators back, because the solitary police officer present was clearly insufficient to the task.[12] Indeed, in the first inning, Butler, the regular left fielder for Columbus, went back to track a long fly ball and ran full-speed into a member of the grandstand crowd who had wandered onto the field. Butler was knocked out cold for close to 10 minutes, and had to leave the game. More officers arrived shortly thereafter to keep the crowd in check.[13]

With the stands full to overflowing, the crowd was eager for the contest to begin. But before there could be a ballgame, there were celebrations to attend to. Tigers owner Van Derbeck had arranged that earlier in the day, trolleys would carry the players of each team as well as several dignitaries through the streets of Detroit before finally delivering them to the field for the 3:30 P.M. game. A cannon was fired "every few minutes to let the natives know it is a day to celebrate, even if it is not the Fourth of July."[14] As game time approached, the two teams lined up on either side of home plate, and County Treasurer Alex McLeod, standing in for Detroit Mayor Hazen Pingree, strode to the mound, received the ball from the umpire, and spoke briefly. He then threw the first pitch to Detroit baseball legend Charlie Bennett, the much-admired catcher for the 1887 National League champion Detroit Wolverines, for whom Bennett Park was named.[15] Bennett's career had come to an unceremonious end in 1894 when a railroad accident led to the amputation of both his legs, though he remained well-regarded around the country.[16] With a roar of the crowd for Bennett, the ceremonies concluded, and the game could begin.

Unexpectedly, the game itself proved not to be very exciting, as Detroit took an early lead, and Detroit's pitcher, Fifield, "was a mystery to the Senators, and only when he began lobbing them up, late in the game, did they do any team hitting."[17] Nonetheless, "in spite of the one-sided game the people were yelling loudly all through and seemed as deeply interested when the last hit was made as when the guiding spirit of the team [player-manager George Stallings] infused life by cracking out a homer [the first in the new park] in the first inning."[18]

Detroit went first to bat, and scored four runs in the first inning on a single by Nicholson, a triple by Dungan, a double by Whistler, and the home run by player-manager Stallings (the play on which Butler of Columbus was knocked out). Columbus hoped to get back in the game when Campbell, their leadoff hitter, hit a single, but he was doubled off base on the next play when right fielder Cantillon's fly ball was caught, much to Campbell's surprise. Cantillon, seeing the catch, bumped hard into Detroit first baseman Whistler to disrupt the play at first, but the umpire saw the tactic, and declared Campbell out in returning to the base due to Cantillon's interference. After a walk to Sharpe and an error on a fly ball by Detroit shortstop Corcoran, Columbus first baseman Morrissey lined out to Detroit's third baseman, Gillen, to end the first. Detroit scored three more in the second, then went silent until they put up eight runs in the sixth against Columbus twirler Bumpus Jones, and then two more in the seventh. Columbus scored one each in the seventh and the ninth. After 2 hours and 26 minutes, the first official game at Michigan and Trumbull was done.

Bales before balls: The corner of Michigan and Trumbull when it was a hay market

There were criticisms, to be sure — the field was not yet in good shape (and, in fact, never really would be throughout the history of Bennett Park, with cobblestones from the earlier hay market occasionally pushing up through the infield).[19] Additionally, the *Free Press* noted that "there was enough kicking on both sides to cause the umpire to toss fines around like a drunken sailor his coin,"[20] and a separate column that same day stated, "Mr. Snyder [the umpire], you cannot enforce the 'conduct' rules too strictly."[21] Some of that kicking may have been because Snyder had negated Detroit pitcher Fifield's second home run of the day when Snyder said he did not see the Columbus third baseman, Collopy, blatantly interfere with Fifield as he rounded the base, allowing Fifield to be thrown out at home. But in general, the crowd went home happy (Columbus left fielder Butler being a likely exception).[22]

Detroit would go on to finish the 1896 season in third place, 10 games behind the Minneapolis Millers, with a record of 80-58.[23] Popular player-manager George Stallings left Detroit at the end of the season to take over the National League Phillies.[24] As the 1896 season ended, owner Van Derbeck scheduled a September 24 exhibition doubleheader at Bennett Park against Cincinnati to raise money for the players, including a night game under electrified lights — the last Tigers night game in Detroit until 1948.[25]

But on April 28, 1896, all of that was in the future — as were over 100 more years of baseball to be played at "The Corner." That day's unexpected 17-2 win was an auspicious start to professional baseball at Michigan and Trumbull.

NOTES

1 "For Lovers of Various Sports," *Detroit Free Press,* March 13, 1896, 6.

2 "A Grand Finale: Brilliant Ending of the Base Ball Season in Detroit," *Detroit Free Press,* October 25, 1887, 2.

3 Jim Hawkins, Dan Ewald, and George Van Dusen, *The Detroit Tigers Encyclopedia.* (Champaign, Illinois: Sports Publishing, 2003).

4 "Sunday Ball Playing," *Detroit Free Press,* October 6, 1895, 24.

5 Richard Bak, Charlie Vincent, and the Free Press staff, *The Corner: A century of memories at Michigan and Trumbull.* (Chicago, Illinois: Triumph Books, 1999).

6 "For Lovers of Various Sports." *Detroit Free Press,* February 21, 1896, 6.

7 *The Detroit Tigers Encyclopedia;* "Bennett Park Historical Analysis," baseball-almanac.com/stadium/st-bp.shtml.

8 "For Lovers of Various Sports." *Detroit Free Press,* April 11, 1896, 6.

9 "For Lovers of Various Sports." *Detroit Free Press,* April 12, 1896, 6.

10 "It Was a Narrow One," *Detroit Free Press,* April 28, 1896, 6.

11 Scott Ferkovich, Bennett Park (Detroit). sabr.org/bioproj/park/336604.

12 "17 to 2!!," *Detroit Free Press,* April 29, 1896, 1, 8.

13 Ibid.

14 "Bennett Park Opening," *Detroit Free Press,* April 26, 1896, 7.

15 "Call it Bennett Park," *Detroit Free Press,* January 19, 1896, 6.

16 "Poor Charley Bennett," *Detroit Free Press,* June 23, 1894, 4.

17 "17 to 2!!"

18 Ibid.

19 Ferkovich. Bennett Park (Detroit); Lowry, *Green Cathedrals,* 82-83.

20 "17 to 2!!"

21 "Hits Along the Line," *Detroit Free Press,* April 29, 1896, 8.

22 "17 to 2!!"

23 "Western League." baseball-reference.com/bullpen/Western_League.

24 "George Stallings." baseball-reference.com/bullpen/George_Stallings#Year-by-Year_Managerial_Record.

25 Richard Bak. The first night game at Michigan and Trumbull was played in 1896. blog.detroitathletic.com/2011/08/31/the-first-night-game-at-michigan-trumbull-was-played-in-1896/; Bill McGraw. "Falling Stadium Lights Have History," *Detroit Free Press,* July 22, 2008. freep.com/apps/pbcs.dll/article?AID=/20080722/COL27/80722064.

WELCOME TO THE BIG LEAGUES, DETROIT

April 25, 1901: Detroit Tigers 14, Milwaukee Brewers 13 at Bennett Park

By Richard Riis

WHEN CHARLES COMISKEY AND OTHER investors purchased the minor Western League in 1894, it was with the express intent of transforming the loop into a major league on a par with the well-established National League. Aggressively signing major-league-caliber players and shifting franchises from smaller markets such as Grand Rapids and St. Paul to Cleveland and Chicago, the league, re-organized as the American League of Professional Baseball Clubs in the fall of 1899, declared itself a bona-fide major-league beginning with the 1901 season. Among the Western League holdovers now a charter member of the new American League: the Detroit Tigers.

The largest crowd ever to attend a baseball game in Detroit[1] streamed into Bennett Park to see the Tigers make their major-league debut against the Milwaukee Brewers. A parade complete with bands, city officials in carriages, local fraternal organizations, and the players from both teams had traveled up Michigan Avenue, while at Bennett Park a crowd of 10,023—some 1,500 greater than seating capacity—was spilling over from the stands into the outfield.

A band of heavy rain that lingered for days across the Northeast provided the upstart loop with an in-auspicious start, causing postponement of three of the four season openers scheduled for April 24, including the game in Detroit. But the next day offered a bright, clear sky and a modest breeze, and although the field was still wet and the basepaths muddy, a fine day for a ballgame.

Pregame ceremonies began with the visiting Brewers marching onto the field, followed by the Tigers, who paraded before the grandstand in bright red wool coats and doffed their caps to the cheering crowd. "Oom Paul," the club's unofficial mascot and good-luck charm since the previous year, when the Tigers won 21 of 22 with the dog in attendance, was brought out to home plate to a roar of delight from the stands. There were a handful of speeches and the presentation of an oversized cup to team owner James Burns and manager/co-owner George Stallings. Finally, City Council President Jacob J. Haarer, filling in for Mayor William Maybury, tossed out the ceremonial first pitch to Charlie Bennett, the beloved catcher for the old National League Detroit Wolverines. The Wolverines had folded 13 years ago, but Detroit baseball fans still held the heroes of the 1887 world champions in high regard.

The umpires, in consideration of a rope stretched across the outfield to corral the fans standing or sitting on the outfield grass, informed both clubs that a ball hit into the crowd would be ruled a double. As the band struck up "There'll Be a Hot Time in the Old Town Tonight," the Tigers sprinted onto the field. Roscoe Miller, a 24-year-old right-hander who had won 19 games the previous year in Detroit's final season as a minor-league club, took the mound.

Whether it was the sodden field, the team's inability to practice for a week due to the unrelenting weather, or simply Opening Day jitters, from the moment the game began the Tigers hardly looked to be ready for the major leagues. Kid Elberfeld, who'd played two seasons in the National League, for Philadelphia and Cincinnati, made a "gorgeous fumble"[2] on a ball hit to short by the first Milwaukee batter, Irv Waldron, and was charged with an error. Although Detroit managed to escape the opening frame without sur-

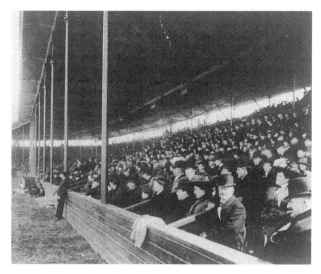

Fans take in a game at Bennett Park

rendering a run, three more errors in the second inning handed Milwaukee a 2-0 lead. The Tigers, for their part, couldn't get anything going against Pink Hawley, who had jumped to the new league after compiling an 18-18 won-lost record for the last-place New York Giants in 1900.

The third inning saw the Brewers score five runs on an error, four hits, a walk, and a sacrifice. This was the end for Miller, who was replaced by Emil Frisk during the inning. Miller had not pitched particularly well, but five errors behind him, including three by Elberfeld, had also let him down. The inning ended with the Brewers up 7-0.

Detroit finally got on the scoreboard in the bottom of the fourth on an error followed by a ground-rule double into the crowd by Frank "Pop" Dillon. Elberfeld drove Dillon home with another ground-rule double. The Tigers added another run in the fifth when Doc Casey scored on a Kid Gleason double.

After six innings the score stood at 7-3, but the Brewers struck again in the seventh, scoring three more runs on two doubles and a single after two men were out.

At this point Milwaukee player-manager Hugh Duffy, perhaps thinking the game was safely in hand, took out Hawley, replacing him with Pete Dowling. Hawley had been pitching well, having surrendered only five hits and walking one in his six innings on the mound, but Dowling had been "Detroit's Jonah all last season,"[3] beating the Tigers four times, twice

by shutout. Dowling retired the Tigers without a hit in the seventh inning.

Milwaukee continued its assault in the eighth, plating three more runs on two walks, three hits, and another Detroit error. The Tigers stirred a bit in their half of the inning, as Dowling gave up four hits and one run, thanks to another ground-rule double by Pop Dillon.

The Brewers were retired in order in the top of the ninth, and with the score now 13-4 the Tigers came to bat for a final time. Many in the grandstand were already heading for the exits, "growling profanely,"[4] as Doc Casey stepped into the batter's box.

Casey drove the ball into the overflow crowd in the outfield for a ground-rule double. Jimmy Barrett followed by beating out a slow roller to third. Kid Gleason then singled to center, scoring Casey. Renewed enthusiasm swept the stands, and the roar of the crowd increased in volume with each successive blow by the Tigers. Ducky Holmes followed with a double, scoring Barrett. Dillon hit his third double of the game, scoring Gleason and Holmes. Kid Elberfeld stroked another double to right field, pushing Dillon across the plate. Five runs had now scored with none yet out.

Hugh Duffy came in from center field and removed Pete Dowling in favor of Bert Husting. Husting immediately uncorked a wild pitch, allowing Elberfeld to advance to third, before retiring Kid Nance on an infield grounder for the first out of the inning.

The charged crowd in the outfield pressed closer toward the diamond. The game was delayed a few minutes as the Detroit players ran out to push the throng back behind the ropes to afford the Milwaukee outfielders a fair chance at getting to long drives. When the game resumed, Husting walked the next batter, Fritz Buelow. Pitcher Emil Frisk followed with a single to left, scoring Elberfeld for the Tigers' 10th run and sixth of the inning.

"Hats were being thrown in the air, coats were flying and everyone was yelling themselves hoarse. One man in the bleachers threw up his coat and when it came down it was in two sections, but he didn't care so long as Detroit was hitting the ball, and the chances are that he forgot he ever had a coat."[5]

Doc Casey, batting for the second time in the inning, laid down a bunt, reaching first just ahead of the throw by diving head-first into the bag. With the bases now loaded, Jimmy Barrett came to bat but went down on strikes for the second out. Kid Gleason then hit a savage grounder that Brewers third baseman Jimmy Burke fumbled, allowing Buelow to score and keeping Detroit's improbable rally alive. The Tigers pulled within one run when Ducky Holmes beat out a slow roller to Burke that scored Frisk.

It was now up to Frank Dillon. The first baseman already had three ground-rule doubles, including one earlier this inning. With the count at two balls and two strikes, Dillon drove a pitch down the left-field foul line and into the crowd, while Casey and Gleason raced home with the tying and winning runs.

With Dillon's hit, pandemonium broke loose at Bennett Park. "Roaring, howling and screaming,"[6] the crowd poured out of the stands onto the field. "The crowd almost tore [Dillon] to pieces, and finally he was picked up and carried around the field on the shoulders of some of the excited spectators."[7]

The Detroit Tigers were winners in their American League debut by the virtue of, as one account described it, "the most magnificent batting rally ever seen."[8]

SOURCES

Books

Bak, Richard, *A Place for Summer: A Narrative History of Tiger Stadium* (Detroit: Wayne State University Books, 1998).

McCollister, John, *The Tigers and Their Den: The Official Story of the Detroit Tigers* (Boulder, Colorado: Taylor Trade Publishing, 1999).

Newspapers

Detroit Journal.

Detroit News.

Detroit Tribune.

Evening Wisconsin (Milwaukee).

Milwaukee Daily News.

Milwaukee Journal.

Milwaukee Sentinel.

Minneapolis Journal.

Sporting Life.

The Sporting News.

NOTES

1   "Ten Runs Won in the Ninth," *Detroit Free Press*, April 26, 1901, 10.

2   Ibid.

3   Ibid.

4   "Detroit Is a Baseball Town," *Detroit Free Press*, April 27, 1901, 4.

5   "Ten Runs Won in the Ninth," *Detroit Free Press*, 1.

6   "Detroit Is a Baseball Town," *Detroit Free Press*, 4.

7   "Big Game in Detroit," *Boston Herald*, April 26, 1901, 1.

8   "On the Diamond," *Augusta Chronicle*, April 26, 1901, 8.

"I NEVER SAW ANYTHING LIKE IT"

July 16, 1909: Washington Senators 0, Detroit Tigers 0 (18 Innings) at Bennett Park

By Phil Williams

DETROIT'S BENNETT PARK HOSTED A four-game series between the Senators and Tigers in mid-July 1909. Detroit won the first three games of the set, with the finale set for Friday, July 16. The Tigers began that day atop the American League, with a 50-28 record. Washington lay in last place, at 23-52. Detroit was pursuing its third straight pennant and, since the beginning of the 1907 season, had compiled a 41-13 record against the Senators.

Yet, a certain anxiety can stalk fans of a winning team, and it may have been evident in the stands that warm, sunny afternoon. Detroit had lost three of four games to Philadelphia immediately before the Senators arrived, and the Athletics had closed to within a half-game of the lead on July 11. The Tigers could not let up against the second division; 11 games with Philadelphia remained.

All the more reason the bugs focused on Ed Summers as he warmed up. As a rookie, in 1908, he had paced the Tigers' staff with 24 victories. Yet by midseason 1909 his rheumatic knees threatened to shut him down. Summers had started only two of the Tigers' previous 15 games, and had not looked particularly good in either. But one of these, on July 10, was the sole victory Detroit managed against Philadelphia in the previous series.[1] Manager Hughie Jennings considered Summers his chief weapon against the Athletics; in the right-hander's year and a half of major-league service, he had compiled a 9-1 record against the Mackmen.

Meanwhile, as badly as the Senators had stumbled, they weren't lying down. At the end of the 1908 season, after the Tigers edged out the Naps (and the White Sox) for the pennant, ugly rumors surfaced from Cleveland. Namely, that the Senators, per the direction of manager Joe Cantillon, had not put forth their best efforts in a final series at Detroit.[2] In early July 1909, Cantillon announced "that for the balance of the season he will lose no opportunity to try out promising young players."[3] But wisely, the Senators' skipper would not experiment in Michigan. The only nonregular in the Washington lineup that afternoon was rookie Speed Kelly, called up to replace an injured Wid Conroy at third base.

Granted, Washington's offense was anemic: in 1909 the team finished dead last in the major leagues with 2.45 runs scored per game. (Combined, the leagues averaged 3.54 runs per game.) But their pitching staff showed some promise, and the Tiger faithful must have looked out with some concern at the two rookies Cantillon had throwing on the sidelines. Both came from the Pacific Coast League, changed speeds well, and could hit corners with biting curves. Right-hander Bob Groom, after losing 7-4 at Detroit on May 25, beat the Tigers 6-2 in Washington on June 12. Southpaw Dolly Gray had emerged as Cantillon's first choice to counter the strong Detroit left-handed bats. Although he had won only once in his four starts against Detroit, Gray pitched well in each, including the 3-0 Tiger victory that opened the series three days earlier.[4]

Cantillon went with Gray. At approximately 3:30, with Tigers catcher Oscar Stanage and umpire John Kerin behind the plate, Senators left fielder George Browne stepped into the box to face Summers.

Browne flied out. Speedy Clyde Milan bunted his way on, and Jack Lelivelt followed with a single. Detroit right fielder Ty Cobb made a "sensational catch" of Bob Unglaub's "long foul, almost out of sight behind the first base bleachers," with Milan and Lelivelt advancing.[5] Summers struck out Jiggs Donahue to retire the Senators.

Washington threatened again in the third. Leading off, Gray doubled past left fielder Matty McIntyre. Shortstop Donie Bush caught Browne's liner. Gray had started to third, but Tigers second baseman Germany Schaefer wasn't near his bag. "Bush started after Gray, made a flying dive and reached him, and had a double play all alone."[6] Milan grounded out to finish the half-inning.

After these early-inning hiccups, the fast-working Summers settled into an efficient groove. Although famed for his "fingernail" ball, a modern-day knuckleball under a different name, Summers didn't throw the pitch exclusively, instead mixing it among his fastballs and curves.[7]

Gray was equally impressive. The only real threat he faced that day occurred in the bottom half of the first inning. McIntyre led off with a single, and was sacrificed to second by Bush. Sam Crawford followed with "a smash that threatened to be a home run" before going "just foul."[8] He then grounded out to second baseman Unglaub, and Washington catcher Gabby Street threw out Ty Cobb trying to bunt his way aboard.[9]

As the two pitchers cruised along, Summers started each inning by digging a hole on the slope of the pitcher's mound for his front (left) foot to land in. Then Gray would kick dirt into the hole and stamp it down. "But in the ninth," the Senators pitcher recalled, "I neglected to do this, and as he has a shorter stride than me, my right foot, after the first ball I pitched, landed right square in Summers's pitching space, and I felt a sharp pain in my left side and thigh."[10]

Gray managed a couple more pitches to leadoff hitter McIntyre, but after the third, "reeled and would have fallen, but for first baseman Donahue, who caught him in the arms." After initially joshing the pitcher, but then seeing the legitimacy of his injury, "the Detroit fans rose in a body and cheered Gray" as he was assisted off the field.[11] In his eight innings of work, the only hit Gray surrendered was McIntyre's single in the first.

Groom took over, and promptly walked McIntyre. Bush bunted to move him to second, and Donahue couldn't handle Street's throw to first. Bush was safe, and Washington had runners at first and second with

none out. Crawford sacrificed the two runners over. Cobb hit a comebacker to Groom, who threw to home plate, where Street tagged out McIntyre. Groom then struck out Claude Rossman.

The affair thus moved into extra innings, and Summers continued to mow down the Senators. Only in the 12th inning did real difficulty arise. With two out and the fast Lelivelt on first, Donahue smashed a line drive to right. "Cobb tore in, staked all on a desperate plunge, and came up with the ball."[12]

But Groom found himself in almost continuous trouble. In four of the five frames after the eventful ninth, Detroit runners got into scoring position. The finest opportunity came in the 15th inning. Stanage led off and singled, and Jennings sent Red Killefer in to pinch-run. Summers bunted, Groom picked up the ball and, aiming for the lead runner at second, unleashed a wild throw past the bag. Killefer scampered to third. Summers reached first.

With the bases loaded and none out, Bush popped up weakly to Kelly. Crawford grounded to Groom. The pitcher was a bit slow on the play and by the time he threw to the catcher, Killefer had apparently crossed the plate safe. Street, believing the game at last over, headed for the clubhouse. The Washington infielders and the Detroit baserunners also started off the field. But umpire Kerin stayed put "and when asked by the incoming players what was the matter, replied tersely, 'Runner's out.'"[13] Everyone scurried back to their positions, the infielders unable (or unthinking) to double up any baserunner. Then "Cobb took three jerky, hectic swings" at Groom's offerings, "and walked to the field, his head hanging."[14]

As a "colossal joke" to cap the inning, one of the Detroit dailies was alerted to the winning run that wasn't, and an extra edition proclaiming the Tigers 1-0 victors flew off the presses.[15]

In the next inning Detroit threatened yet again, with Rossman and Schaefer singling and standing on first and second with one out. Nothing came of it. The 17th and 18th innings were uneventful. By this point the fans, accustomed to seeing their high-octane offense bully opposing pitchers out of the box, saluted Groom's resilience by cheering him when he came to bat.

After the 18th inning, and 3:15 of play, Kerin called the game. It was near 7 P.M., with enough light still to accommodate one, maybe two, more innings. Players from both sides were upset with the decision, probably none more than Summers, who had pitched the entire game for Detroit with nothing to show for it.

Washington's Bob Unglaub spoke for many when he said, "Why do they want to keep us out here so long and then not let us have a chance to finish the game?"[16] The crowd of 3,078 streamed out of the park, back home towards cooling dinners, abuzz with talk of what they had seen. One of them, the great Sam Thompson, who starred for the Detroit Wolverines a generation earlier, remarked, "I never saw anything like it."[17]

NOTES

1   In addition to his 9-5 win over visiting Philadelphia on July 10, Summers lost 6-0 at Cleveland on July 6.

2   "Ban Johnson May Try to Oust Cantillon From American League," *Cleveland Plain-Dealer*, October 20, 1908, 8; "Joe Cantillon Says He's Been Asked to Come Back," *Detroit Times*, July 15, 1909.

3   "Colts for Washington," *Detroit Times*, July 8, 1909.

4   For background on Groom, see Catherine Petroski and John Stahl, "Bob Groom," The Baseball Biography Project, sabr. org/bioproj/person/cbf60399, accessed September 11, 2014. For background on Gray, see "'Dolly' Gray Declares the Terms are Satisfactory," *Washington Herald*, February 9, 1909, 11. Gray's previous starts against the Tigers: a 4-2 loss at Detroit on May 23, a 3-1 victory at Detroit on May 26, a rain-shortened five-inning 1-0 loss at Washington on June 14, and the 3-0 loss at Detroit on July 13.

5   "Nationals Play for 18 Innings," *Washington Herald*, July 17, 1909, 1.

6   Joe S. Jackson, "All Records Broken for Scoreless Play," *Detroit Free Press*, July 17, 1909, 8.

7   For background on Summers, see Phil Williams, "Ed Summers," The Baseball Biography Project, sabr.org/bioproj/person/bb06e-aee, accessed September 11, 2014.

8   "Told About the Tigers," *Detroit Free Press*, July 17, 1909, 9.

9   Play-by-play accounts of first four innings may be found in Paul H. Bruske, "Cantillon Depends on Gray to Stop Tiger Rally—Lilivelt, Tigers' New Recruit, Will Report Tomorrow Ready for Work," *Detroit Times*, July 16, 1909, 1.

10   William Peet, "Gray to Pitch Soon," *Washington Herald*, July 24, 1909, 8.

11   "Get Together Fans! And Play Over Nationals-Tigers Great Game in 1909," *Washington Herald*, July 29, 1912, 7.

12   "Nationals Play for 18 Innings," 8.

13   "Get Together Fans!"

14   "Nationals Play for 18 Innings," 8.

15   Paul H. Bruske, "Detroit Dots," *Sporting Life*, July 24, 1909, 25.

16   "Gray in Bad Way," *Washington Post*, July 17, 1909, 8.

17   "Nationals Play for 18 Innings," 8.

AN HONEST SLIDE, OR A CASE OF MALICIOUS INTENT?

August 24, 1909: Detroit Tigers 7, Philadelphia Athletics 6 at Bennett Park

By Jeff Samoray

IN BASEBALL'S ROUGH-AND-TUMBLE Deadball Era, no player was more vilified for spiking his opponents than Detroit's Ty Cobb. While there's no doubt he spiked many players during his 24-year career, a large part of Cobb's reputation as a vicious baserunner stems from an incident that occurred in the heat of the 1909 American League pennant race. The play in question not only endangered the Tigers' chances of winning the league title, it also threatened to end Cobb's blossoming Hall of Fame career.

The Tigers and Philadelphia Athletics began a fierce rivalry in 1907 as Detroit rose from mediocrity and became a league force. The Tigers played some tense games with the Athletics that season, including a memorable 17-inning tie in late September during a tight pennant race. Detroit captured its first American League pennant by 1½ games over the Athletics. Cobb also emerged as the league's biggest star, winning his first batting title and leading the junior circuit in hits, RBIs and stolen bases.

The enmity between the teams extended into 1909. Detroit set out to capture its third straight pennant while Philadelphia kept pace in the standings. By late August, the Athletics had a one-game lead over the Tigers when they began a three-game set in Detroit. Sportswriters anticipated a tense series and felt its outcome would have a major impact on the pennant race. At that point in the season, Detroit had won just four of 15 games against Philadelphia.

The Athletics arrived with a five-game winning streak and rookie third baseman Frank Baker. He had already earned a reputation as a powerful hitter by socking the first home run to clear the fence in Philadelphia's Shibe Park.

Sparks started flying in the first inning of the series' first game, played on August 24 before a near-capacity crowd of 9,711 at Bennett Park.

Philadelphia scored two runs off Tigers starter Ed Summers in the top of the first. Detroit tried to counter against Athletics left-hander Harry Krause in the bottom of the inning. With two outs, Cobb walked, stole second, then attempted to steal third as batter Sam Crawford took ball four.

Athletics catcher Patrick "Paddy" Livingston threw Cobb out to end the inning. The play wasn't close, but Cobb spiked Baker while sliding into the base. Cobb's spikes cut Baker on his inner forearm about three inches below the right elbow. The *Detroit Free Press* mentioned the play briefly:

"Cobb spiked Baker's right forearm in sliding into third back in the first inning. Baker was aggrieved, regarding the injury as premeditated. Cobb was out easily, but went into the bag feet first, only to be tagged."[1]

The *Detroit News* simply stated: "Cobb was easily thrown out. There was no doubt about his being out."[2]

The Tigers scored four runs in the seventh to take a 7-5 lead. Cobb tied the game with a two-run double that exemplified his no-holds-barred playing style. As the throw came in from the outfield, Cobb knocked second baseman Eddie Collins head over heels while sliding into the bag. The *Detroit Free Press* noted that Collins was in the baseline while receiving the throw. He made no appeal to the umpires.[3]

The Athletics added a run in the ninth and loaded the bases with one out. But Tigers right-hander Bill Donovan retired the final two batters to seal the 7-6 victory for Detroit. Fans rushed onto the field in joyous celebration after outfielder Crawford caught an easy fly for the final out.

While Tigers fans enjoyed the thrilling victory, protests from Athletics manager Connie Mack overshadowed the outcome. Mack angrily criticized Cobb, claiming he deliberately spiked Baker in the first inning:

"Cobb is the greatest ball player in the world, but he is also one of the dirtiest. He boasted before the game that he would get some of the Athletics before the game was over, and he made good by spiking Baker and all but cutting the legs off Collins. ... Such tactics ought to be looked into by the American League, and I intend to see to it that the matter is taken up. ... [Cobb] may be a great player, but he is a pinhead in this respect. Organized base ball ought not to permit such a malefactor to disgrace it."4

Cobb fired back, stating that the spiking was unintentional:

"Mack knows that I have never spiked a man deliberately, and he also knows that the runner is entitled to the line, and if the baseman gets in his way, he is taking his own chances. When I slid I made for the bag. If the man with the ball is in the way he is apt to get hurt. But that is his lookout, he has no business on the line."5

Baker's injury seems to have been minor, as he remained in the game with a small plaster dressing over the wound and played every inning of the series. However, American League President Ban Johnson weighed in on the matter, implicating Cobb directly:

"There's been altogether too much of this sort of game at Detroit, and somebody is going to be made a shining example of if I hear of another such affray. Cobb seems to be the chief offender, and a word of advice should go a long way. He must stop this sort of playing or he will have to quit the game."6

Controversy swirled for several days as the Tigers swept the Athletics to take a two-game lead in the standings. Would Johnson banish Cobb from baseball? Or was Cobb's slide clean?

Then a serendipitous photograph surfaced. *Detroit News* photographer William Kuenzel had been stationed near third base with his camera during the series'

first game. He wasn't aware of the debate surrounding Cobb's slide until the sports department asked if he had a photo of the play. Kuenzel didn't, but retrieved an undeveloped glass plate negative he set aside because it was scratched.7

The photo first appeared on the front page of the August 27 *Detroit News*. It shows Cobb in the baseline sliding feet first into third with his right leg extended about 10 inches above the ground toward the base. Baker is reaching across the bag to tag Cobb with the ball in his bare hand. The *News* presented the image as evidence that Cobb attempted to avoid Baker's tag and reach third safely. Cobb added:

"This picture plainly shows that I did not spike Baker intentionally. ... Baker is mighty nice about it and said yesterday that he did not think I tried to spike him intentionally. He looks at it as an accident and lets it pass at that. Connie Mack, naturally sore at losing to us, is inclined to look at the matter more seriously as he naturally would, being a hard loser."8

Johnson backtracked after reviewing the image, stating that if Cobb had violated the rules of the game the umpires would have settled the matter promptly.9

Kuenzel's photo is one of the most widely reproduced images from Cobb's career, appearing in countless publications through the years. Cobb, Baker and Mack came to terms about the incident. But the play became a notorious part of the Cobb legend, seemingly gaining embellishments with each passing decade, much to his chagrin.

In a 1953 article, former player Al Schacht said Cobb spiked Baker so badly, he had to be carried off the field.10 When Baker was elected to the National Baseball Hall of Fame in 1955, Cobb was present at the induction ceremony. According to *New York Herald Tribune* sportswriter Tommy Holmes, an attendee wondered aloud if Cobb would "slide across the dais in front of [Baseball Commissioner Ford] Frick, spike Baker again and start another riot."11

As late as 1961, the year of his death, Cobb defended his actions, maintaining in his autobiography that he slid away from Baker in order to hook the base with his foot.12

Was Cobb completely innocent, or was Mack right in his assertions? Regardless of intent and photographic evidence, the Cobb-Baker incident remains one the most controversial and widely discussed plays of the Deadball Era.

SOURCES

In addition to the sources cited in the notes, the author also consulted:

Alexander, Charles C. *Ty Cobb* (New York: Oxford University Press, 1984).

Baseball-reference.com.

Cobb, Ty, ed. William R. Cobb. *My Twenty Years in Baseball* (Mineola, New York: Dover Publications, Inc., 2009).

Jones, David, ed. *Deadball Stars of the American League* (Dulles, Virginia: Potomac Books, Inc., 2006), 546-550, 620-624.

Lieb, Frederick G. *The Detroit Tigers* (New York: G.P. Putnam's Sons, 1946).

Macht, Norman L. *Connie Mack and the Early Years of Baseball* (Lincoln and London: University of Nebraska Press, 2007).

Sparks, Barry. *Frank "Home Run" Baker: Hall of Famer and World Series Hero* (Jefferson, North Carolina: McFarland & Company, Inc., 2006), 28-33.

NOTES

1   "Told about the Tigers," *Detroit Free Press*, August 25, 1909.

2   "Fighting Spirit Is Again a Prominent Feature of Playing," *Detroit News*, August 25, 1909.

3   "Told about the Tigers," *Detroit Free Press*, August 25, 1909.

4   "One More Regrettable Athletic-Detroit Controversy," *Sporting Life*, September 4, 1909.

5   Ibid.

6   "One Way to Beat the Tiges," *Detroit Free Press*, August 27, 1909.

7   William W. Lutz. *The News of Detroit: How a Newspaper and a City Grew Together* (Boston: Little, Brown & Company, 1973), 159-160.

8   "The Disputed Play on Account of Which Philadelphia Now Wants Ban Johnson to Drive Ty Cobb From Organized Base Ball," *Detroit News*, August 27, 1909.

9   "Told About the Tigers," *Detroit Free Press*, August 28, 1909.

10 Al Schacht, "Mr. Mantle and Mr. Moore," *Rome* (Georgia) *News-Tribune*, September 13, 1953.

11 Tommy Holmes, "Cooperstown Ceremony Recalls Old Stories of Baseball Greats," *St. Petersburg Times*, August 2, 1955.

12 Ty Cobb with Al Stump, *My Life in Baseball: The True Record* (Garden City, New York: Doubleday & Company, 1961), 114-115.

"THE MOST EXCITING WORLD SERIES GAME EVER"

October 14, 1909: Detroit Tigers 5, Pittsburgh Pirates 4 at Bennett Park (Game Six of the World Series)

By Mitch Lutzke

THE THIRD TIME WAS SUPPOSED TO BE the charm for manager Hughie Jennings and the Detroit Tigers. The skipper had led the Detroiters to the World Series in each of his three seasons at the helm, but unfortunately had dropped the first two against the Chicago Cubs. The 1909 Series pitted two of the best players in the game, Triple Crown winner Ty Cobb and the Pittsburg Pirates' Honus Wagner. On a brisk fall day in Detroit, others would join this pair of baseball heroes as Game Six was "without a doubt….the most exciting World Series game ever."[1]

Pittsburgh needed only one more victory to wrap up the title, leading the series three games to two, as the Pirates were coming off a dominating 8-4 win in their hometown on Wednesday. The Detroit weather forecast for Thursday, October 14 called for possible snow flurries. A crisp morning saw the temperature hover around the freezing mark, but by the 2 o'clock game time it had soared to 47 degrees. The skies eventually cleared and it would have been a "perfect autumn day" if it weren't for the high winds that buffeted the players and fans at Bennett Park.[2] The weather played a role in keeping the attendance to just over 10,000 fans, about half of the Series average, and also as to who would pitch for Detroit that day. Manager Jennings went with his Midwestern-born George Mullin over his other pitching star Wild Bill Donovan. Mullin had a reputation as a cold-weather pitcher, and had proved it in 1909 when he ran off 11 straight victories to begin the season. Demonstrating a workhorse mentality, Mullin had pitched a complete-game victory on Tuesday and tossed eight innings in the Series opening loss just six days earlier. Before the game, Jennings had asked Mullin if he was strong enough to go again. "The arm feels fine," Mullin replied. "I think I can tie that Series up for you."[3]

Pittsburgh started the considerably fresher veteran Vic Willis, a 23-game winner, who in this series had pitched only once in long relief in the Game Two loss to Detroit.

Manager Jennings' upbeat personality and his motto "Today is the day, boys," had been a recurring theme throughout the 1909 season.[4] It did look as though it would be Detroit's day when Mullin fired a strike from his right arm with the game's first pitch. But, quickly, Jennings' words rang hollow. The partisan Detroit fans sat by nervously as the visitors racked up four straight hits to begin the game, including two that narrowly evaded Tigers fielders. When cleanup batter Wagner laced a two run double, and Pittsburgh raced to a 3-0 lead, they appeared to be on their way to a World Series championship.

According to one scribe, when the Tigers managed to score in the bottom of the first inning, "that one run changed the whole outlook."[5] Wahoo Sam Crawford drilled a double to centerfield that plated Donie Bush from second and cut the Pirates' lead to two runs. Mullin settled down on the mound, holding Pittsburgh hitless and scoreless until the sixth inning. In the meantime, Detroit managed to tie the game with a pair of scores in the fourth and then took the lead with a run in the fifth inning. When Cobb managed a two-out double into the right-field corner in the sixth, fellow outfielder Davy Jones crossed home plate and the Tigers saw their margin grow to 5-3.

The fact that Cobb was still playing in the World Series became a story in and of itself. Earlier that summer, while the team was in Cleveland for a series with the Naps, the short-tempered superstar had allegedly stabbed a hotel worker during an argument. Secret grand-jury testimony had been leaked and the plan was that when Cobb traveled with the Tigers through Cleveland to Pittsburgh, he would be arrested and charged with a felony. So, Detroit's management put Cobb on a different train than the team, one that chugged through Canada to Buffalo and then south to Pittsburgh. The same tactic was employed for his return trip to Game Six in Detroit. While controversy surrounding Cobb was nothing new, he'd showed up considerably late for Game Five in Pittsburgh, leading to some anxious moments.

A couple of head-turning defensive plays highlighted the game's middle innings. While Detroit managed to tally twice in the fourth inning, a rifle throw from Pirates right-fielder Chief Wilson to Wagner covering third base cut down a Tiger and helped to limit the scoring damage. For Detroit, catcher Boss Schmidt, who had seen the Pirates run at will so far in the Series with 13 stolen bases, turned a neat double play in the Pittsburgh sixth. The Pirates had broken Mullin's stranglehold with a one-out single by rookie Dots Miller. Then, Bill Abstein hit a towering foul ball behind home plate. Schmidt had a long run in foul territory and, with his back to the infield, corralled the pop up in front of the grandstand. Miller, sensing that the Tigers' catcher had forgotten about him at first base, dashed for second. Schmidt wheeled and fired high to Bush covering second. Bush jumped and snared the errant throw and while coming down, dropped a tag on Miller, who was attempting to slide under the airborne shortstop. The next inning, after Pittsburgh had advanced a runner to second base with two outs, Bobby Byrne hit a line drive on the left side of the infield. The "screecher" was nearly past shortstop Bush, but he lunged and stabbed the ball out of the air, ending a Pittsburgh threat.[6] These three plays had the Bennett Park crowd buzzing, but it was simply a hint of what was to come.

The ninth inning was "perhaps the most spectacular inning of any World's Series game ever played," according to Malcolm Bingay of the *Detroit News*.[7] Mullin needed three more outs to get his second

Bennett Park's "wildcat" stands

victory of the Series and force a deciding Game Seven at Bennett Park. Pittsburgh and Detroit had exhibited "plain cold nerve" throughout the day and the visitor was ready to play "right up to the death of the last Pirate."[8] Pittsburgh began the ninth with Miller singling to right, while Abstein followed with a base rap to center. On Wilson's bunt, Schmidt scampered from behind the plate and chucked the ball errantly to first base. First baseman Tom Jones reached for the wild toss near the baseline, just as Wilson arrived at first. The collision jarred the ball loose, knocking Jones unconscious, and he dropped like he'd been "shot."[9] Some feared that Jones, having landed on his head, was killed on the play. As Tigers' second baseman Jim Delahanty scrambled for the rolling ball, Miller scored and Abstein raced to third, while Wilson, remained at first base. Jones was so badly injured that a doctor dashed from the crowd to render aid, while the Tigers trainer sprinted from the dugout, and players from both sides surrounded the prone Jones. To add insult to injury, he was charged with an error on the play. He was carried off the field by his teammates, and manager Jennings had to replace the slick-fielding first baseman with outfielder Crawford.

Jones's right arm and experience were seen as strengths of the infield, far outstripping the skills of Crawford, a veteran of less than a season's time at first base, over his lengthy career. As luck would have it, however, the next batter, Pittsburgh's George Gibson, hit a Mullin curve ball to the newly-planted Crawford.

In one elegant motion, the left-hander scooped the ball up and fired a strike to home. Catcher Schmidt dropped down on both knees to block the plate, as Abstein crashed into the burly Tiger. Despite inflicting a 6-inch gash with his spikes on Schmidt's thigh, Abstein was out.

With runners now on first and second, relief pitcher Deacon Phillippe was scheduled to bat, but Pittsburgh manager Fred Clarke sent Ed Abbaticchio to pinch hit. Fans back home crowded the streets in front of the Pittsburgh newspaper offices, following posted game updates, and yelled, "Get a hit, Abby!"[10] Abbaticchio battled with Mullin and managed to reach a full count. On the payoff pitch, both base runners were off with the delivery. Abbaticchio swung and missed for the second out and the inconsistent Schmidt was called on again to throw to a base. He fired to third baseman George Moriarty, who sprawled to catch the peg, block the bag, and attempt to tag Wilson. Both men dove for the base and crashed into each other. Out of a cloud of dust umpire Bill Klem waved his arms and signaled the game's final out. Detroit had won 5 - 4 and lived to play a Game Seven.

(On Saturday, October 16, the Tigers lost Game Seven, 8- 0, and the World Series title to Pittsburgh. Detroit hurler George Mullin made yet another appearance and pitched six innings of relief)

SOURCES

Reichler, Joseph L., ed., *Baseball Encyclopedia*, 4th Ed, (New York: MacMillan Publishing Company, 1979).

New York Times

Sporting News

NOTES

1   R.W. Lardner, "Tigers 5-4 Victory Costs Three Men," *Chicago Daily Tribune*, October 15, 1909, 8.

2   H.G. Salsinger, "Men of Jennings and Clarke Line-up in Sixth Battle," *Detroit News*, October 14, 1909, 1.

3   Fred Lieb, *The Detroit Tigers* (Kent Ohio; Kent State University Press, 2008), 134.

4   H.G. Salsinger, "Today is the Day Boys, Slogan of H. Jennings that Landed Pennant, *Detroit News*, October 1, 1909, 22.

5   Lee Anderson, "Best Game Ever Played, Verdict of 10,535 Fans," *Detroit News*, October 15, 1909, 21.

6   M.W. Bingay, "Just Gameness Won Yesterday's Battle for Detroit Team," *Detroit News*, October 15, 1909, 21.

7   Ibid.

8   Bingay,8.

9   Lardner.

10 "Gloom Pervades Pittsburg," New York Times, October 15, 1909, 12; "Pittsburg Is a Sad City," *Detroit Free Press*, October 15, 1909, 8.

FRANK NAVIN'S FIELD OF DREAMS

April 20, 1912: Detroit Tigers 6, Cleveland Naps 5 at Navin Field

By Jim Wohlenhaus

THE FIRST GAME TO BE PLAYED AT Navin Field was scheduled for Thursday, April 18, 1912, with the Detroit Tigers hosting the Cleveland Naps. To commemorate this special Opening Day of the season, many activities were scheduled, all to take place on the 18th. A parade featuring both teams was to work its way from the middle of downtown Detroit to the new ballpark at the corner of Michigan and Trumbull Avenues. After the game the Tigers and Naps were to attend a banquet in their honor at the elegant Hotel Pontchartrain, sponsored by the Detroit Board of Commerce. However, once again, the best plans did not occur as planned. It rained hard on April 18 and the game was postponed.

The baseball park the Tigers had played in in 1911 was called Bennett Field. Immediately after the last game of the 1911 season, the small wooden structure was demolished, and Navin Field was erected on the same plot of ground. Made of steel and concrete, a new construction concept at the time, it was reported to have cost around $300,000 to build.

The rain started during the evening of Wednesday, April 17, and lasted most of Thursday, causing the rainout. On Friday the game was also postponed; officially the reason was unplayable grounds. This was plausible, considering that the field was so new and had taken on a lot of water. This was largely the result of the park's new tarpaulin: It was hailed as a perforation-type (rather than a solid sheet), which was supposed to make it less vulnerable to wind. Unfortunately, excessive amounts of rainwater drained through the perforated tarp's holes, causing a muddy field. But another possible reason for the postponement (which was never listed as official) was that Frank Navin was a superstitious gambler who did not want to start the season on Friday, which he referred to as the hoodoo day of the week.

There was some talk that the game would be shifted to Cleveland, which had a dry field. In fact Ban Johnson, president of the American League, had bought off on this idea. The opening game was originally scheduled as the start of a four-game series with the Naps. It turned into a two-game series. If these games had been shifted to Cleveland, the first game at Navin Field would have been pushed back until April 27, another reason for trying to play the games in Detroit.

Despite the delays, the banquet went off as originally scheduled on Thursday evening. The parade and game took place on Saturday. The first pitch was thrown out by Mayor William Barlum Thompson of Detroit, who threw it to Charley Bennett, a popular ex-Tiger catcher from the 19th century, and the namesake of old Bennett Park.

The starting lineups were:

Cleveland

Jack Graney	left field
Ivy Olson	shortstop
Joe Jackson	center field
Nap Lajoie	second base
Buddy Ryan	right field
Eddie Hohnhorst	first base
Terry Turner	third base
Ted Easterly	catcher
Vean Gregg	pitcher

Detroit

Ossie Vitt	left field
Baldy Loudon	third base
Ty Cobb	center field
Sam Crawford	right field
Jim Delahanty	second base
Del Gainer	first base

Donie Bush	shortstop
Oscar Stanage	catcher
George Mullin	pitcher

As can be seen, the starting lineups included three future members of Baseball's Hall of Fame: charter member Ty Cobb, Wahoo Sam Crawford, and Nap Lajoie. Many might argue that a fourth player, Shoeless Joe Jackson, should be in the Hall of Fame, too.

Detroit manager Hughie Jennings—himself a future Hall of Famer—gave right-hander George Mullin the game ball. Mullin was starting his ninth home opener in 10 years.

The first pitch by Mullin was a called strike to Jack Graney, the game was finally started, and the history of Navin Field had begun.

Cleveland wasted little time scoring the first run at the new park, although the Naps did get help from the Tigers. The game's third batter, Shoeless Joe Jackson, reached first on a base on balls, immediately stole second, and raced home on an error by Tigers second baseman Jim Delahanty on Nap Lajoie's grounder. The run was unearned.

Left-hander Vean Gregg, 23-7 with a league-leading 1.80 ERA the year before, was Cleveland manager Harry Davis's starter. In the first inning, Ossie Vitt singled and was sacrificed to second by Baldy Loudon. On the very first pitch he saw at Navin Field, Cobb rapped a base hit, scoring Vitt. The Georgia Peach

An early photo of Navin Field's main entrance at Michigan and Trumbull

went to second on Crawford's single. Then it got exciting. Cobb and Crawford performed a double steal as Delahanty struck out. While on second and third, Cobb and Crawford performed yet another successful double steal. The aggressive baserunning produced Cobb's first run at Navin Field—on his steal of home.

The game went back and forth for the next seven innings. Cleveland scored two in the third on an infield single and a bases-loaded hit batsman to take a 3-2 lead, but Detroit came back in its half to tie it up, and might have scored more but the bold and daring Cobb was thrown out at home plate trying to score from second base on Delahanty's grounder back to the pitcher.

In the fifth Cleveland went ahead by two runs on a single, a double, and a bad error by second baseman Delahanty. The score stayed 5-3 until the bottom of the eighth, when Detroit tied the game on Cobb's single, Crawford's double, and Delahanty's two-run single past third baseman Terry Turner.

The game went into extra innings. In the top of the 11th, Cleveland put runners at second and third with just one out, thanks to an error and Joe Jackson's ground-rule double into the overflow crowd in center field. Because of the huge throng in attendance (according to the turnstile count it was 24,382, but estimates put it at closer to 26,000), many hundreds of fans had to stand in the nether reaches of the outfield in a cordoned-off area. This had resulted in five ground-rule doubles, four by Cleveland and one by Detroit. The *Cleveland Plain Dealer* said that Jackson's drive would likely have gone for a triple had it not been for the ground rule that held him at second—and more importantly, held Olson at third.

Mullin issued an intentional walk to Lajoie, which loaded the bases. The strategy paid off: The next two batters grounded out without a run being able to score.

In the Detroit half of the 11th, Del Gainer grounded out, but Donie Bush singled and Oscar Stanage followed suit. Bush went to third as Stanage was out at second trying to take an extra base. That made it two outs with Bush on third. Even though Mullin had already given up 13 hits and walked four, Jennings elected to let him hit for himself—he was a good hitter, having batted .286 in 1911. Mullin came through. He singled to left, scoring Bush with the winning run. It was quite a way to inaugurate a new ballpark.

SOURCES

Cleveland Plain Dealer

Detroitathletic.com

Detroit Times

Myfoxdetroit.com

Retrosheet

SABR BioProject

Sporting Life

GEORGE MULLIN TOSSES FIRST TIGER NO-HITTER

July 4, 1912: Detroit Tigers 7, St. Louis Browns 0 at Navin Field

By Mitch Lutzke

AN AGING VETERAN, WHO HAD BATTLED weight problems all season and was placed on waivers a few weeks before was an unlikely choice to hurl the Tigers' first no-hitter. But that is what George Mullin did on his birthday, no less, as he redeemed himself and mowed down the St. Louis Browns to make Detroit baseball history.

The Wabash Mauler was a long-time pitching star for the Tigers. In consecutive trips to the World Series in 1907 and 1908 against the Chicago Cubs, Detroit won only one game, Mullin earning that victory. He almost single-handedly led Detroit to the 1909 AL pennant, then won two games in a World Series the Tigers lost to the Pittsburgh Pirates. But by three years later his right arm and his body were showing the wear and tear of baseball.

In June 1912 the team waived Mullin and pitcher Eddie Summers, blaming them in part for the Tigers' lackluster fifth-place standing. With the waiver request, players were in limbo and waited for a club to claim them. Reportedly, Mullin had his eye on the Cleveland team, which would keep him near his home in Toledo, Ohio.

The 1912 season had already begun to unravel for the Tigers. With the team mired well out of first place, the fans accustomed to the three straight World Series appearances a few years earlier began to show their displeasure. Star outfielder Ty Cobb was publicly critical of the fans, saying the players hadn't quit on each other, but that the fans had quit on the team. To make matters worse, a few days later Cobb left the dugout during a game and took off his uniform, only to see his batting spot in the line-up make it up to the plate. Manager Hughie Jennings summoned Mullin, also known for his slugging, to pinch-hit for Cobb. Detroit owner Frank J. Navin was very critical of Jennings, saying the team wasn't motivated and had lost confidence in the skipper. It was against that backdrop that Mullin returned to the team and fired the franchise's first no-hitter.

While in waiver limbo Mullin worked out to lose weight. When no team claimed him, the Tigers activated him and returned him to the starting rotation. The Tigers won the morning game of the July 4 doubleheader against the Browns, and Mullin was the starter for the afternoon contest. It was his 32nd birthday, according to baseball-reference.com.

Sportswriters covering the game described Mullin as effectively wild. In the first inning he walked a batter and then encountered trouble in the second inning. With runners on first and second and none out, after an error and another walk, the Browns threatened to score. A sacrifice by Willie "Happy" Hogan was foiled when Mullin snared the airborne bunt and fired to Tigers first baseman George Moriarty, hoping to double off the runner. Moriarty then fired a strike to shortstop Donie Bush covering second base, as the Tigers attempted a triple play. However, the base-runner returning to first was called safe, though the runner going back to second was out, for a nifty double play. An infield pop out ended the threat.

The third, fourth, and fifth innings were uneventful as the last-place Browns were set down in order. By the end of the fifth inning, the Navin Field crowd sensed that history was being made and became much louder. In the sixth inning the Browns' Burt Shotton walked. But he was thrown out at second trying to steal and that ended any Browns' threat. Mullin then retired the Browns in order in the seventh inning.

Earlier that spring, Mullin had told a reporter that he would be the "happiest man in baseball" if he could throw a no-hitter.[1] He had come close in the 1909 season, when he tossed a one-hitter against Chicago on Opening Day, the first of 11 straight wins to open the season. In that game the only hit was a bloop single that narrowly evaded an infielder. Mullin had clearly been the ace of the staff in the team's World Series appearances, but that was far from the club's mind when they tried to dump him in mid-June.

In terms of mound artistry, this was not a perfect pitching performance for the hurler, but his "lack of control was an advantage rather than a defect. The big curve was just wild enough to keep the aliens guessing and hitting at bad balls," wrote E.A. Batchelor, the *Detroit Free Press* sportswriter, who also doubling as the game's official scorer.[2]

Between innings Tigers trainer Archie Tuthill worked on Mullin's arm, massaging it to keep it loose and ready for more pitches.

The final two innings saw the tenor of the game change. Until then, the Browns had not managed any good swings against Mullin. To lead off the eighth, Mullin threw Jimmy "Pepper" Austin three balls that "were too high, wide or low."[3] Then he sent two down the middle that Austin didn't even flinch at, for called strikes. The full-count pitch was a "trifle off," and Austin got a base on balls.[4] Pinch hitting for Hogan, Pete "Bash" Compton worked Mullin into a full count. The pay-off pitch was a fastball and Compton hit one hard. His blast was headed into the gap between right fielder Sam Crawford and Ty Cobb. "After a hard run" into "far" center field, Cobb caught up with the ball and out number one was recorded.[5] Browns catcher Jim "Little Nemo" Stephens then followed Compton's effort with "another tough fly" that Cobb also ran down for the second out.[6] Player-manager George Stovall pinch-hit for the pitcher and got himself out to end the inning.

In the meantime, Mullin was also doing damage with his bat. He wound up with three hits in four at-bats, including an RBI double in the second inning. The Tigers scored single runs in the first three innings off rookie Willie Adams. They exploded for four runs in the eighth inning to lead 7-0, and a Detroit victory was no longer in doubt. Strolling to the mound to begin the crucial final inning, Mullin yelled, "Hey Batch," and put up three fingers in an effort to confirm that his last at-bat had been ruled a hit and not an error.[7] When Batchelor, the official scorer, nodded in agreement, Mullin took his place on the mound for the ninth inning.

The crowd sat quietly, but burst into applause as the outs were recorded. Mullin faced Shotton to begin the final inning. The Browns' lead-off hitter was considered the fastest man in the league and some feared that any type of ground ball might wreck the no-hit bid. Mullin wasn't even close with his pitches and the Browns speedster walked on four straight balls. Then rookie Heinie Jantzen hit a rocket to right-center field that Cobb ran down for the first out.

Next up was slugger Joe Kutina, who had hit .374 the previous summer for the Saginaw Krazy Kats of the Southern Michigan League. He was known for being inconsistent, but "hammering the ball" when he did connect.[8] The first baseman put up a weak foul ball that Tigers catcher Oscar Stanage corralled in front of the grandstand for out number two. After that grab the crowd erupted like "Niagara," Batchelor wrote.[9] The Browns' last gasp was rookie shortstop Del Pratt, who took the first two pitches outside for balls. Mullin then laid one over the plate and Pratt took a mighty cut. The ball rocketed off his bat and streaked on a line to left-center field. The Georgia Peach, as he had done twice in the eighth inning, robbed the Browns one last time that afternoon. He snagged Pratt's drive and Mullin had the Tigers' first no-hitter.

Mullin was far from perfect that day, walking five, while striking out five. But, he was good enough for the Tigers to forget about releasing him, or assigning him to the minor leagues. Wabash George, the birthday boy, was for one day, at least, again, the ace of the Tigers' staff.

SOURCES

Detroit News Tribune

New York Times

The Sporting News

NOTES

1   Ralph L. Yonker, "Mullin Has Realized the Dearest Ambition of His Baseball Life," *Detroit Times*, July 5, 1912, 6.

2   E. A. Batchelor, "Maumee George is Numbered with Game's Immortals," *Detroit Free Press*, July 5, 1912, 11.

3   H.G. Salsinger, "Mullin Pitches Himself to Fame in No-Hit Game," *Detroit News*, July 5, 1909, 24.

4   Ibid.

5   Ibid.

6   Ibid.

7   Batchelor, 11.

8   Ibid.

9   Ibid.

SMOKY JOE SEEKS A 17TH STRAIGHT WIN

September 20, 1912: Detroit Tigers 6, Boston Red Sox 4 at Navin Field

By Rich Bogovich

FOR BOTH MAJOR LEAGUES 1912 "WAS a banner year for streaks by pitchers," as noted at the start of a SABR article on such accomplishments.[1] Future Hall of Famers in each league had already tied or set records for consecutive wins as the Tigers prepared to face Red Sox ace Joe Wood during the second half of September. In the NL, Rube Marquard of the New York Giants started the season with 19 consecutive wins to tie Tim Keefe's record, set in 1888 with the same franchise. In short order, Washington's Walter Johnson broke the previous AL record of 14 straight and got as far as 16 by beating the Tigers on August 23.

Almost immediately, Howard Ellsworth "Smoky Joe" Wood, in his fourth full AL season at age 22, had a streak reach 13. As a result, strong interest built for a game on September 6 when it was announced that he would start a day ahead of schedule and counter none other than Johnson. "On September 6 a circus-like crowd estimated at 35,000 packed every crevice of Fenway Park — filling the stands, outfield and even foul territory along the right- and left-field foul lines — and cheered wildly with every strike Joe burned across," wrote Michael Foster, Wood's SABR biographer. "In the end, Joe prevailed 1-0, a victory made possible when back-to-back fly balls by Tris Speaker and Duffy Lewis (which would have been playable under ordinary circumstances) fell untouched into the crowd and were ruled doubles. Nine days later, Joe tied Johnson's record with a 2-1 victory over St. Louis."[2] That game against the Browns also impressed. "Wood won in one of the greatest pitching engagements ever staged in any ball park," *The Sporting News* enthused.[3]

Many fans across America would be eager to learn the outcome of Wood's next start, in Detroit on Friday, September 20. The big game's crowd of 3,115 was about 2,000 below the average for the new Navin Field, though a day earlier just 558 watched the Tigers defeat New York.[4] Boston arrived two days after clinching the pennant. The Tigers began play with a record of 67-75.

Detroit manager Hughie Jennings had recently been starting pitchers who made their major-league debuts that month. The assignment opposite Wood went to William Wilkes "Tex" Covington, 25. His major-league career began in 1911 with a record of 7-1. He had already started eight games for the Tigers in 1912 and earned a complete-game victory six days earlier. Jennings' lineup included four regulars in the first six slots, plus Bobby Veach, at the start of a 14-year career.

Boston was retired in order in the first inning. Donie Bush started the bottom of the inning by beating out a ball hit to 23-year-old rookie Marty Krug at shortstop, who was subbing for Heinie Wagner. Red Corriden then grounded to Krug to begin a double play, and Sam Crawford was retired for the third out.

Boston's first baserunner came with two out in the second when Covington walked Clyde Engle, who was subbing for player-manager Jake Stahl at first base because Stahl was serving a three-game suspension after a dustup with an umpire in Cleveland the day before. However, Covington picked Engle off to end the inning. In the bottom of the second, Ty Cobb grounded out to Wood and the next two hitters struck out.

Boston was again retired in order in the third inning. In the bottom half, Wood struck out Eddie

Smoky Joe Wood won 34 games in 1912

Onslow and retired Eddie's older brother Jack on a grounder. That brought up Covington with the bases empty. After having had no trouble with the first eight batters, Wood walked four in a row—the opposing pitcher and the next three batters—forcing in a run. This set the stage for a pivotal moment. As a Boston reporter put it, "Krug muffed a puny fly raised by Cobb and two more runs came across."5 Wood was finally able to induce a groundout by Veach.

Leadoff man Harry Hooper started the fourth frame for Boston by beating out an infield hit. Covington caught Hooper napping at first base but his pickoff throw got past Eddie Onslow and the runner took second. Hooper advanced to third on a groundout; another by future Hall of Famer Tris Speaker enabled Hooper to score. One more groundout ended the inning. Wood retired the Tigers in order in the bottom half, notching another strikeout in the process.

In the top of the fifth inning, bases on balls again led to a run, this time enabling Boston to battle back. Larry Gardner drew the first walk. He moved to second on a passed ball and then Engle walked. That brought up Krug. Soon enough, Covington complained loudly enough about a call by umpire Frank "Silk" O'Loughlin on a pitch to Krug and was ejected (by the first umpire ever to eject Cobb, in 1908). Jennings had to bring in a new hurler, and chose veteran Joe Lake.

On Lake's first offering, Krug singled to center, though Gardner stopped at third. Catcher Hick Cady came up with the bases full and none out. He hit sharply to Bush, who stepped on second to force Krug but threw wildly to first when trying to double up Cady. That allowed the two lead runners to score and tie the game, 3-3. Wood batted next, and singled to left. Hooper followed by hitting a ball that drew Eddie Onslow away from first but neither Lake nor Louden covered that bag so the bases were loaded again with just one out. After a popup for the second out, up strode Speaker. He grounded to Louden at second but a poor throw drew Onslow's foot off the bag, and the Red Sox had taken the lead. Lake succeeded in striking out Gardner to end the rally.

Lake then started the bottom of the inning with a single. Wood retired Bush on a popup to Krug, but Corriden singled to center and Lake advanced to third as Speaker had trouble controlling the ball. Corriden then stole second. Crawford followed by singling right up the middle to plate both runners and put the Tigers back on top, 5-4. Crawford took second on Speaker's throw homeward and stole third while Cobb batted, but Wood ultimately struck out Cobb and retired Veach.

Except for a two-out walk to Krug, Boston went quietly in the top of the sixth. Louden led off the bottom half by walking, but Eddie Onslow grounded to Krug, who started another double play. Wood then struck out Jack Onslow. In the top of the seventh, the Red Sox were retired in order. In the bottom half Lake again led off by singling. He was bunted into scoring position but Wood struck out Corriden and Crawford popped out to Krug.

Speaker began Boston's eighth by drawing a free pass. Lake struck out Lewis. Gardner then worked the count full, and Speaker took off for second just before Gardner knocked a fly toward Crawford in right field. Whether a coach or Speaker was to blame, Crawford made the catch and easily doubled Speaker off first to end the inning.

Cobb led off the bottom of the eighth by beating out an infield hit but he slid into first and hurt his ankle. Thus, when Veach smashed a line drive over Speaker's head, Cobb only reached third and Veach settled for a double. Smoky Joe secured the first out when Louden hit a fly right back to him. Next up was

Eddie Onslow, who grounded to Gardner at third. Gardner may have been overconfident about Cobb's ankle, and threw to first only to have Cobb suddenly sprint for home. With a skillful slide, Cobb gave the Tigers an insurance run before Wood recorded the third out.

Boston was retired in order in the ninth, and the contest ended with Wood on deck. "American league (*sic*) history will have to struggle along without the immediate establishment of any new records," began the story in the *Detroit Free Press* the next day by Edward A. Batchelor.[6]

Under the scoring standards of the time, Tex Covington was credited with the victory. The game would prove to be Covington's major-league finale, so his career concluded with an ejection. Wood made two more regular-season starts and won both, for a record of 34-5. He then won three of the eight World Series games as Boston defeated Marquard's Giants.

Wood never enjoyed such success again. His pitching career went downhill after he broke his thumb at Navin Field on July 18, 1913, after slipping on wet grass while fielding a ball. Wood was sold to Cleveland in 1917 and converted to the outfield, which extended his career through 1922. The record shared by Johnson and Wood was tied in 1931 by Lefty Grove of the Philadelphia Athletics and in 1934 by the Tigers' Schoolboy Rowe.

NOTES

1   Ronald G. Liebman, "Winning Streaks by Pitchers," research. sabr.org/journals/winning-streaks-by-pitchers.

2   Michael Foster, "Smoky Joe Wood," sabr.org/bioproj/person/9f244666. Foster's biography of Wood originally appeared in David Jones, ed., *Deadball Stars of the American League* (Washington, D.C.: Potomac Books, Inc., 2006). See also Emil Rothe, "The War of 1912—The Wood-Johnson Duel," research. sabr.org/journals/war-of-1912.

3   "Wood Had to Win It," *The Sporting News*, September 19, 1912, 4.

4   Many box scores at the time omitted attendance totals, but examples of ones that reported it include the *Washington Herald*, September 21, 1912, 10, and the *San Francisco Call*, September 21, 1912, 16, which printed very different accounts of Wood's attempt to break the newly set record. In addition, attendance data was reported daily in the "Told in a Nutshell" chart of the *Boston Post*.

5   Charles E. Young, "Tigers Put End to Joe's Record," *Boston Post*, September 21, 1912, 6. Many play-by-play details are paraphrased from Young's account. Others are from "Champion Red Sox Pay Final Visit," *Detroit Times*, September 20, 1912. Though its overview of the game was terse, the paper documented every play through the top of the eighth inning.

6   E.A. Batchelor, "Detroit Breaks Up Joe Wood's Winning Streak," *Detroit Free Press*, September 21, 1912, 1. Batchelor had become a charter member of the Baseball Writers Association of America about four years earlier and held membership card number 1 for many years.

COBB SINGLE IN 18TH DEFEATS BIG TRAIN

August 4, 1918: Detroit Tigers 7, Washington Nationals 6 at Navin Field

By Richard Riis

THE DECISION HAD COME DOWN BARELY a week before: baseball was closing up shop and going to war. Suddenly, in the middle of summer, the 1918 baseball season was drawing to a close.

On May 23 General Enoch Crowder, provost marshal and director of the draft, decreed that by July 1 all eligible men aged 21 to 30 employed in "non-essential" occupations must apply for work directly related to the war effort or be prepared to be called into military service.

Despite the fervent pleas of team owners for an exemption, Secretary of War Newton Baker agreed with Crowder, announcing on July 20 his decision that playing baseball qualified as "non-essential" employment. On July 26 Baker agreed to delay the "work or fight" deadline for Major League Baseball by two months, to September 1. With no decision yet on the American and National Leagues' petition for a further extension to allow the playing of a World Series, a sense of urgency had fallen over the August schedule.

For all practical purposes, the season was already over for the Detroit Tigers. When the Washington Nationals arrived in Detroit on Friday, August 2, for a four-game weekend series, the Tigers were in sixth place, 43-53 and 16½ games behind the league-leading Boston Red Sox. Outside of Ty Cobb's league-leading .388 batting average, the team had been punchless all season and their pitching poor. "They [can't] quit any time too soon to suit me," Tigers owner Frank Navin scoffed to the press.[1]

Washington, on the other hand, was enjoying a competitive season. After putting up a 74-79 record in 1917, the Nationals found themselves this season in a bona-fide pennant race with a 52-44 record, good enough for third place, 7½ games out of first and a scant two games behind Cleveland for second place. A first pennant for the club did not seem to be out of reach.

Washington's improved fortunes rested almost exclusively on the phenomenal pitching arm of Walter Johnson. Johnson's 18-11 won-lost record scarcely reflected his formidable presence on the mound. Coming into the series with the Tigers, Johnson had completed his last 29 starts, including all 23 so far in 1918. His earned-run average for the season was a microscopic 1.30, and had been as low as 0.76 on June 30. On May 15 Johnson had pitched all 18 innings of a 1-0 shutout of the defending world champion Chicago White Sox, one of seven extra-inning complete games the Big Train had pitched already this season. His most recent, a 15-inning, 1-0 shutout of the St. Louis Browns and a 10-inning, 3-2 win over the New York Yankees, had come in his last two starts.

Friday's series opener saw the Nationals rough up George "Hooks" Dauss for 14 hits in eight innings in taking the game 5-0 behind a six-hit shutout by Harry Harper. Detroit's bats continued their slumber on Saturday as the Nationals pummeled the Tigers 10-1, the loss dropping the hapless Tigers into seventh place behind the Browns.

Nonetheless, nearly 10,000 fans[2] passed through the turnstiles at Navin Field on the brutally hot afternoon of August 4 for a Sunday doubleheader. In the first game, the Nationals scored six runs in the first three innings off rookie right-hander Rudy Kallio and coasted to a 7-0 victory. But the day's big attraction was the opportunity to see the extraordinary Walter Johnson pitch in the nightcap.

The Tigers' sacrificial lamb, so to speak, was right-hander Carroll "Deacon" Jones, making his first start of the season after 14 games of mostly mop-up work, which included a scoreless sixth inning in the previous day's Nationals rout. Curiously, the Tigers had announced Jones's unconditional release, along with that of pitcher Harry Coveleski, after Friday's game, but quickly retracted Jones's release the following day.[3]

Whether Johnson, having pitched 26⅔ innings in the past eight days (including a short relief appearance on July 29), was just off his game, or the Tigers had called upon some heretofore untapped collective resolve in taking on the most renowned hurler in baseball is uncertain, but the Tigers appeared to find the immortal Johnson decidedly human that afternoon. Detroit's bats were as hot as the weather, hitting Johnson hard; even more uncharacteristically, Johnson was walking more batters than he struck out. The Tigers reached Johnson for three runs on three hits and a walk in the third inning and, after spotting Washington two runs in the sixth, added three more runs in the seventh on five singles, an error, and a wild pitch. The scrappy Nationals pushed across two more runs in the eighth to narrow the gap to 6-4.

Jones, who walked two batters in the eighth, may have been tiring—his longest outing of the season had been 5⅓ innings of relief in a game back in June—but manager Hughie Jennings allowed him to take the mound in the top of the ninth inning. Howie Shanks promptly opened the inning with a single and the next batter, Doc Lavan, followed with another base hit. Jennings pulled Jones and sent in Hooks Dauss.

Dauss had fared badly in his start against Washington on Friday, but seemed sharper this day, retiring the first two Washington batters he faced. But when Burt Shotton drilled a triple to tie the score and put the go-ahead run on third, the sweltering crowd might have been forgiven a sense of despair. Dauss retired Eddie Foster for the third out, but the damage had been done, and when Detroit failed to score in the bottom of the ninth, the game, knotted now at 6-6, went into extra innings.

What followed from that point seemed to those in the stands and the press box to be an entirely different game. The Tigers, "seem[ing] to have finally become ashamed of themselves,"[4] began to play some very fine baseball. On the mound, Dauss was almost unhittable, setting down Washington batters inning after inning. Back in the game, Johnson had recovered from his poor start and was now mowing down the Tigers, matching Dauss scoreless frame for scoreless frame.

Although their offense had suddenly been stalled, Detroit's defense was keeping the Tigers alive in spectacular fashion. A mighty heave by Cobb in the 13th inning, "one of the best throws from the meadows ever made,"[5] cut down the speedy Clyde Milan attempting to score from second on a single by Lavan. In the 14th inning, shortstop Donie Bush threw two runners out at the plate on balls batted directly at him with the infield drawn in.

Finally, after Dauss had set the Nationals down scoreless for the ninth straight inning, the Tigers came to bat in the bottom of the 18th. "In the golden mellow of the setting sun,"[6] Donie Bush led off with a single. Bob Jones moved Bush to second with a sacrifice bunt. Into the batter's box stepped Cobb, who lined Johnson's final delivery of the afternoon off the glove of Eddie Foster at third for a two-base hit, scoring Bush and giving the Tigers an improbable 7-6 win over the greatest pitcher in baseball.

Johnson's pitching line for the afternoon: 17⅓ innings, 16 hits (only five of them after the eighth inning), eight bases on balls, five strikeouts, and seven runs, all but one of them earned. Hooks Dauss, the winner in relief, had pitched 10 innings, surrendering but five hits and three bases on balls to go with six strikeouts and no runs scored. It was, in the words of one sportswriter, "one of the prettiest duels between pitchers that it has ever been the good fortune for patrons of Navin Field to witness."[7]

Amazingly, all eight position players for Washington played all 27 innings of that day's doubleheader. The same was true for Detroit, except for the catching position: Oscar Stanage started the first game behind the plate, while Tubby Spencer spelled him in the finale.

"For an exhibition of the national pastime in which the ultimate winners had nothing to gain but a worthless victory and the losers were hysterical to win," according to one lyrical account of the game, "the contest was, without question, the greatest ever for the edification of Detroit fandom."[8]

SOURCES

Books

Devereaux, Tom, *The Washington Senators, 1901-1971* (Jefferson, North Carolina: McFarland, 2001).

Kavanagh, Jack, *Walter Johnson: A Life* (South Bend, Indiana: Diamond Communications, 1995).

Thomas, Henry W., *Walter Johnson: Baseball's Big Train* (Washington, D.C.: Phenom Press, 1995).

Newspapers

Flint Daily Journal.

Jackson (Michigan) *Citizen Patriot.*

New York Times.

Saginaw (Michigan) *News.*

Washington Herald.

Washington Post.

NOTES

1   *The Sporting News*, August 8, 1918, 7.

2   Harry Bullion, "Tigers Beat Washington in Eighteenth Inning of Sensational Diamond Bout," *Detroit Free Press*, August 5, 1918, 9.

3   *The Sporting News*, August 8, 1918, 7.

4   Ibid.

5   Bullion.

6   Ibid.

7   Ibid.

8   Ibid.

CHARLIE ROBERTSON'S PERFECT GAME

April 30, 1922: Chicago White Sox 2, Detroit Tigers 0 at Navin Field

By David L. Fleitz

ON SUNDAY, APRIL 30, 1922, MORE than 25,000 fans packed Navin Field to see the Tigers play the Chicago White Sox. Since the crowd exceeded the park's stated capacity of 23,000, Tigers management stretched rope barriers in front of the outfield fence to accommodate the overflow. Special ground rules were instituted for the contest, in which a batter was awarded two bases on a fly ball hit into the standing-room area behind the ropes. With two inexperienced starting pitchers, Detroit's Herman Pillette and Chicago's Charlie Robertson, on the mound, the crowd no doubt expected a high-scoring game.

Charlie Robertson had compiled a mostly uneventful career up to then. He made his debut in 1919, starting one game for the White Sox and lasting only two innings. Robertson spent 1920 and 1921 in Minneapolis, going 18-16 and 17-15 and pitching more than 300 innings each year. This performance earned him an invitation to training camp the following spring, and Robertson pitched so well that White Sox manager Kid Gleason put the 26-year-old in the starting rotation. Robertson's assignment against the Tigers on April 30 was only his fourth start, and fifth appearance, in the major leagues.

The contest started uneventfully, with the crowd hooting its usual insults at the White Sox in general and the rookie pitcher in particular. Robertson ignored the commotion and breezed through the first, striking out Lu Blue, getting George Cutshaw on a popup, and retiring Detroit's player-manager Ty Cobb on a grounder to third. The next three innings followed the same script, with the ever-dangerous Cobb ending the

fourth with a weak fly to Johnny Mostil in left. The rookie pitcher had retired the first 12 batters.

Detroit's Herman Pillette, who like Robertson was pitching in his fifth major-league game, gave up two runs in the second when he walked Harry Hooper, watched Mostil beat out a bunt, and retired Amos Strunk on a sacrifice. Earl Sheely then drove a shot off the glove of Bob Jones at third, scoring both Hooper and Mostil and giving the White Sox a 2-0 lead. There would be no more scoring in the game.

Staked to a lead, Robertson kept the hard-hitting Tigers off the bases. Said Robertson to a reporter several weeks later, "I never was going better in my life than that day. Everything worked properly. I was able to put the ball right where I wanted it. ... You see, it was just perfect concentration of mind and body."[1] Robertson did not know the hitters, but catcher Ray Schalk, who had already caught three no-hitters in his 11-year career, did. He gave the signals and Robertson hit the mark, pitch after pitch.

In the fifth, the trouble started. Robertson disposed of Bobby Veach for his 13th out in a row, but the next batter, Harry Heilmann, protested to home-plate umpire Frank Nallin that Robertson was either discoloring the ball or using some foreign substance. Heilmann demanded that Nallin inspect the ball, but the umpire found nothing wrong. Heilmann went out on a weak bounder to the pitcher, which only made him complain louder. One inning later, Cobb stalked to the mound to examine Robertson's clothing, but once again Nallin and first-base umpire Billy Evans saw no cause for concern. "The irrepressible Tyrus inspected all parts of Robertson's uniform," wrote Irving Vaughan in the *Chicago Tribune*. "He was foiled again, but even after it was all over he still insisted there was something wrong. To a spectator it sounded like the squawk of a trimmed sucker."[2] The Tigers continued to argue, and in the eighth the Detroit manager demanded that Evans check the glove of first baseman Sheely. Evans found nothing and the game resumed, though Cobb took a ball out of play to send to the league office for inspection.

The mood of the Detroit crowd changed markedly by the start of the eighth inning. Until then the fans had booed the rookie pitcher with their usual lusty exuberance, but after the Chicago right-hander had retired the first 21 Tigers in succession, they did an about-face. Now the Detroiters started pulling for Robertson to complete the rarest of pitching feats. When Veach opened the eighth by taking a called third strike and Heilmann rolled a weak grounder to Eddie Collins at second, the crowd became strangely quiet. Jones drove a grounder to Sheely at first to end the inning, bringing an excited cheer rolling from the stands. The fans had shifted their allegiance to Robertson, and waited impatiently for Pillette to retire the White Sox in the top of the ninth.

Cobb, anxious to break the spell, sent two left-handed pinch-hitters to the plate in the ninth. Danny Clark, batting for shortstop Topper Rigney, struck out, Robertson's sixth whiff of the game. Clyde Manion popped out to Collins, and then Johnny Bassler, batting for Pillette, stepped to the plate.

Robertson said later that he did not fully realize that he was one out from perfection until Bassler stepped in. "It suddenly dawned on me," Robertson said, "that I was standing right on the brink of the thing. … I turned and walked over to [Eddie] Mulligan, who was playing on the infield in that game. 'Do you realize that that funny little fat guy is the only thing between me and a perfect game?'"[3] Mulligan turned the pitcher around and gave him a push back to the mound. "I went in and served one up," he said, "the fat guy swung and the ball sailed into Mostil's hands in the outfield."[4] The fifth perfect game in major-league history was complete.

Onlookers claimed that they had never heard such a roar for an opposing player. Some of the Detroit fans gave Robertson the ultimate honor when they caught up to the pitcher before he had crossed the first-base line on the way to the dugout. They hoisted Robertson on their shoulders and carried him off the field.

Most no-hitters require at least one spectacular fielding play to keep the streak of hitless batters alive, but Robertson's effort did not. Only six balls were hit to the outfield, and the only mild threat came in the second inning, when Mostil reached into the roped-off section of the crowd in deep left and snagged a fly off the bat of Bobby Veach. Many later game accounts credit Mostil with a spectacular catch, but as Harry Bullion of the *Detroit Free Press* reported, "The crowd in that sector spread to make the Sox left fielder's feat easy to perform."[5] Fifteen batters were retired on the infield, and six Tigers struck out, including Cobb. According to Irving Vaughan of the *Chicago Tribune*, "When Cobb was at bat in the seventh, he did a lot of talking about the alleged soiled ball, and he was so centered on that subject that he neglected to connect when the third strike went floating by."[6]

Unofficially, Robertson threw only 90 pitches, and as Bullion wrote, "He never was in the hole to a batter and consequently did not feel obliged to groove a pitch to avoid passing a man."[7] Though Cobb, still complaining to anyone who would listen, delivered some game balls to the league office, the baseball world celebrated the rookie's feat. Robertson's total dominance led historian John Thorn to call his performance "perhaps the most perfect game ever pitched."[8]

Robertson ended his rookie season with a 14-15 record for the fifth-place White Sox. He never came close to matching his one spectacular game, and by 1924 a chronic sore arm spelled the eventual end of his career. He struggled for several years, bouncing from the majors to the minors, and after losing 19 games for Milwaukee in 1930, Robertson left the game and returned to his native Texas. He ended his major-league stay with 49 wins and 80 losses, easily one of the least impressive career logs of any perfect-game pitcher.

Thirty-four years went by before another major leaguer matched Robertson's feat. When Don Larsen threw his perfect game in the 1956 World Series, fans naturally wondered whatever became of Charlie Robertson. A reporter for the *New York Times* located Robertson in Texas, where the ex-pitcher was self-employed as a pecan broker. Robertson, then 60, had long since left baseball behind. "My game didn't make much of a lasting impression on me," he said. "If I had known then what I know now it would never have happened to me. I wouldn't have been in baseball. … There's nothing wrong with professional athletics as such, you understand. But when they get through with an athlete he has to start over at an age when it's the wrong time to be starting."[9]

Charlie Robertson, who threw major-league baseball's fifth perfect game, died in Texas in 1984 at the age of 88. Five weeks later, Mike Witt of the California Angels threw baseball's 11th perfect game, against the Texas Rangers.

SOURCES

Websites

Chicago Baseball Museum (chicagobaseballmuseum.org)

NOTES

1 Robert F. Kelly, "The Perfect Game That Rookie Robertson Pitched," *Literary Digest*, May 27, 1922, 54.

2 *Chicago Tribune*, May 1, 1922.

3 Kelly, 54-56.

4 Kelly, 56.

5 *Detroit Free Press*, May 1, 1922.

6 *Chicago Tribune*, May 1, 1922.

7 *Detroit Free Press*, May 1, 1922.

8 James Buckley Jr., *Perfect: The Inside Story of Baseball's Twenty Perfect Games* (Chicago: Triumph Books, 2012), 52.

9 *New York Times*, October 10, 1956.

THE DAY ALL HELL BROKE LOOSE

June 13, 1924: New York Yankees 10 (9), Detroit Tigers 6 (0) at Navin Field

By Mike Lynch

ON JUNE 10, 1924, THE NEW YORK Yankees and Detroit Tigers stood only a game apart in the standings, the Yankees tied for first place with the surprising Boston Red Sox, the Tigers in third place only a game back. The Tigers were eight games into a 21-game homestand when they hosted the Yankees for the first time all season on June 11. Earl Whitehill, a 25-year-old left-hander in his first full season, tossed a complete-game gem at the Bronx Bombers, beating them 7-2, and pulled the Tigers into a virtual tie for first place, only .008 percentage points behind Boston and New York.

The game on the 12th was a different story; Detroit manager and center fielder Ty Cobb tabbed another left-hander, Bert Cole, to stifle the Yanks, but Babe Ruth belted his 15th home run of the season to lead New York to a 10-4 rout, and Cole was out of the game after only five batters.

The match-up of the 13th pitted New York's Sad Sam Jones, a 21-game winner in 1923, against Ulysses Simpson Grant "Lil" Stoner, a slight right-hander who had won 27 games in the Texas League in 1923 after a brief and unsuccessful stint with Detroit in 1922. Stoner went into the game with a 7-4 record but had struggled in his previous eight starts, pitching to a 5.43 ERA in 61⅓ innings since May 6. Jones, on the other hand, had lost his last start on June 9 to fall to 3-3, but had reduced his earned run average from 27.00 on April 16 to 4.37 on June 9.

There was animosity between the teams that had festered since late May when Tigers first baseman Lu Blue and Yankees infielder Mike McNally nearly came to blows at Yankee Stadium after Blue accused McNally of interfering on a play at first. The combatants were separated by a Tigers coach but Yankees first sacker Wally Pipp also intervened in case Blue

threw a punch. Tigers third baseman Fred Haney took exception to Pipp's involvement and "leaped at" Pipp's neck before both benches emptied on to the field. Blue and McNally were ejected and the game continued without further incident.[1]

The Tigers were led by two-time batting champ Harry Heilmann, who was batting .366 and had two more batting titles ahead of him, and Ty Cobb, who at 37 was still among the best hitters in baseball and proving it with a .356 mark. Ruth paced the Yankees at .365 and Bob Meusel came into the contest batting .350.

According to the *New York Times*, the 18,000 at Navin Field on the 13th were already in a foul mood when the game began. "The temper of the crowd had not been good from the first inning," wrote the *Times*.[2] The Yankees scored three runs in the top of the second, but the Tigers countered with two in the bottom of the inning. New York plated three more in the third to take a 6-2 lead and knocked Stoner from the box.

Cobb called on Bert Cole for the second straight game and Cole was fantastic until the seventh inning. Two more runs in both the fifth and sixth innings pulled Detroit even, and Jones was sent to the showers. Milt Gaston took the hill for the Yanks and stifled Detroit's offense, allowing one hit over the final three innings. Cole was solid in his 6⅓ innings of work, surrendering four runs on four hits and three walks, while fanning three.

He also hit a batter and that's where things went sideways.

From the *New York Times*:

"The game between the New York Yankees and Detroit Tigers came to an unexpected end this afternoon when 18,000 spectators stormed the field and started a riot which involved the police, the players and the employees of the park. It was a free-for-all fight, with the police, endeavoring to distinguish rival fighters, only making the fight more complicated and more intense."[3]

The Yankees pushed four runs across in the top of the seventh and held a 10-6 lead going into the ninth when all hell broke loose. During New York's seventh-inning rally Ruth stiff-armed Cole on a play at first, and Cole took exception. When Ruth came to bat in the ninth, Cole hurled two offerings that The Bambino barely escaped, including one aimed at his head. He fouled out to Blue and that brought up Meusel. Depending on whom you believe, Meusel either took a Cole pitch to the back or the ribs and "the storm broke."[4]

The *Los Angeles Times* wrote that Meusel "threw down his bat and strode slowly out to the pitcher's eminence," at which time words were exchanged before Meusel threw a wild punch that missed Cole, who smiled and ducked under a second wild swing.[5] The *New York Times* reported that Meusel "dashed" to the mound, took a swing at Cole and was restrained by umpires Billy Evans and Red Ormsby before he could throw a second punch.[6]

Both benches entered the fray. Ruth "crashed into the group of players and arbiters, swinging both his fists," and exchanged heated words with Cobb[7] before being pushed toward his dugout by Ormsby and dragged away by Yankees skipper Miller Huggins and other Yankees.[8] Police left the stands and jumped onto the field just in case things got out of hand, which they eventually did.[9] The full-throated crowd gave the Yankees a tongue-lashing as Meusel, having been ejected from the game, left the field with his glove in hand.[10]

Fans from the lower levels were practically begging for a reason to get involved and they needn't wait long. Meusel, escorted from the field by teammate Bullet Joe Bush, made his way to the Tigers' dugout where he started another fight. Fred Haney, who stuck up for Lu Blue in the May fracas, countered with a punch at the much larger Yankee.[11]

"By this time the disorder was general and all Yankee and Tiger players were fighting among themselves," wrote the *Chicago Tribune*.[12] Players from both

Ruth and Cobb in a lighter moment

teams rushed to the Tigers' dugout to get their licks in. Wally Pipp allegedly brought a bat with him.[13]

Fans began streaming onto the field and engaged police. "The fans had now started to fight with the bluecoats," wrote the *New York Times*, "and the mob, ever increasing in numbers, completely covered the diamond."[14] The police were outnumbered and barely contained the throng, described as a "surging mass of bobbing straw hats and swinging fists,"[15] but were able to clear a path so the Yankees could safely reach the clubhouse.

Reserves were called in to help quell the uprising, and arrests were made, but fans refused to leave the field and Billy Evans determined that the game couldn't continue. He declared a forfeit, giving the Yankees a 9-0 win.

Ruth insisted that Cole was purposely throwing at the Yankees.[16] The *Boston Globe's* Mel Webb speculated that the Yankees were feeling pressure from the Red Sox and Tigers, had "chips on their shoulders," and were so used to receiving postseason checks that they'd do just about anything to keep getting bonuses.[17] "Every time it looks as if the going would be hard and that someone else might get the pennant the New York players don't like it a bit. You bet they don't," wrote Webb.[18]

Meusel and Cole were suspended indefinitely by American League President Ban Johnson and neither played again until June 24.

NOTES

1 *New York Times*, May 26, 1924.

2 *New York Times*, June 14, 1924.

3 Ibid.

4 One article in the *New York Times* claimed Meusel was hit in the ribs, while another in the same paper reported he was hit in the back. The *Los Angeles Times* said it was in the ribs, but the *Chicago Tribune* said it was in the back.

5 *Los Angeles Times*, June 14, 1924.

6 *New York Times*, June 14, 1924.

7 *Los Angeles Times*, June 14, 1924.

8 *New York Times*, June 14, 1924.

9 Ibid.

10 Ibid.

11 *Chicago Tribune*, June 14, 1924.

12 Ibid.

13 *Los Angeles Times*, June 14, 1924.

14 *New York Times*, June 14, 1924.

15 Ibid.

16 *Chicago Tribune*, June 14, 1924.

17 *Boston Globe*, June 14, 1924.

18 Ibid.

"...WILD AS BEDLAM."

June 2, 1925: Detroit Tigers 16, Chicago White Sox 15 at Navin Field

By Gregory H. Wolf

IN WHAT WAS DESCRIBED BY BERT Walker of the *Detroit Times* as "one of the most vicious slugfests seen on the local diamond this year," the Detroit Tigers and the Chicago White Sox combined for 43 hits and 31 runs at Navin Field in the Motor City on Tuesday, June 2, 1925. The Tigers enjoyed a seemingly insurmountable 15-5 lead at the end of six innings, until the White Sox made what James Crusenberry of the *Chicago Daily Tribune* called "one of the greatest uphill fights ever seen" to tie the game in the ninth. The stage was set for the Bengals' 38-year-old player-manager Ty Cobb. "The prayers of the fans were answered," wrote Walker, as the Georgia Peach blasted a walk-off homer to give the home team an exciting 16-15 victory.

Detroit entered the game in sixth place with a disappointing 19-26 record, but was arguably the hottest team in baseball. They had won 10 of their last 13, averaging an eye-popping 9.6 runs per game in their victories. The Tigers continued their offensive juggernaut against player-manager Eddie Collins's South Siders. Chicago had finished in last place in 1924, but was a surprise team in 1925 with a record of 23-19, good for third place. Following an exciting conclusion to the first contest of the clubs' three-game series the day before (Detroit's Frank O'Rourke belted a walk-off, two-run clout in the ninth),[1] the Tigers jumped on Chicago starter Sloppy Thurston, considered the "star of the Sox staff," for four runs in the first inning, highlighted by RBI doubles by O'Rourke, Cobb, and right fielder Harry Heilmann, who had blistered opponents for a .553 average (21-for-38) in his previous 10 games.[2] (Heilmann finished the 1925 season with a .393 batting average to capture his third crown in five years.)

Detroit's starter, Hooks Dauss, a 35-year-old right-hander in his 14th campaign, was aiming for his 200th career victory. He breezed through the first four innings, yielding only one run when third baseman Willie Kamm smashed a towering solo shot "over the scoreboard" in left field in the fourth.[3] Dauss helped his own cause in the bottom of the fourth by belting a two-run double to increase the Tigers' lead to 6-1, and later scored on left fielder Al Wingo's single for a six-run cushion.[4]

Chicago made the game interesting in the top of the fifth when 38-year-old manager and second sacker Eddie Collins smashed a double off the scoreboard, driving in two runs. Following a one-out walk to left fielder Bibb Falk, right fielder Harry Hooper and Kamm belted consecutive run-scoring singles to make it 7-5 and drive Dauss from the mound. With two on and one out, lefty Ed "Satchelfoot" Wells set down the next two batters to put out the fire.

The Tigers' onslaught continued in the fifth and sixth innings. Heilmann led off with a walk, moved to second on a sacrifice, and scored on catcher Larry Woodall's two-out single.[5] Reliever Wells and third baseman Fred Haney followed with run-scoring triples to make the score 10-3 and send Thurston to the showers. O'Rourke greeted right-handed reliever Frank Mack with a monstrous blast to "deep center" for two more runs. (Thurston was charged with a career-high 11 runs, 10 earned.)[6] Wingo and Cobb followed with singles, but the inning ended when Cobb was caught in a rundown on what Bert Walker described as an attempted double steal.[7] After Wells held the visitors scoreless in the sixth, the Bengals went back to work, loading the bases with two outs. Haney singled, his fourth hit of the game, driving in two runs. O'Rourke followed with a run-scoring single for a 15-5 lead.

But the game was far from over. "The desperate Sox kept battling back against heavy odds," wrote Walker.[8] "A lot of folk," noted Crusinberry, "had gone home to supper thinking the Tigers were so far ahead, they couldn't be caught," and consequently missed an exciting comeback in the top of the seventh when Chicago exploded for seven runs. Four of the first five White Sox batters of the inning clouted extra-base hits off Wells, accounting for three runs. The beleaguered hurler was finally removed after surrendering consecutive two-out singles with the score 15-9. "The pitchers seemed equally bad," quipped H.G. Salsinger of the *Detroit News*, and added, "(T)he heat must have effected *(sic)* the pitchers."[9] The White Sox had no mercy on reliever Lil Stoner, who could not register an out. Cleanup hitter Earl Sheely rapped an RBI double and Falk slashed a single over second base, scoring two more runs to pull within three, 15-12. "Pitchers came and went all afternoon," wrote Crusinberry. "One felt sorry for them." Lefty Bert Cole relieved Stoner and erased Hooper to end the inning.

The ninth inning began with the score 15-12, but Cole could not close the deal. With the bases loaded and one out, Hooper hit a long sacrifice fly to Heilmann in right field to drive in Collins and end Cole's afternoon. In a career day, Willie Kamm greeted Detroit's fifth pitcher, Jess Doyle, with his fourth hit, a double, to drive in his fourth and fifth runs and tie the score.

Due to bat second in the ninth inning was Ty Cobb. Once the game's biggest attraction, Cobb had seen his star eclipsed by Babe Ruth, whose home-run-hitting exploits had singlehandedly changed baseball and demonstratively announced the end of the Deadball Era. The two had a heated rivalry that reached its nadir when they brawled during a game at Navin Field on June 13, 1924. "The Babe was a great ballplayer," once said Hall of Famer Tris Speaker, "but Cobb was even greater. Babe could knock your brains out, but Cobb would drive you crazy."[10] In his fifth season as player-manager, Cobb announced before the season that he planned to play in only 75 to 100 games (down from

155 in 1924) to conserve his body. In spring training he suffered from a severe case of the flu and made only one appearance, as a pinch-hitter, in the Tigers' first 12 games. It had seemed as though Cobb were on his last legs. Ever competitive, Cobb once claimed he could be a home run hitter like Ruth, but preferred to hit for average.[11] Almost as if to prove his point, Cobb belted five home runs and drove in 11 runs in two games on May 5 and 6, 1925. It was the first time a big leaguer hit five homers in consecutive games since Cap Anson in August 1884.

With the score tied and fans eerily quiet, Cobb stepped to the plate in the ninth inning with one out and promptly took three balls from Chicago reliever Ted Blankenship. After looking at two strikes, Cobb moved his bat on the sixth pitch. Cobb "swung from his hips to his shoulders," exclaimed Crusinberry. "The ball went on a straight line to right center and cleared the screen" for a dramatic walk-off solo shot.[12] Cobb's blast was "undoubtedly the longest hit he has ever made on the Detroit lot," opined Detroit sportswriter Salsinger.[13] The fans were "wild as bedlam," wrote Crusenberry.[14] Reported Bill Walker, Cobb "trotted around the bases, being halted at intervals on the way by a crowd that thronged on the field to shake hands with him."

Cobb's "heroic homer," the Tigers' 22nd hit of the game, gave the victory to Doyle (3-1) and saddled Blankenship with the loss (1-5) in the highest-scoring game (combined runs for both teams) of the season for both clubs.[15] Newspapers remarked about the game's length, 3 hours, 2 minutes, which proved to be the longest nine-inning game in the AL in 1925. The Tigers played only two games that were longer and the White Sox one; all three were extra-inning games. "Despite the huge score," opined Walker, "it was not a badly played game. Some clever fielding was done and only one error was made by each side. Either the pitching was bad or the hitting sensational."[16] Coincidentally, the Tigers had defeated the White Sox by the same unusual score at Navin Field about 14 years earlier, on June 18, 1911.

Staying true to his promise to play less in 1925, Cobb played in 105 games in the outfield, and also added 16 pinch-hit appearances. In just 415 at-bats, he tied his career high with 12 home runs, arguably none as big as his game-winner on June 12, and finished fourth in batting average (.378).

NOTES

1   James Crusinberry, "O'Rourke's Long Homer in the 9th Beats Faber and Sox, 8 To 6," *Chicago Daily Tribune*, June 2, 1925, 20.

2   John C. Hoffman, "Detroit Crushes Sox; Thurston Driven Off," *Chicago Daily News*, June 3, 1925, II 23. This article provides a play-by-play summary of the entire game and was an invaluable resource.

3   Hoffman.

4   Although the box score for the game on Baseball-Reference.com credits Dauss with just one RBI, contemporary papers credit him with two on his double.

5   Woodall replaced backstop Johnny Bassler in the first inning when the latter injured his hand on a foul tip by cleanup hitter Earl Sheely.

6   Hoffman.

7   Bert Walker, "Tigers Play Sox in Last Game Today," *Detroit News*, June 3, 1925, 18.

8   Walker.

9   H.G. Salsinger, "Tigers Drive Out 99 Hits for 125 Bases in Six Games," *Detroit News*, June 3, 1925, 38.

10 Jim Hawkins, Dan Ewald, and George van Dusen, *Detroit Tigers Encyclopedia* (Champaign, Illinois: Sports Publishing, 2003), 44.

11 Hawkins et al, 45.

12 Crusinberry.

13 Salsinger.

14 Crusinberry.

15 Crusinberry.

16 Walker.

"I'M GLAD TO BE BACK HERE..."

May 10, 1927: Philadelphia Athletics 6,
Detroit Tigers 3 at Navin Field

by Richard Riis

FORTY THOUSAND FANS TURNED OUT at Navin Field on a cloudy and chilly Tuesday afternoon to witness an extraordinary homecoming: Ty Cobb, the greatest Tiger of them all, was returning to Detroit—in the uniform of the visiting team.

The Tigers had fallen from fourth to sixth place in 1926, and to many it may have seemed as if age were finally catching up with the mighty Ty Cobb. Cobb had recovered from eye surgery in March to hit .339, but had played in only 79 games. It was no secret that his managerial style didn't always sit well with his players and that he was often at odds with club owner Frank Navin. Still, it took the baseball world by surprise when Cobb announced on November 3 that he was retiring from the game.

Sportswriters and editorial columnists were still rhapsodizing about Cobb's illustrious career when on November 29 the Cleveland Indians' celebrated player-manager, Tris Speaker, announced that he also was retiring. At 38, Speaker was still a productive player, and had just managed the Indians to a second-place finish, three games behind the New York Yankees. "I am taking a vacation from baseball," Speaker said, "that I suspect will last for the remainder of my life."[1]

A few weeks later the reason for the sudden retirement of two of the game's biggest stars became apparent. Baseball Commissioner Kenesaw Mountain Landis made public the shocking claim of Dutch Leonard, a former Tigers pitcher: Leonard, along with Cobb, Speaker, and Cleveland outfielder Joe Wood, had conspired to fix a game between Detroit and Cleveland on September 25, 1919.

The most suggestive evidence came in the form of two letters, one from Wood and one from Cobb, written to Leonard in the fall of 1919 alluding to wagers. In a hearing before Landis, Cobb and Wood admitted to having written the letters, but the gambling references, they claimed, involved horse racing. Leonard's accusations, Cobb contended, were in retaliation for his having waived Leonard to the Pacific Coast League back in 1925. Speaker denied any wrongdoing, but under considerable pressure from American League President Ban Johnson, Cobb and Speaker agreed to retire.

The alleged fix became major news across America. Newspapers were filled with stories and speculation. A few sports columnists castigated Cobb and Speaker, but many, many more attacked Leonard for sullying the good names of two of baseball's most lionized figures. Humorist Will Rogers put it for like-minded baseball fans across the country in a piece he wrote for the *New York Times*: "If they'd been selling out all these years I would have liked to have seen them play when they wasn't selling."[2]

Cobb professed his innocence in no uncertain terms. "I have been in baseball for 22 years. I have played the game as hard and square and clean as any man ever did. All I thought of was to win. My conscience is clear."[3]

When Leonard refused to travel to Chicago in January to face Cobb and Speaker at another hearing, Landis, having no good evidence upon which to ban the two stars, and undoubtedly feeling the pressure of a decidedly pro-player public and press, ruled that the pair had been officially cleared, stating, "These players have not been, nor are they now, found guilty of fixing a ball game. By no decent system of justice could such finding be made."[4]

Landis reinstated Cobb and Speaker to their former clubs, but the Tigers and Indians, in turn, chose to give each his unconditional release. Speaker signed with the Washington Senators. Cobb accepted an offer from

Philadelphia Athletics owner and manager Connie Mack for a salary reported at $40,000, with a $25,000 signing bonus and $10,000 in other bonuses,[5] making Cobb, at $75,000, the highest paid player in baseball.[6] Cobb was quoted as saying he returned only to seek vindication, and so that he could say he left baseball on his own terms.[7]

If it was vindication he was seeking, Cobb was surely finding it in Philadelphia: A month into the season he was hitting a robust .408, the second highest average in the league, and was averaging better than one run scored per game. He had hit safely in 10 straight games coming into the series with Detroit.

An on-field dust-up in Philadelphia involving Cobb, teammate Al Simmons, and members of the Boston Red Sox had moved Ban Johnson to fine and suspend Cobb and Simmons on May 6. Public outcry, however, and pressure from highly placed individuals planning for Cobb's homecoming, persuaded Johnson to lift the ban on the morning the Athletics arrived in Detroit.

And so it was that a delegation of dignitaries led by Detroit Mayor John W. Smith was there to greet Cobb and the Athletics as they stepped off a steamer from Cleveland on the morning of May 10. A testimonial luncheon honoring Cobb was held at noon, followed by a parade to the ballpark headed by a police motorcycle escort and a military band.

In pregame ceremonies broadcast by a local radio station, Cobb was presented with an assortment of gifts including a giant floral horseshoe, a silver serving set, and a new automobile. A handful of speeches from dignitaries and a few words of appreciation from Cobb were boomed to the crowd through a microphone placed at home plate. As the players warmed up, Cobb clinched his warm welcome when, after catching a fly ball, he tossed it over the screen into the bleachers in right field.

Cobb, batting third in the lineup, stepped into the batter's box in the first inning to a lusty roar from the crowd. He responded by driving a pitch from Earl Whitehill down the right-field line for a double, moving Eddie Collins, who had walked to lead off the game, to third. Collins and Cobb then scored on a single to center by Simmons, giving the Athletics a 2-0 lead. The game had to be held up for several minutes in the bottom half of the inning as Cobb walked back and forth in front of the bleachers, signing autographs and soaking up applause.

In the third inning Cobb drew a base on balls but advanced no further than second; in the fourth he struck out to retire the side. In the field, Cobb thrilled the crowd with two catches that were "distinctly spectacular,"[8] once going into the overflow crowd to pull down a high fly off the bat of Jack Warner and again in snaring a liner off the bat of Lu Blue while running at top speed diagonally across the field.

In the seventh inning Cobb drove the ball hard between short and third, but Tigers shortstop Jackie Tavener got a glove on it and threw out Bill Lamar, who was steaming toward third. Cobb, safe at first, was removed from the game to thunderous applause. Walter French came in to run for Cobb and afterward replaced him in right field.

Lefty Grove had the game well in hand for Philadelphia most of the afternoon, surrendering one run in the third inning and little else as the Athletics breezed to a 3-1 lead. Whitehill had recovered after the first inning, being touched for only one more run until he was removed for a pinch-hitter in the bottom of the eighth. Philadelphia roughed up reliever Rip Collins for three runs on four hits, so that it mattered little that Grove struggled a bit in the bottom of the ninth. The Tigers, entering the inning with a five-run deficit, bunched two hits, an error, and a walk for two more runs before Grove regrouped and retired the last three batters to seal a 6-3 victory for the Athletics.

"I'm glad to be back here, even if I do appear with the visiting team," Cobb told the assembled press corps. "I will always have a soft spot for Detroit fandom and my many fine friends here who have done so much for me."[9]

SOURCES

Books

Alexander, Charles C., *Ty Cobb* (New York: Oxford University Press, 1985).

Holmes, Dan, *Ty Cobb: A Biography* (Westport, Connecticut: Greenwood Press, 2004).

Rhodes, Don, *Ty Cobb: Safe at Home* (Guilford, Connecticut: Globe Pequot Press, 2008).

Newspapers

Detroit Free Press.

Detroit Tribune.

Philadelphia Inquirer.

Websites

Baseball-reference.com.

NOTES

1   Henry P. Edwards, "Happy Jack Best Bet to Follow Speaker as Next Indian Pilot," *Cleveland Plain Dealer*, November 30, 1926, 1.

2   Will Rogers, "Will Rogers' Christmas Advice and a Tribute to Ty and Tris," *New York Times*, December 24, 1926, 12.

3   "Baseball Scandal Up Again, With Cobb and Speaker Named," *New York Times*, December 22, 1926, 17.

4   "Cobb and Speaker Cleared by Landis in Baseball Probe," *New York Evening Post*, January 27, 1927, 1.

5   "Athletics Get Cobb for $75,000 for Year," *New York Times*, February 9, 1927, 14.

6   Ibid.

7   Ty Cobb and Al Stump, *My Life in Baseball: The True Record,* (New York: Doubleday, 1961), 248.

8   Sam Greene, "Cobb Is Still Cobb, Detroiters Agree," *The Sporting News*, May 19, 1927, 1.

9   William M. Anderson, *The Glory Years of the Tigers: 1920-1950* (Detroit: Wayne State University Press, 2012), 71.

HEILMANN TAKES TITLE ON SEASON-ENDING SPREE

October 2, 1927: Cleveland Indians 5, Detroit Tigers 4 at Navin Field (Second Game of Doubleheader)

By Chip Mundy

HARRY HEILMANN ENTERED THE FINAL day of the 1927 regular season in a tight race for the AL batting championship. He had been in a similar situation just two years earlier.

In 1925 Heilmann surpassed veteran Cleveland Indians center fielder Tris Speaker with six hits in a season-ending doubleheader at Sportsman's Park in St. Louis to jump his average from .388 to .393. Speaker, who did not play the final day, finished second to Heilmann at .389.

On October 2, 1927, it was Al Simmons of the Philadelphia Athletics who was in the batting race with Tigers right fielder Heilmann, and the season-ending doubleheader was played against the Indians at Navin Field in Detroit. The Tigers were playing a doubleheader because the game the previous day had been rained out. Meanwhile, Simmons was closing out his season with a game against the Senators in Washington.

Simmons, in his fourth major-league season, had led the league in hitting for most of the year, but he missed six weeks from late July until early September with a groin tear. He was hitting .393 when he sustained the groin injury sliding into second base on July 24, and Heilmann was at .364 that day.

Heilmann, a 33-year-old right-handed hitter in his 13th big-league season, was known as Slug. Heilmann was a notoriously slow runner, which made his batting averages all the more impressive, and that triggered the nickname.

Slug worked his way into the batting race with a torrid August while Simmons was out with the injury. Heilmann hit an eye-popping .505 (49-for-97) and had 19 walks and just one strikeout as he posted an unbelievable slugging percentage of .814 and an off-the-charts OPS of 1.401 in August. (The OPS figure is retrospective; OPS, the sum of a player's on-base percentage and slugging average, was not a compiled at that time.)

Heilmann caught and passed Simmons on Sept. 17, but his lead lasted for just three days as Simmons regained the lead. Heilmann grabbed the lead again for three days in the final week, but Simmons took charge with five hits in a doubleheader the day before the season finales to boost his average to .392. Heilmann was a shade back at .391 going into the final day.

Simmons stayed at .392 on the final day by going 2-for-5 against the Senators. Meanwhile, Heilmann went 4-for-5 with six RBIs off Indians right-hander George Grant in the first game of the doubleheader. Grant, 24, had been used exclusively in relief for three months and had not started a game since July 1, when he lasted 2⅓ innings against the Tigers in a 10-5 Detroit victory.

Heilmann touched Grant quickly with an RBI double in the first inning and a three-run double in the third. He grounded out to third in the fifth, reached base on a bunt single in the sixth, and belted a two-run homer in the eighth to cap the Tigers' 11-5 victory.

The six RBIs established a career high for Heilmann. It also was the 53rd time he collected at least four hits in a game, and it was the eighth time he accomplished it in 1927. At the end of the first game, Heilmann's average, at .395, had surpassed Simmons's .392, making it possible for Harry to sit out the second game of the doubleheader and win the batting title.

Heilmann decided to play, and the Detroit fans loved the decision.

"Every man, woman, and child in the park cheered him as he went out to right field at the start of the game," Frederick G. Lieb wrote two decades later.[1]

The Indians had 29-year-old left-hander Garland Buckeye on the mound for the second game. Buckeye — there could be no better name for a player on a team in Ohio — had made five starts against the Tigers in 1927 before the season finale. He was 2-3 with a 4.25 ERA against Detroit, including a tough 1-0 loss to Rip Collins on May 31.

Heilmann had enjoyed some success against Buckeye in 1927, and he came into the game hitting .432 (63-for-146) against left-handers in 1927. In five previous games against Buckeye in 1927, Heilmann had hit .375 (6-for-16), including a three-run homer in their most recent meeting, on July 3.

Buckeye, like George Grant in game one, was no match for Heilmann on this Sunday afternoon in Detroit.

Heilmann walked in the first, singled to left in the third, smacked a two-run homer in the fifth, and ripped an RBI double in the seventh. Still, the Indians held a 4-3 lead going into the bottom of the ninth inning.

The Tigers quickly tied it when second baseman Charlie Gehringer reached on an error by shortstop Joe Sewell and scored when Buckeye messed up a sacrifice bunt by Art Ruble. That brought Slug to the plate with the game on the line.

The stage was set for a final heroic act by Heilmann, who was a triple away from the cycle. Ruble was on first base as the potential winning run, and a home run would put an exclamation point on Heilmann's great final day of the season.

It was one of just two times in 10 plate appearances that day that Heilmann failed to come through.

Perhaps trying to hit the game-winning homer, Heilmann swung mightily at a pitch and lined a grounder back to Buckeye, who started a 1-4-3 double play. Meanwhile, Heilmann had fallen to his knees in pain; he had hurt himself while swinging. At first it was feared that he had broken his leg, but he managed to limp back to the dugout with assistance, and an

examination after the game showed that the injury was not serious.

But the game wasn't over. It was still tied with two out and nobody on base. Now the Tigers had some magic of their own left. Bob Fothergill and third baseman Jack Warner hit consecutive doubles with Warner's hit giving Detroit a 5-4 victory.

The Tigers had used pitchers recently out of college to start both ends of the doubleheader. Josh Billings, 19, in his first pro season out of Brown University, had been called up in August, and he pitched a complete game in the opener of the doubleheader to bump his record to 5-4.

Left-hander Rufus Smith, 22, from Guilford College in Greensboro, North Carolina, made his major-league debut in the second game and hurled eight innings. He left the game after Al Wingo pinch-hit for him in the bottom of the eighth inning. Ownie Carroll, a 24-year-old right-hander in just his second major-league season out of Holy Cross, pitched a scoreless ninth inning for the Tigers and picked up the win to improve to 10-6.

The sweep, however, was secondary to the fans. It clearly was Heilmann's day.

"The crowd realized that victory or defeat meant nothing to the final standing and concentrated their cheering on behalf of Heilmann," *The Sporting News* wrote. "Whenever he came to the plate he was applauded, and when he responded with a base hit the applause became more general. Once the crowd rose to boo Garland Buckeye because they thought he was going to pass Heilmann purposely and then deprive him of the opportunity for a base hit."[2]

Heilmann had an amazing seven hits in the doubleheader and reached base eight times in 10 plate appearances as he won his fourth AL batting championship — and led both leagues — with a .398 average. One more hit during the season would have raised his average to .400 for the second time in his career. (Heilmann had hit .403 in 1923.)

Heilmann's batting title was the 16th in 21 years won by a member of the Tigers. Ty Cobb led the way with 11, while Heilmann had four and Heinie Manush one. Heilmann became the first right-handed hitter to win four batting championships, breaking a tie with Nap Lajoie.

Each of Heilmann's four batting titles came in successive odd-numbered years (1921, 1923, 1925, and 1927).

"(Tigers owner) Mr. (Frank) Navin gives me contracts on a two-year basis," Heilmann told a reporter who pointed out his habit of winning batting titles every other year. "I always bear down real hard when a new contract is coming up."[3]

It was fitting that Heilmann enjoyed his big day during a doubleheader sweep at Michigan and Trumbull. He hit .471 in games won by the Tigers and .434 at Navin Field in 1927.

SOURCES

Alexander, Charles C., *Ty Cobb* (New York: Oxford University Press, 1984).

Lieb, Frederick G., *Detroit Tigers* (New York: G.P. Putnam's Sons, 1946).

Skipper, James K., Jr., *Baseball Nicknames: A Dictionary of Origins and Meanings* (Jefferson, North Carolina: McFarland & Company, 2011).

Detroit Times

NOTES

1 Frederick G. Lieb, *Detroit Tigers* (New York: G.P. Putnam's Sons, 1946), 186.

2 "Heilmann Upholds Detroit Tradition," *The Sporting News*, October 13, 1927, 7.

3 "Heilmann Is Dead; Baseball Star, 56," *New York Times*, July 10, 1951.

THE G-MEN PULL OFF THE MIRACLE ON MICHIGAN

July 14, 1934: Detroit Tigers 12, New York Yankees 11 at Navin Field

By Jeffrey Koslowski

THE 1934 SEASON BEGAN WITH MINIMAL fanfare for the Detroit Tigers outside of Corktown. The Washington Senators were projected to repeat as American League champions with the Bengals expected to come in behind the New York Yankees and Boston Red Sox in fourth place. Despite this, new player-manager Mickey Cochrane was entirely optimistic. "We have as good a chance as any club," he insisted.[1] Second baseman Charlie Gehringer reiterated his manager's optimism, calling the 1934 squad "the best in ten years."[2]

A 6-2 start saw the Tigers near the top of the American League at the end of April. By the 13th of May they had slipped to 5½ games behind New York. But a 14-7 stretch enabled them to catch the Yankees on June 5.

The two teams then swapped the lead back and forth for the next month. But with Lou Gehrig, Babe Ruth, and Lefty Gomez still producing, Detroit would have to play determined baseball to keep pace. A key four-game series in Detroit starting on Thursday, July 12, could prove decisive in determining the fates of both clubs. The Tigers were only a half-game behind the Yankees.

The series lived up to its potential from the start. The Tigers took the first game, 4-2, with Schoolboy Rowe giving up only six hits for his 10th win of the season. Babe Ruth went 0-for-4 and was said by a writer covering the game to have been lacking his "old wrist slap."[3] The Yankees fought back the next day, however, with a 4-2 victory of their own that saw Gehrig leave in the second inning with "an attack of lumbago."[4] Ruth shook off the previous game by

hitting his 700th home run. As Saturday approached, the Yankees still held a half-game lead over the Tigers.

A crowd of 22,500 crammed into Navin Field with some even sitting in temporary bleachers set up along the warning track, which meant special ground rules had to be established. The *New York Times* sportswriter covering the game was not pleased with this special arrangement, stating that Babe Ruth was "almost impaled on one of the temporary fence posts," and referring to the seating as "unnecessary" and "only complicating matters."[5]

Lou Gehrig had a short day's work on Saturday, starting at shortstop instead of his usual first base, leading off with a single, then being lifted for a pinch-runner so he could return "to his hotel quarters."[6] This was Gehrig's 1,427th consecutive game. It was clear that the lumbago that had been hampering him the day before had not yet subsided. The Yankees followed Gehrig's hit with three more and scored four runs before the inning was out. Tigers starting pitcher Vic Sorrell, who pitched his entire major-league career wearing an Old English D, was relieved after just one-third of an inning and replaced with Elden Auker.

"Ruppert's Riflemen" continued their offensive onslaught in the third inning when third baseman Frankie Crosetti singled in two more runs to extend the Yankees' lead to 6-0. After a Charlie Gehringer single brought in Goose Goslin with the Tigers' first run, Babe Ruth returned to bat for the Yankees in the fourth inning and, with two men on, sent an Auker offering into the Tigers faithful to give the Yankees a 9-1 advantage. The home run was the 701th of his career and the last one he hit at Navin Field.

With an eight-run cushion, all seemed to be going the Yankees' way, especially with their ace, Lefty Gomez, on the mound. The 1934 campaign was Gomez's finest as he finished the year with career records in wins (26-5) and earned-run average (2.33). When the fourth inning began, however, the tide turned in favor of Detroit. Hank Greenberg led off with a double and helped the Tigers tally three runs to cut the Yankees' lead to five runs. The fifth inning started just as well for the Tigers as Gehringer and Billy Rogell led off with doubles. Yankees manager Joe McCarthy, having seen enough, replaced Gomez with reliever Jimmie DeShong. Gomez complained of having a cold and, as the *New York Times* reported, "pitched as if he had one."[7] DeShong, in his first full season with the Yankees, induced Greenberg to pop out to first and Cochrane, who had inserted himself into the lineup as a pinch-hitter, to ground into a double play and end the Tigers' threat. With another run in, however, Detroit had reduced the Yankees lead to four runs, at 9-5.

The sixth inning saw the third hit of the game by Tigers center fielder Gee Walker. Known for his speed and tenacity on the bases, Walker was labeled by Cochrane as "my type of ball player."[8] His speed could get him into trouble, however, and only two weeks earlier, it nearly cost him his job. On June 30 Walker was picked off of second base in a loss to the St. Louis Browns, causing Cochrane to suspend him and nearly cut him from the roster.[9] The Tigers players voted to bring Walker back despite their manager, who was "angry and sputtered like a wagon load of lighted cannon crackers" at Walker's recent play.[10] Gee's presence in the lineup benefited the Bengals this day, however, as not only did his double score two runs, but he came home later, capping a three-run Tiger sixth inning.

With the seemingly insurmountable eight-run lead cut to a single tally, Cochrane sent pitcher Chief Hogsett to the mound. Hogsett, who was given the nickname "Chief" because he roomed with a Kiowa Indian,[11] gave up a double to Bill Dickey, threw a wild pitch, and watched Frankie Crosetti drill a home run into the stands before giving way to Firpo Marberry.

Greenberg and Gehringer starred on the '34 team

The Yankees threatened but Marberry held them scoreless the rest of the game. The score read 11-8 in favor of the Yankees going into the bottom of the eighth inning, but the Tigers, who the *Free Press* reported won a game "simply because they refused to stay licked," were not ready to give up.[12]

The Tigers seemed poised to take the lead in the eighth inning when they loaded the bases. On third was leadoff hitter Ervin Fox, whose nickname, Pete, was borrowed from Peter Rabbit, a reference to his speed.[13] On second was Goose Goslin, acquired by Cochrane from Washington before the season started in the hopes that his veteran experience on three championship teams would rub off on the young Tigers.[14] Walking to first was Billy Rogell, who would go on to have a personal-best season with 114 runs scored, 100 runs batted in, and 175 hits.[15] Stepping to the plate was perhaps the most dangerous of the Tigers' "G-Men," Hank Greenberg. The team could have used one of Greenberg's home runs during this at-bat, but he could only muster an inning-ending groundout to shortstop Red Rolfe. Despite this setback, the Tigers had one inning left.

Yankees reliever Russ Van Atta started the ninth and surrendered back-to-back hits to Marv Owen and Mickey Cochrane. In the pitcher's position of the lineup, Marberry was removed in favor of another pitcher, Schoolboy Rowe, who delivered a single that loaded the bases. A Pete Fox fielder's choice brought Owen home to close the gap to 11-9. New York, in need of a stopper, inserted veteran Burleigh Grimes, one of the few remaining pitchers in major-league baseball still allowed to throw a spitball. After Walker sacrificed, Goslin lifted a double that tied the game. With the crowd still in a fever pitch, Gehringer was walked for an attempted force out of Goslin, who stood on second base as the winning run. Billy Rogell, who had been stranded on first the previous inning, now had the chance to become the hero. The Tigers shortstop delivered by slapping a base hit through the left side. "I only got to first base. I was jumping up and down, yelling, 'Run Goose! Run, Goose!'"[16] Goslin scored the final run of the game to give the Tigers an incredible 12-11 victory and sole possession of first place in the American League, a position they would not relinquish for the remainder of the season as they advanced to their first World Series since 1909.

After the game, H.G. Salsinger of the *Detroit News* called this "the most exciting game ever played at Navin Field."[17] The *Detroit Free Press* reported that "old men wept and muttered 'not since 1909.'"[18] The *New York Times* reported that Tiger fans went home "joyous to the point of delirium with hopes of the city's first pennant in twenty-five years."[19] On this day, the Tigers had showed that 1934 would indeed be their year. They had shown "by anyone's count that they were champions for the day, if not for the season."[20]

SOURCES

Anderson, William. *The Detroit Tigers: A Pictorial Celebration of the Greatest Players and Moments in Tigers History, fourth edition* (Detroit: Wayne State University Press, 2008).

Bak, Richard. *A Place for Summer: A Narrative History of Tiger Stadium* (Detroit: Wayne State University Press, 1998).

Bak, Richard. *Cobb Would Have Caught It* (Detroit: Wayne State University Press, 1991).

Pattison, Mark, and David Raglin. *Detroit Tigers: Lists and More—Runs, Hits, and Eras* (Detroit: Wayne State University Press, 2002).

Websites

Baseballhall.org.

NOTES

1   *Detroit Free Press*, April 15, 1934.

2   *Detroit Free Press*, April 17, 1934.

3   *Detroit Free Press*, July 13, 1934.

4   *Detroit Free Press*, July 15, 1934.

5   *New York Times*, July 15, 1934.

6   *New York Times*, July 15, 1934.

7   *New York Times*, July 15, 1934.

8   *Detroit Free Press*, March 29, 1934.

9   *Detroit Free Press*, July 5, 1934.

10 *Detroit Free Press*, July 2, 1934.

11 Richard Bak, *Cobb Would Have Caught It*, 252.

12 *Detroit Free Press*, June 29, 1934.

13 Mark Pattison and David Raglin, *Detroit Tigers: Lists and More—Runs, Hits, and Eras*, 216.

14 William Anderson, *The Detroit Tigers: A Pictorial Celebration of the Greatest Players and Moments in Tigers History, fourth edition*, 63-64.

15 Anderson, 71.

16 Richard Bak, *A Place for Summer: A Narrative History of Tiger Stadium*, 157.

17 *Detroit News*, July 15, 1934.

18 *Detroit Free Press*, July 15, 1934.

19 *New York Times*, July 15, 1934.

20 *Detroit Free Press*, July 15, 1934.

HAPPY NEW YEAR, HANK!

September 10, 1934: Detroit Tigers 2, Boston Red Sox 1, at Navin Field

By Matt Keelean

AT THE END OF THE DAY ON SEPTEMBER 8, 1934, the Detroit Tigers, who had not been to the World Series since 1909, stood 4½ games ahead of the powerful New York Yankees. This lead had been constricting around the neck of the Tigers since September 5, when the lead stood at 6 games. Fans of the team grew more nervous with each day—was the pressure of the pennant race starting to consume them? Prior to splitting a doubleheader with Connie Mack's lowly Philadelphia Athletics on that day, the Tigers had won only two games in the early days of September. And now the Boston Red Sox, a middling .500 unit that season, were arriving in town for a four-game series. If they couldn't do better than take two of five games from the A's, how disastrous would an engagement with the Red Sox prove to be?

On Sunday, September 9, the Tigers tried to allay the fears of their hometown faithful with a victory in game one against the Sox, prevailing 5-4 in 10 innings. Despite the win, in which the Tigers coughed up the lead in the top of the ninth, then secured victory in the bottom of the 10th, the Yankees continued to make things interesting, taking a doubleheader from the St. Louis Browns. The Tigers' lead shrank further, from 4½ games ahead to 4 games.

To make matters even more worrisome for Detroit rooters, Hank Greenberg, the Tigers' young slugging sensation, and the hero of the day in the September 9 contest, was struggling with his own decision regarding his availability on the following day. September 10, 1934, was Rosh Hashanah, the Jewish New Year and the traditionally observed start of the High Holy Days of the Jewish calendar. Greenberg, who never viewed himself as particularly observant of Jewish rituals and traditions, nonetheless wanted to be respectful of his parents' wishes. And yet he was also a key run producer in a lineup that had not been producing many runs of late.

Complicating matters further were the larger sociopolitical events of the day. In Europe, Adolf Hitler had risen to power in Germany, and was now well on the way to scapegoating Jews for the country's ills and reducing their status in their native land to that of second-class citizens, a mere inkling of what was to come. Jews also were under attack in the United States, courtesy of Detroit's own Henry Ford and Father Charles Coughlin. Through his own publications and through the influence that his wealth brought him, Ford time and again railed against Jews as the source of so many ills plaguing the United States before and during the Great Depression. Father Coughlin, the Catholic priest and radio show host, echoed these sentiments in his anti-Semitic broadcasts every week to millions of listeners.

There were, however, sympathetic and learned voices available to Greenberg, including local rabbis. When asked, they offered interpretations of Jewish law and custom for his consideration, taking into account Greenberg's professional obligations to his teammates and fans, as well as to his faith. In the end, after arriving at Navin Field, and after talking with his manager, Mickey Cochrane, as well as several teammates, Greenberg reached into his locker for his uniform, dressed, and joined his team on the field.

Starting for the Red Sox on that Monday was Gordon Rhodes, a journeyman pitcher not known for his blazing heater; in 1934 he would average 3.2 strikeouts per nine innings, and would allow 247 hits and 98 walks, leading to a WHIP (walks plus hits per inning pitched) of 1.575. Surely the Tigers could make short work of Rhodes, despite their recent offensive struggles. Countering Rhodes would be Elden Auker, the young hurler for the Tigers enjoying something of a breakout season.

Auker immediately got into trouble against the Red Sox, as he gave up a walk to leadoff hitter Max Bishop, followed by a fielder's choice to Billy Werber, which advanced Bishop to second base. Mel Almada, the rookie center fielder for the Red Sox, followed with an RBI bloop single to drive Bishop in from second. Auker then settled in and retired the next three Sox batters in order, but the early damage had been done. And with that began the fretting of the Tiger faithful.

The game remained 1-0 Red Sox into the bottom of the seventh inning, with only one Tiger advancing as far as second base between the second and seventh. Up first for the Tigers, shortstop Billy Rogell led off with another weak infield groundout. Next came Hank Greenberg. He had done the same in his first two at-bats as Rogell had just done, and opportunity to improve on that was getting to be in short supply.

Greenberg swung late at Rhodes' first offering for strike one, but was able to work the count to two balls and two strikes. Then Rhodes went with a breaking ball, and Greenberg let the ball travel into his hitting zone. At the precise moment that a great hitter knows instinctively to let loose with a mighty cut, Greenberg did just that, launching Rhodes' offering deep into left field. The Red Sox outfielders did not pursue the projectile, and the Tigers faithful, waiting nervously for something—anything—to cheer about, roared their approval as the ball sailed well over the scoreboard in left.

Marv Owen followed Greenberg's home run with a single, and Gee Walker drew a pass from Rhodes. Red Sox skipper Bucky Harris panicked, sending the venerable Lefty Grove, this season a shadow of his former self with the Athletics, down to the bullpen to warm up. Rhodes recovered, sending Auker down on strikes and coercing a weak groundball out from White to retire the side. Nevertheless, Greenberg's homer had done the job, and the score was now knotted at one run apiece.

Auker continued to contain the Red Sox hitters, putting them down in order in the top of the eighth inning. In the bottom of the inning, Cochrane once

again reached base, preserving a perfect 2-for-2 day in four total plate appearances. Despite being on base for the fourth time in the game (single, double, walk, and hit-by-pitch), once again Black Mike could only watch as the heart of the order failed to deliver for the home team. Auker came back out in the top of the ninth, and dispatched the Red Sox hitters as efficiently as he had done from the second inning.

Now came the bottom of the ninth, and leading off—Hank Greenberg. As he climbed out of the dugout and stepped on to the field, he found himself in a position seemingly unexpected to him, given his struggles over whether to play on this day. Because of the decision to play, he now had the opportunity to provide a struggling team, and an anxious fan base, with a victory.

Rhodes, still in the game, started Greenberg off with a slow curve down in the zone. Greenberg let it go by, despite its being very similar to the pitch he had launched into the left-field bleachers in the seventh inning. Rhodes' next offering was the last pitch thrown that day—Greenberg launched the ball into deep left-center. It was still rising in its flight as it sailed over the wall and beyond the confines of Navin Field. Much as the exterior confines of the ballpark could not contain Greenberg's clout, the interior confines could not contain the frenetic masses of Tigers fans as he rounded the bases for home. Fans and photographers alike welcomed Greenberg at the plate, and his teammates showered him with appreciation in the clubhouse for his choice to play, and for his singular effort in the victorious outcome.

Hank had struck two blows in the game itself, one to tie the score, and one to win the game. He had also struck a larger blow for the Tigers' pennant chances, which improved to a 4½-game lead over the Yankees, rained out that day in St. Louis. But perhaps the greatest blow that day was against the steady expression of anti-Semitism heard and read about in American daily life. In the backyard of that vitriol, Hank Greenberg, already one of the best known and most beloved of Jewish athletes, became one of the most beloved of Detroit baseball stars by both Jew and gentile alike. And while the Tigers' lead in the

American League vacillated over the next few weeks before the team clinched the pennant, the questions of whether the team would fold down the stretch, and whether Greenberg would be there to help see the team to that goal, were laid to rest in the minds of the Tigers and their fans.

SOURCES

Auker, Elden, with Tom Keegan. *Sleeper Cars and Flannel Uniforms* (Chicago: Triumph Books, 2006).

Greenberg, Hank, with Ira Berkow. *The Story of My Life* (Chicago: Ivan R. Dee, 2001).

Levine, Peter. *From Ellis Island to Ebbets Field: Sport and the American Jewish Experience* (Oxford: Oxford University Press, 2002).

Rosengren, John. *Hank Greenberg, the Hero of Heroes* (New York: New American Library, 2013).

Detroit Free Press

Detroit News

Detroit Times

Grand Rapids (Michigan) *Herald*

Grand Rapids (Michigan) *Press*

The Sporting News

ROWE TAKES THE CARDINALS TO SCHOOL

October 4, 1934: Detroit Tigers 3, St. Louis Cardinals 2 (12 innings) at Navin Field (Game 2 of the World Series)

By Gregory H. Wolf

DETROIT TIGERS RIGHT-HANDER Lynwood Thomas "Schoolboy" Rowe "gave one of the most courageous exhibitions of pitching ever seen in World Series," wrote H.G. Salsinger of the *Detroit News*."[1] After the Tigers' demoralizing 8-3 loss to Dizzy Dean and the St. Louis Cardinals in Game One of the 1934 fall classic at Navin Field in the Motor City, the 24-year-old Rowe hurled an inspiring 12-inning complete game to pick up the victory, 3-2, on Goose Goslin's walk-off single. Sportswriters gushed in their praise of the wildly popular, 6-foot-4 Rowe. "[He] stands today alongside the pitching giants of World Series history," exclaimed AP sportswriter Alan Gould.[2] "A towering giant, playfully called Schoolboy," wrote John Drebinger of the *New York Times*, "strode into the world series today and by the sheer power of his mighty right arm changed its course."[3] Former big-league umpire, syndicated sportswriter, and then Cleveland Indians general manager Billy Evans added, "It was a great dramatic game, full of excitement, and packed with expectancy."[4]

Described by Westbrook Pegler as a "tall, loose-jointed rustic from El Dorado, Arkansas," Rowe took the American League by storm in 1934, his second season in the big leagues. A torn muscle in Rowe's right arm had prematurely ended his rookie season in July of 1933 and cast doubts on his future. With a dismal 1-3 record after five weeks of the 1934 season, the hard-throwing Rowe hit his stride, winning 23 of his next 26 decisions en route to a career-best 24-8 record, including 20 complete games in 30 starts and

266 innings. More importantly, the Tigers captured their first pennant since 1909 with a record of 101-53.

Sportswriter James Isaminger of the *Philadelphia Inquirer* noted that Rowe had momentarily "replaced Babe Ruth as baseball's biggest drawing card."[5] Colorful and superstitious, Rowe had a folksy personality and his success appealed to baseball fans' imagination during the hardships of the Great Depression. Long before another Tigers pitcher—Mark "The Bird" Fidrych—captured the attention of fans for his animated antics on the mound in 1976, Rowe was known for talking to the baseball, which he often called Edna in honor of Edna Mary Skinner, whom he married after the 1934 World Series. "Just eat a lot of vittles, climb the mound, wrap my fingers around the ball and say to it, 'Edna, honey, let's go,'" he once said of his preparation for pitching.[6]

On a sunny, crisp, yet windy autumn afternoon, Navin Field was packed with 43,451 screaming fans on Thursday, October 4, to see Rowe face St. Louis's vaunted Gas House Gang, who had overcome a seven-game deficit to the New York Giants on September 6 to take the pennant on the last weekend of the season. There were lingering concerns about Rowe, whose dislike of pitching in cooler temperatures was well documented. He had struggled at the end of the season, yielding 10 earned runs and 25 hits in his final 15 innings "Rowe had a sore arm," wrote George Moriarity of the *Detroit News*, "and willingly tackled his task under a great handicap."[7]

The Cardinals came out swinging at the Schoolboy, who yielded six hits and two runs in the first three innings, and things could have been worse. Pepper

Martin led off the game with a liner on Rowe's first pitch. Although center fielder Jo-Jo White made a routine catch, the hard-hit ball put the partisan crowd on edge. With one out in the second inning, catcher Bill DeLancey hit a sharp grounder that glanced off second baseman Charlie Gehringer's knee and was ruled a hit. The next batter, center fielder Ernie Orsatti, hit Rowe's first pitch over Goose Goslin's head in left field. The ball "hooked away from the Goose and rolled into corner for a triple" to drive in DeLancey.[8]

With Orsatti 90 feet from home, Rowe retired the next two hitters, shortstop Leo Durocher and pitcher Bill Hallahan. Martin led off the third inning with a single and moved to second on a sacrifice. With two outs, cleanup hitter Joe "Ducky" Medwick singled to left. Goslin fielded the ball cleanly and threw home, but not in time to peg the speedy Martin at the plate. Medwick moved up to second, setting the stage for the defensive play of the game.

Ripper Collins, who had led the Redbirds in home runs (35), RBIs (128), and batting average (.333), lashed a single to Goslin. The Goose threw a strike to Mickey Cochrane at the plate to nail the charging Medwick, who bowled over the MVP player-manager. "Nothing but a tonic such as Goslin's throw could have kept the Schoolboy in the arena," wrote Edward Burns of the *Chicago Tribune*.[9]

Unlike his counterpart, Cardinals southpaw Wild Bill Hallahan cruised through the first three innings yielding only two singles. An eight-year veteran with a 76-58 record, Hallahan was considered among the NL's hardest throwers. He had paced the circuit in strikeouts in 1930 and 1931 and was one of the heroes, with two complete-game victories, in the Cardinals' stunning defeat of the Philadelphia Athletics in the 1931 World Series; however, his record had fallen to 8-12 in 1934. The Tigers caught their first break with one out in the fourth inning when shortstop Billy Rogell hit a "flukey" double on what H.G. Salsinger considered an easy out.[10] Orsatti lost the ball in the sun and, according to Irving Vaughan, "failed to make allowances for the wind" as the ball dropped for a double.[11] With Rogell on third, right fielder Pete Fox doubled down the third-base line, driving in the Tigers'

first run. Cardinals player-manager Frankie Frisch protested that the ball was foul, but was rebuffed.

The game looked bleak for the Tigers, who began the bottom of the ninth trailing 2-1, but the gods of fate were on their side. Fox led off the frame with a single, the team's first hit off Hallahan since his double in the fourth, and moved to second on Rowe's sacrifice bunt. Gerald "Gee" Walker, pinch-hitting for White, lofted a "high twisting fly between home and first."[12] As if mesmerized, neither Hallahan nor DeLancey broke for the ball, and Collins was too late as the routine popup landed in fair territory, but rolled foul as Walker scampered to first. After a discussion among the umpires, the ball was ruled foul and Walker was sent back to the plate. Given a second chance, he singled to center, driving in Fox to tie the score. Southpaw Bill Walker relieved Hallahan, picked off Walker at first, and punched out Cochrane to send the game into extra innings.

"We doubt that whether any pitcher ever delivered nine innings of pitching in a World Series compared to the nine that Rowe pitched," wrote Salsinger.[13] From the fourth inning through the 12th, Rowe retired 27 of 28 batters, including a record-tying 22 in a row. According to Drebinger, the only hard-hit ball during that stretch was DeLancey's "low screaming liner" to left field in the seventh inning when Rogell made a "spectacular diving catch."[14] "[Rowe] was very fast," wrote Salsinger, "[H]is curve ball was breaking and his change of pace had the Cardinals batters swinging off stride."[15] Pepper Martin's one-out double in the 11th finally broke Rowe's spell, but Schoolboy got the next two batters.

With one out in the bottom of the 12th inning, Gehringer and Hank Greenberg drew consecutive free passes off Walker, an overlooked hurler of the era who had led the NL in ERA in 1929 and 1931 as a member of the New York Giants. Goslin, whom the Tigers had acquired in the offseason, stepped to the plate. In his 14th season with a career .321 batting average, the future Hall of Famer had been one of the Washington Senators heroes in their World Series victory over the Giants in 1924, clouting three home runs among his 11 hits. Walker, who had not yet surrendered a hit in three

Schoolboy Rowe was dominant in '34

innings, threw a "fastball, waist high and through the heart" which the Goose belted to center field, driving in Gehringer for a dramatic 3-2 victory.[16]

Salsinger hailed Detroit's victory as "one of most thrilling ever played in the World Series."[17] "There was none of that panicky, jittery feeling that confounded the Tigers in Game One," wrote Drebinger.[18] Notwithstanding Goslin's momentum-changing throw in the fourth inning and his walk-off, game-winning hit, the story of the game was the Schoolboy. Rowe admitted after the game that he had been nervous early in the contest. But he settled down to toss 132 pitches (99 for strikes), yielding just seven hits; he whiffed seven and did not issue a walk. It was "as brilliant an exhibition of pitching as ever was witnessed in world series competition," opined Drebinger.[19]

NOTES

1 H.G. Salsinger, "Rowe's pitching Vastly Superior To Dean's," *Detroit News*, October 5, 1934, II, 1.

2 Alan Gould, "Rowe Stands Today Among the Greats," *Detroit News*, October 5, 1934, II, 27.

3 John Drebinger, "Tigers Beat Cards in Twelfth, 3 To 2, And Square Series," *New York Times*, October 5, 1934, 1.

4 Billy Evans, "Tigers Change To Waiting Game To Down Cardinals," *Detroit News*, October 5, 1934, 29.

5 James C. Isaminger, "Rowe, Killed by Kindness and Hindered By Handshakers, Missed A.L. Hill Record," *Philadelphia Inquirer*, September 2, 1934, 1.

6 Associated Press, "Schoolboy Rowe, Pitcher, 48, Dies," *New York Times*, January 9, 1961, 39.

7 George Moriarity, "Schoolboy Unhittable After Third Inning," *Detroit News*, October 5, 1934, 30.

8 Irving Vaughan, "Detroit Wins, 3 to 2; Even Series," *Chicago Daily Tribune*, October 5, 1934, 1.

9 Edward Burns, "Rowe and Goslin Head Detroit Hero Roll," *Chicago Daily Tribune*, October 5, 1934, 31.

10 Salsinger.

11 Vaughan.

12 James P. Dawson, "Play-By-Play Story Of Detroit Battle," *New York Times*, October 5, 1934, 30.

13 Salsinger.

14 Drebinger.

15 Salsinger.

16 Evans.

17 Salsinger.

18 Drebinger.

19 Ibid.

"THIS IS A CASE FOR JUDGE LANDIS"

October 9, 1934: St. Louis Cardinals 11, Detroit Tigers 0 at Navin Field (Game Seven of the World Series)

By Brent Heutmaker

THE TIGERS' DREAMS OF THEIR FIRST World Series title were evaporating after a tough 4-3 Game Six loss in the 1934 World Series. The St. Louis Cardinals were favored in Game Seven and ticket demand wasn't as strong. The sun shined bright and a cool northeast wind blew in over the right-field wall at Navin Field.

Detroit player-manager Mickey Cochrane complained about Game Six: "The Cards did not beat us, Umpire Owens did. I was safe at third in the sixth, but Owens had me out before I hit the bag. That was the turning point in the game. We had Daffy Dean on the run and would have finished him. But the umpire stopped us. We were beaten by an umpire and hitters like Durocher and Dean."[1]

After Game Six, both Cochrane and pitcher Lynwood "Schoolboy" Rowe were treated at a hospital. Numerous reports circulated about Cochrane's ailments. He had been spiked for the second time. "They want to play that way, we're ready to fight back, he said."[2]

Rowe's right hand had swelled after a dispute with a door. Apparently the bruise was made worse after Rowe shook hands with comedian Joe E. Brown. Management's story was that Rowe had a swollen hand from stopping a ball. The problem was that no one remembered a play where Rowe stopped a ball. There was also a rumor that Rowe had tried to punch a Cardinals player.

The 24-year-old had planned to marry Edna Skinner immediately after Game Six, provided Detroit won. Skinner was writing a guest column for a Detroit newspaper about being the fiancée of a World Series player. The Cardinals bench used it as fodder for taunting Rowe constantly.

Rowe said of the handshake and the taunts, "Joe E. Brown the comedian wasn't so funny when he rushed over to me before the game to shake hands. He gripped my pitching hand like a longshoreman and I fear he dislocated a knuckle. At least it felt that way while I was pitching. The Cardinals didn't bother me in the least by chanting, 'Come on, Edna.' referring to my fiancée."[3]

No pitcher had thrown a complete World Series game and started again the very next day. Until the injury, Cochrane was hoping Rowe could start two consecutive games. Some writers thought General Crowder might start. Instead, the skipper went with Elden Auker.

Cardinals player-manager Frankie Frisch said, "I'll give them Hallahan or Dizzy tomorrow and we'll win the Series."[4] Dizzy Dean wanted to start. "Who's going to pitch for the Tigers?" he said. "They'd better put 'em all in there."[5]

Dean mocked Rowe's injury: "There ain't going to be no alibi, though, understand that. And we ain't shaking hands with nobody."[6]

Not stopping there, Dean ridiculed the American League: "It's too bad they won't let us draft players from the American League like we do from the American Association and other leagues like that. We'd like to have Schoolboy on our side. When I get around to it, I'm going to ask Mr. Rickey if he can't talk the American League into some kind of a draft agreement. We could pick up a good player once in a while from teams like the Tigers."[7]

One of the quirks of Detroit's Navin Field was that all players had to pass through the Tigers dugout to reach the playing field. Numerous Cardinal players stopped in front of Detroit's bench to scrape their spikes on the concrete. They also mocked Cochrane, asking, "How is our stricken leader?"[8]

Already, rough play and disputes with umpires had marred the 1934 World Series. The trend continued in Game Seven. A seven-run third inning by St. Louis removed any doubt about the final outcome.

In the sixth inning, Joe Medwick hit a ball to the center-field fence. Thinking triple all the way, he tore around the bases and slid safely into third base. The cloud of dust that erupted may have caused some of the discrepancies about the incident. Some observers thought Detroit third baseman Marvin Owen stepped on Medwick or kneed him. Medwick may have kicked back with either one or both feet at Owen's legs. Others thought both players kicked at each other.

"Medwick held out his hand to Owen. The Tigers third baseman refused it petulantly and returned to his station, observed sportswriter Paul Gallico."[9]

Medwick later said, "I didn't mean to harm anybody but I don't want anybody to kick me. I offered to shake hands with Owen on the spot but he wouldn't do it. He walked away and turned his back."[10]

A single by Ripper Collins scored Medwick. After the inning ended, Medwick returned to his left-field position, where fans in the temporary left-field bleachers began throwing debris at him. Medwick headed to the safety of the infield and joked with teammates about it. Shortstop Leo Durocher and third baseman Pepper Martin began playing a pepper game with vegetables that had been thrown on the field. Cochrane ran out to left field in an effort to implore the crowd to calm down, but was unsuccessful. Medwick tried several times to return to left field. A loudspeaker announcement stated that the umpires would forfeit the game to St. Louis if the crowd didn't stop throwing items. Head umpire Harry Geisel, however, later told sportswriter James Isaminger that he would have never allowed a forfeit under any circumstances.

After Medwick's third failed attempt to return to left field, Geisel asked Frisch, "This is an exceptional case, so won't you take Medwick out of the game?" Frisch refused. Geisel said, "Well, this is a case for Judge Landis."[11]

During the entire Series, the umpires had made reports detailing players using profanity against each other. Medwick and Owen were called over to speak to Landis. Landis asked both players if the other had sworn at him, which they both denied. Landis told Medwick that he was out of the game and wouldn't listen to Frisch's protests. Chick Fullis replaced Medwick and was cheered when he ran to left field. The entire incident lasted about 20 minutes. Due to an incident in the 1933 World Series, Landis had warned the umpires about ejecting players:

Before the series, the umpires are instructed not to put any player off the field unless the provocation is very extreme. I saw as well as everybody what Medwick did, but when Umpire Klem took no action and the players quieted down I hoped the matter was ended. But when it became apparent that the demonstration of the crowd would never terminate I decided to take action. I did not call Medwick and Owen in any attempt to patch up the difference between the players. I asked Owen whether he knew of any excuse why Medwick should have made such an attack on him. He said he did not, and with that I ordered Medwick off the field. I do not intend to take any further action.[12]

With so much at stake, I feel that only the most extraordinary circumstances should warrant action depriving either team of its full strength in the championship series.[13]

I made my decision in order to avert a demonstration leading to possible riot and injury and to protect Medwick from violence. At the same time Medwick admitted kicking Owen, while Owen denied kicking Medwick.[14]

I do not blame that crowd for what happened today although under the circumstances and due to the uncontrollable outburst I felt it was wisest to remove Medwick from the game. As I saw the incident at third base, Medwick came sliding hard into the bag, then kicked his feet up at Owen. I did not see Owen make any gesture previously toward Medwick but I do not say he didn't. I have yet to find two men who agree on exactly what happened or who was to blame. When I finally called the players, managers and umpires to my box, I simply asked Medwick if Owen had done anything to him or if there was any reason for his kicking at the Detroit player. To both questions Medwick answered 'No,' Thereupon I decided to promptly remove him from the game, particularly as I felt that an even more dangerous outbreak might develop if Medwick continued to play.[15]

Frisch defended Medwick saying, "The kid wouldn't spike anybody. He was just sliding into third base."[16]

Owen later said, "It is all over so far as I am concerned. I'm sorry it happened and I'm sorry Medwick was ordered out of the game."[17]

The game ended with a whimper. Dizzy Dean allowed six hits and struck out Hank Greenberg three times. Dean threw 22 balls out of 98 total pitches. Six Detroit pitchers allowed 17 Cardinals hits including two by Dean. Every Cardinals starting player had at least one hit and scored at least one run.

Many Detroit writers blamed the umpires and Joe E. Brown for the Tigers' loss. Detroit had to wait another year for that long-awaited first world championship.

NOTES

1   James P. Dawson, "Frisch Is Elated; Praises All Hands," *New York Times*, October 9, 1934.

2   Alan Gould, "Champs Slaughter Detroit Hurlers in Wild, Riotous Finish," *Minneapolis Tribune*, October 10, 1934.

3   *Brooklyn Daily Eagle*, October 10, 1934.

4   Dawson.

5   Charles W. Dunkley, "Dizzy Dean Begs to Take Mound Against Tigers in Final Tilt," *Minneapolis Tribune*, October 9, 1934.

6   J. Roy Stockton, "Cardinals Pin Their World Series Hopes on Dizzy Dean," *St. Louis Post-Dispatch*, October 9, 1934.

7   Dizzy Dean, "Rowe Fine Prospect; We Oughtta Draft Him," *St. Louis Post-Dispatch*, October 9, 1934.

8   Stockton.

9   Paul Gallico, "Dizzy Spell Hits Detroit Fandom," *Minneapolis Journal*, October 10, 1934.

10 Charles W. Dunkley, "Tears Fill Frisch's Eyes as Cochrane Congratulates Him," *St. Paul Pioneer Press*, October 10, 1934.

11 James C. Isaminger, "Geisel Cited as Hero of Seventh Game," *The Sporting News*, October 18, 1934.

12 John Drebinger, "Cards Win Series, Beat Detroit, 11-0; Tiger Fans Riot," *New York Times*, October 10, 1934.

13 "Player Kicked at Owen in Sliding to Bag, Judge Says," *St. Paul Pioneer Press*, October 10, 1934.

14 John E. Wray, "Wray's Column," *St. Louis Post-Dispatch*, October 11, 1934.

15 "Landis Blames Medwick for Riot of Tiger Fans," *Minneapolis Tribune*, October 10, 1934.

16 Dunkley, "Tears Fill Frisch's Eyes.".

17 W.J. McGoogan, "Cardinal Would Not Accuse Owen of Giving Him Jolt With Knee," *St. Louis Post-Dispatch*, October 10, 1934.

GOOSE GOSLIN, MONEY PLAYER

October 7, 1935: Detroit Tigers 4, Chicago Cubs 3, at Navin Field (Game 7 of the World Series)

By Scott Ferkovich

THE DETROIT TIGERS HAD BEEN TO THE World Series four times in their 34-year history. Four times, they had suffered defeat. On October 7, 1935, the Tigers, along with the entire city of Detroit, were thirsty for victory, hoping that the fifth time would be a charm. As that Monday morning dawned, the team found itself up three games to two against the Chicago Cubs in the 1935 World Series. Navin Field buzzed with anticipation, as 48,420 giddy Detroit fans jammed their way into the ballpark at the corner of Michigan and Trumbull.

Twenty-one-game winner Tommy Bridges took the mound for Detroit, while Chicago countered with Larry French, who had won 17 during the regular season. If the Tigers were to prevail this afternoon, they would have to once again do it without the services of their young slugger Hank Greenberg, who hadn't played since Game Two after injuring his wrist. This was a star-studded Detroit team, with no less than four future Hall of Famers (Greenberg, Charlie Gehringer, Goose Goslin and catcher-manager Mickey Cochrane). The Cubs, as well, had their own share of stars destined for Cooperstown, including Gabby Hartnett, Billy Herman, Chuck Klein and Freddie Lindstrom (although the latter did not play in this game).

The score was tied at three entering the fateful ninth. Tommy Bridges was still on the mound for Detroit. Stan Hack led off by stroking a long triple over the head of Gee Walker in center, and it looked like Chicago was going to take the lead. Bridges, however, in a gutsy display of pitching, retired the next two batters on a strikeout and a roller back to the mound, Hack remaining on third. Bridges quickly got two strikes on Augie Galan. Then came what Tigers owner Frank Navin later called "the most important play of the Series."[1] Bridges bounced an errant curve ball two feet in front of the plate, but Cochrane got down on his knees and was able to block it—barely. Hack, the potential go-ahead run, was forced to scamper back to third. On the next pitch, Galan swung and hit a high popup into short left field. Shortstop Billy Rogell, third baseman Flea Clifton, and left fielder Goslin all converged on it, while Hack raced for home. It was Goslin who made the catch, dashing toward the infield. The crowd went delirious. No runs, one hit, no errors. Improbably, the score remained tied, 3-3.

Years later, Billy Herman would still lament Cochrane's splendid play: "When I think back to the 1935 World Series, all I can see is Hack standing on third base, waiting for somebody to drive him in. Seems he stood there for hours and hours."[2]

Charles P. Ward wrote in the next day's *Detroit Free Press*, "Those who saw defeat staring the Tigers in the face failed to remember that Bridges is one of the gamest little men that ever came out of the hills of Tennessee. He was sent into the game by Cochrane because Mickey wanted to have somebody on the mound who would show the Cubs plenty of gameness even if he didn't have much on the ball."[3]

And then came the bottom of the ninth. With one out, Cochrane reached on an infield single, Gehringer hit a sharp smash to Phil Cavarretta, the Chicago first baseman, who bobbled the ball momentarily before stepping on first to retire Gehringer. His throw to second was too late to nab Cochrane. Goose Goslin ended the affair with a single into right, just over the head of second baseman Billy Herman. Cochrane raced around third and headed home with the winning run. The Tigers were World Series winners for the first time in their history, and Navin Field erupted into pandemonium.

"They will remember the manner in which the base ball [sic] championship of 1935 was won as long as they remember the team that won it," wrote H.G. Salsinger the next day in the *Detroit News.* "There have been better teams than Detroit in the past but no team ever won a World Series more spectacularly than Detroit won the one that ended with two out in the ninth inning at Navin Field yesterday."[4]

"The greatest exhibition of pitching in the clutch I have ever seen," exclaimed a jubilant Cochrane in the postgame celebration, referring to Bridges' ninth-inning heroics. "I told those Cubs that we'd throw 150 pounds of heart at them out there today, and I guess they realize now that Little Tommy is all of that—after that ninth inning. Pitching! He threw the six greatest curves I ever caught to lick them. ... That Bridges. What a thrill he gave me. That little guy has the heart of a lion. ... What a pitcher, what a heart. Just 150 pounds of grit and courage. That's what he is."[5]

In downtown Detroit, euphoric crowds jammed the streets, dancing and celebrating throughout the afternoon and into the evening. Automobiles clogged the length of Woodward Avenue. A carnival spirit spread everywhere in the city.

The *Detroit Free Press* put it down for posterity the next day:

Police said the crowd was bigger than the Armistice Day crowd of 1918. Even in that glorious moment no such crowds had choked Detroit streets; no such paralysis of transportation had ensued; no such heights of pandemonium had been reached.

Detroit, through the baseball team that is a symbol and the incarnation of its fighting spirit, had won the baseball championship of the world, and the world was to know it.

It was Detroit's salute to America.

Detroit had the dynamite; Mickey Cochrane and his Tigers provided the spark.

Detroit celebrated because it had won the world championship.

It celebrated because it was the city that had led the nation back to recovery.

It celebrated because it was the city that wouldn't stay licked; the city that couldn't be licked.

It was Detroit the unconquerable, ready to tell the world when the moment arrived.

The moment had arrived, and the world was told.

"There's no doubt," Police Inspector William Maloney said, "that it's the biggest crowd in downtown Detroit in my memory." And, he added, he has a very long memory.[6]

Meanwhile, back in the celebratory clubhouse, Cochrane managed to locate Goslin and Bridges among the mayhem. Grasping them both around their necks, he planted a kiss on each of them while flashbulbs popped.

"What a thrill! What a game to win! What a heart that Bridges has! What a money player that Goslin is! What a team the whole damned gang is! I've had many big moments in my life, but none to equal the thrill of crossing the plate with the winning run. Boy, that was great. I thought I never would get there."[7]

NOTES

1   John Rosengren, *Hank Greenberg: The Hero of Heroes* (New York: New American Library, 2013), 126.

2   Charles Bevis, *Mickey Cochrane: The Life of a Baseball Hall of Fame Catcher* (Jefferson, North Carolina: McFarland, 1998), 6.

3   Charles P. Ward, "Detroit Wins World Championship," *Detroit Free Press*, October 8, 1935.

4   H.G. Salsinger, "Cochrane, Goslin Share Hero Role with Bridges," *Detroit News*, October 8, 1935.

5   W.W. Edgar, "Wild Scenes Are Enacted in Tigers' Dressing Room," *Detroit Free Press*, October 8, 1935.

6   "Detroit Hails its Champion Tigers as a Symbol of the City Dynamic," *Detroit Free Press*, October 8, 1935.

7   Edgar, "Wild Scenes."

"WHISTLING JAKE" ONE-HITS TRIBE; STOPS JOHNNY ALLEN'S 15-GAME WIN STREAK

October 3, 1937: Detroit Tigers 1, Cleveland Indians 0 at Navin Field

By Terry W. Sloope

FOR TEAMS ALREADY ELIMINATED from a pennant race, the last game of a season typically means very little. In many of these instances, managers, players, and umpires might be more concerned about bringing the final game to a swift end to facilitate an expedited trip back to their offseason homes. For bench players and untested late-season call-ups, the final game of the season might represent a chance at a start that they otherwise wouldn't have received.

Occasionally, a season's last game might have repercussions for a player trying to achieve a certain statistical landmark. At the end of the 1937 season, Cleveland Indians pitcher Johnny Allen found himself in such a situation.

Johnny Allen reached the major leagues relatively late in life. He was a 27-year-old rookie with the New York Yankees in 1932. A right-handed pitcher, he went 17-4 with the Yankees that year and achieved a record of 50-19 with New York from 1932 through 1935. Traded to Cleveland for pitchers Monte Pearson and Steve Sundra after the 1935 season, Allen won 20 games for the Indians in 1936, the only time he reached that mark in his career. In 1937 the lantern-jawed pitcher had an opportunity to put his name in the record books.

Suffering from a tender arm at the start of the season, Allen was used sparingly the first month. After a start against Boston in Fenway Park on June 18, Allen's record was an unremarkable 4-0 in nine appearances (including eight starts). He was then felled by appendicitis and did not pitch again until August 4, again against the Red Sox at Fenway Park, when he threw one inning of scoreless relief, not figuring in the decision. He tossed 3⅔ innings in relief, with no decision, on August 8 at Yankee Stadium. He won his fifth game of the season, a start on August 14 at home against the Chicago White Sox, and his next four starts as well, including two against the St. Louis Browns and one each against Washington and Boston. He pitched 2⅓ innings in relief on September 6 (he didn't figure in the decision), and then returned to his starting role on September 8 in Detroit, beating the Tigers, 6-1, with a complete-game effort. He then recorded wins in five consecutive starts, all complete games, to finish the month of September with a season record of 15-0. With a win against Detroit at Navin Field on October 3, the last day of the season, Allen could tie the AL record of 16 consecutive winning decisions held by Walter Johnson, Smoky Joe Wood, Lefty Grove, and Schoolboy Rowe.

The game of October 3 meant nothing to either the Indians or Tigers. Detroit had a lock on second place in the American League standings, 13 games behind the pennant-winning Yankees. Despite the sizable gap in the standings that existed between New York and Detroit most of that season, attendance at Navin Field in 1937 was very good as Charlie Gehringer charged toward a batting championship and MVP award, and Hank Greenberg and rookie sensation Rudy York treated Tiger fans to a spirited race for the team home-run title. Cleveland had assured itself of a finish in the first division as well, sitting in fourth place, 1½ games behind the White Sox and two games ahead of the Red Sox. Under normal circumstances, it might have been one of those games in which both teams started a number of their bench players. Whether it was out of a sense of personal pride, or respect for the integrity of a game that could prove important for Allen and the record books, both teams used a full complement of regular players, including stars Earl Averill and Hal Trosky for Cleveland and Greenberg, Gehringer, and York for the Tigers. Whether it was because of the accomplishments of their hometown heroes or the excitement associated with Allen's chase for a record, 22,000 of the Detroit faithful turned out for the final game.

Allen's biggest advantage in his quest for the record that day was his mound opponent. The Tigers tabbed Whistling Jake Wade for the starting assignment against Cleveland. Wade, who epitomized the very definition of lanky (he was listed at 6-feet-2, 175 pounds), was a left-handed pitcher who the Tigers hoped one day would become a fixture in their starting rotation. Since joining the organization in 1932, however, Jake had been unable to tame his wildness on the mound, with an alarmingly high walk-to-strikeout ratio. Entering his closing-day assignment, Wade had a record of 6-10 and a 5.70 ERA, with 103 free passes and just 62 strikeouts in 156⅓ innings pitched. If Allen could pitch just an average game, the odds were good he would get his milestone achievement.

Allen held up his end of the bargain. He surrendered a run to the Tigers in the first inning when Greenberg singled home Pete Fox, who had reached base on a double. From that point on, Allen kept the Tigers off the scoreboard, giving up just three additional hits and four walks while striking out four batters in another complete-game effort.

Jake Wade pitched what may have been the game of his career. With two outs in the seventh inning and Hal Trosky at the plate, Wade had yet to surrender a hit. The fans in attendance were no longer thinking about Allen's winning streak; instead, they were focused on Wade's improbable pitching gem. With Lyn Lary on first thanks to a walk, Trosky hit a hard liner back up the middle that glanced off Wade's glove and continued into center field. It was the only hit Wade gave up all day. He then hit Moose Solters with a pitch, loading the bases. Indians right fielder Bruce

Campbell hit an easy can-of-corn to Gee Walker in right field to end the threat. In the ninth inning Lary walked again to lead off. Second baseman John Kroner sacrificed Lary to second, but Wade got Averill to fly out to Pete Fox, and then Trosky struck out to end the game. Wade struck out seven batters, hit one, and walked four in a complete-game shutout that denied Johnny Allen his place in history.

Doc Holst of the *Detroit Free Press* noted that after the game Allen sat at his locker, cursing to himself. When he spoke to the press, he "was not so polite in his descriptions of the Indians as a whole, and one could hardly blame him."[1] One has to wonder just how hard the Indians, or the Tigers for that matter, were really trying that day. In a game with just six hits and eight walks, the elapsed game time was one hour and 35 minutes.[2]

Jake Wade saw very limited major-league action with a handful of teams over the next 10 years. He finished his career with a record of 27-40 and an ERA of 5.00. He walked 5.9 batters per nine innings while striking out just 3.9 batters per nine innings over the course of his career.

Johnny Allen went on to win 14 games for Cleveland in 1938 and was named to the All-Star team for the only time in his career. He left Cleveland after the 1940 season and subsequently pitched for the St. Louis Browns, Brooklyn Dodgers, and New York Giants, mostly in relief, before retiring after the 1944 season. He finished his career with a record of 142-75 (an excellent winning percentage of .654) and a 3.75 ERA.

SOURCES

Holst, Doc, "Johnny Loses Chance to Tie League Mark," *Detroit Free Press*, October 4, 1937, Sports, 1.

Retrosheet (retrosheet.org) for player game logs, play-by-play accounts and other materials.

Baseball-Reference.com (baseball-reference.com) for player statistics.

NOTES

1 Doc Holst, "Johnny Loses Chance to Tie League Mark," *Detroit Free Press*, October 4, 1937, Sports, 1.

2 In fairness, it must be noted that the previous day's game, which featured 17 runs and 22 hits, is listed on Retrosheet as having lasted just two hours.

WHO IS THAT KID?!

May 4, 1939: Boston Red Sox 7, Detroit Tigers 6 at Briggs Stadium

By Bill Nowlin

RED SOX ROOKIE TED WILLIAMS WAS 20 years old when he first played in a game at Briggs Stadium. It quickly became his favorite ballpark in which to hit.

Williams—"The Kid"—had won the Triple Crown in the American Association in 1938, with 43 home runs among his contributions to the Minneapolis Millers. Williams batted left-handed and was a pull hitter. The overwhelming number of home runs he hit went to right field, or right-center. Thus far, his only major-league home run had been hit on April 23, off Bud Thomas of the Philadelphia Athletics at Fenway Park.

Williams faced right-hander Roxie Lawson of the Tigers on May 4, 1939, at Briggs Stadium, the 10th game of the season for Boston. Lawson was pitching in his eighth year in the big leagues and had more than 600 innings of experience under his belt. Del Baker was managing the Tigers.

Jim Bagby, Jr. started for the Red Sox but he never made it through the third inning; the Tigers scored twice in the first and added two more in the third. Denny Galehouse came in and worked the next four innings.

His first time up, in the first inning, Williams hit one out of Briggs Stadium—up and over the right-field roof, but "foul by inches."[1] He then lined out to center.

Hitting a ball over the right-field roof was quite a feat in itself, even if foul. It was 325 feet to right field and 440 feet to straightaway center, with right-center listed at 375 feet.[2] A second deck in right had been added after the 1935 season. It overhung the lower deck by 10 feet, and there was a "315" marker attached to the second deck.

On a 3-and-2 count in the fourth inning, with Boston player-manager Joe Cronin on base, Ted's "towering smash landed atop the right-field roof, nearer center field than right, and bounded back into the playing field only because the eaves of the roof slant downward in that sector. As the crow flies, that belt was good for 360 feet without even figuring altitude."[3] The *Boston Herald* agreed: The ball had "landed on top of the 120-foot-high third and last deck of the grandstand in right-center, above a spot on the field 360 feet from home."[4] In perspective, 120 feet is about triple the height of Fenway Park's "Green Monster."

It was a dramatic drive, a two-run homer that halved the Tigers' lead to 4-2.

Ted came up again in the fifth inning. Lawson had walked Doc Cramer, given up a single to Joe Vosmik, and walked Jimmie Foxx. Cronin hit a bases-loaded single to score two runs and tie the game. Bob Harris was brought in to relieve. He had only 15⅔ innings of major-league experience, but had been with Toledo in the American Association in 1938 and certainly knew about Ted Williams. The righty, who had turned 24 just three days earlier, pitched around Williams, and the count went to 3-and-0.

Harris likely had seen "Titanic Ted's" first two drives out of the park, one foul and one fair. Tigers catcher Rudy York certainly saw them. Harris, on in relief with the score 4-4, had to worry about Foxx and Cronin on base. On the 3-and-0 count, John Kieran of the *New York Times* wrote that as York "signed for a fast ball, he looked up at Ted and said, 'You wouldn't think of hitting this one, would you?' 'Hit it?' says Ted, 'If it's near the plate I'll hit it outta the park.'"[5] And so he did.

Williams recounted the story to reporters after the game: "When the count was three and no, I got the sign from Joe to take a shot at the next one, cripple though it was. York was kidding me all along. Now he says, 'Three and nothing, kid. What are you going to do? Hit?' and I answered him that I always told the truth and that I was going to hit the next pitch. He didn't believe it, called for the fast one, it was in there and I hit it."[6]

This one hadn't landed on the roof; it went clear out of the park. The *Globe* described it: "It was a climbing liner — as much a liner as a drive could be which cleared a 120-foot barrier, straight as a string, over the whole works in right field, about a dozen feet fair. According to eye-witnesses outside the park, it landed across adjoining Trumbull av. and bounded against a taxi company garage on the other side on the first hop."[7] Think Tigers pitchers were a little intimidated? Think the word didn't spread around baseball very quickly? "So you weren't kidding, after all?" said York as Williams crossed home plate.[8]

At 120 feet, the Briggs Stadium upper deck was the "tallest barrier in either league to clear and one that the game's greatest sluggers from Babe Ruth down had tried and never accomplished."[9] The Detroit writers called it the longest homer ever hit at the stadium.

Detroit fans were sufficiently impressed that, the *Boston Herald* reported, "a tremendous, unanimous 'O-O-O-Oh' of amazement arose from the stands and practically all the spectators stood and applauded as Ted made the circuit and tagged the plate."[10]

The three-run homer gave the Red Sox a 7-4 lead. Detroit scored one run in the fifth and one in the seventh. The final was 7-6 Boston, and Ted Williams had the first game-winning home run of his career, to be followed by 105 more. A little over 20 percent of the homers he hit won ballgames for Boston.[11]

It was reportedly 17 years before another batter hit one out of Detroit's ballpark. That batter was Mickey Mantle.

Williams hit 521 homers, 248 of them at Fenway Park. Of the 273 he hit on the road, more than 20 percent were hit in Detroit. The 55 home runs he hit at Tiger Stadium far outpaced the 35 he hit at Shibe Park and the 35 he hit at Cleveland Stadium. Only one visiting player hit more; Babe Ruth hit 60 home

Ted Williams loved hitting at Briggs Stadium

runs in Detroit. It's no wonder Ted called Detroit his favorite park in which to hit. One wonders how many homers he would have hit had he been a Tiger his whole career.

Detroit sportswriter Joe Falls remembered a late-career batting practice in the Motor City. There was already a large crowd in the park. Williams stepped into the cage to take his seven swings. "The first one he lines down the right-field line just inside the foul pole. Crash! Home run into the upper deck. The second one went a little further into the upper deck. The third one a little further. And now the crowd starts to pick up on this. The fourth one — BOOM, a little further. He did it seven straight times — seven times in the upper deck, each one a little longer than the last one and by the time the seventh ball went out, the place was up in uproar. I'd say 25,000 were roaring because they saw what he was doing. He turned around, went back to the dugout, went down the steps, didn't say hello, good-bye, kiss my ass, tip his hat, nothing. That's a true story."[12]

NOTES

1 *Boston Globe*, May 5, 1939.

2 All ballpark measurements are from Philip J. Lowry, *Green Cathedrals* (New York: Walker & Company, 2006), 83, 84.

3 *Boston Globe*, May 5, 1939.

4 *Boston Herald*, May 5, 1939.

5 *New York Times*, January 9, 1949.

6 *Boston Herald*, May 5, 1939.

7 *Boston Globe*, May 5, 1939.

8 *New York Times*, January 9, 1949.

9 *Boston Globe*, May 5, 1939. The reporter may have not realized that Ruth's last year in the American League was 1934, before the upper deck was built following the 1935 season.

10 *Boston Herald*, May 5, 1939.

11 The full story of Williams's home runs can be found in Bill Nowlin, *521 — The Story of Ted Williams' Home Runs* (Cambridge, Massachusetts, 2013).

12 Jim Prime and Bill Nowlin, *Ted Williams: The Pursuit of Perfection* (Champaign, Illinois: Sports Publishing, 2002), 195.

NEWSOME'S PERFORMANCE MARKED WITH EXTRAORDINARY EMOTION

October 6, 1940: Detroit Tigers 8, Cincinnati Reds 0 at Briggs Stadium (Game 5 of the World Series)

By William M. Anderson

THE 1940 FALL CLASSIC FEATURED THE National League champion Cincinnati Reds, who won 100 games and outpaced their nearest rival by 12 games, and the Detroit Tigers, who captured the AL flag by a mere one-game margin over Cleveland. The Bengals were in a dogfight until the very end as only eight games separated the first five teams in the final American League standings.

If one believed Connie Mack's axiom that good pitching will overcome good hitting, victory by the Reds in the World Series was where the bettors should place their money. Cincinnati had a strong pitching staff headed by Bucky Walters (22-10) and Paul Derringer (20-12), both right-handers. Walters led the National League in wins, earned-run average, and complete games. Yhe Reds' number two man in the rotation, Paul Derringer, tied for the second most victories and ranked second in innings hurled and complete games. But on the offensive side of the game, Detroit held a decided advantage with a league-leading .286 team batting average against Cincinnati's average of .266, and in Hank Greenberg and Rudy York, the Tigers had two premier sluggers, with Greenberg soon to be chosen the Most Valuable Player in the American League.

In the first contest, waged in Cincinnati on October 2, ace Detroit hurler Bobo Newsom, a 21-game winner, outdueled Derringer, winning 7-2. Newsom's father was in the stands to see his son win the opener. Sadly for both, his father died early the next morning. A shaken son said, "I'll win the next one. I'll pitch it for Dad."[1]

In the next three games, the opponents took turns winning in alternate games with the Reds prevailing 5-2 in Game Four, in Detroit, and knotting the Series at two wins apiece.

The winner of Game Five would need only one more victory to become baseball's world champion. Reds manager Bill McKechnie called on second-year big leaguer Junior Thompson to pitch. Thompson had his career year in 1940, winning 16 games with a solid 3.32 ERA. Tigers skipper Del Baker countered by sending Newsom, the AL's second-winningest pitcher, to pitch on very short rest.

This game was all Detroit and all Bobo Newsom as the home team won, 8-0. When the fifth game in the Series concluded, the hot bats of Hank Greenberg, Bruce Campbell, and Barney McCosky had struck 24 hits over five games. In this game, the Tigers scored seven runs in the third and fourth innings combined, and chased the Reds starting pitcher after he retired only one hitter in the fourth inning. Thompson pitched 3⅓ innings and gave up eight hits and six runs.

McCosky led off the third with a single and raced around to third on Charlie Gehringer's base rap. On a 2-and-1 count, Greenberg launched a drive that carried into the second deck in left field for a three-run homer.

The Tigers sent nine men to the plate in the fourth frame. Catcher Billy Sullivan walked to start the productive inning and advanced to second when Newsom laid down a sacrifice bunt with two strikes on him. Dick Bartell doubled to left, driving in Sullivan. A passed ball moved Bartell to third and Thompson walked McCosky. McKechnie summoned Whitey Moore from the bullpen. Moore immediately walked Charlie Gehringer, loading the bases. Greenberg hit a deep fly ball that plated Bartell and sent McCosky scooting to third. York then drew a free pass, again loading the bases. Campbell came through again with a single, driving in two lead runs as Detroit built its lead to 7-0.

Cincinnati managed just three hits, all singles: Frank McCormick led off the second with a hit and died there; Mike McCormick led off the fourth and advanced to second on a groundout but didn't go any further; Bill Werber repeated the scenario by driving out a base hit leading off the sixth but was quickly erased when Mike McCormick hit into a double play. Newsom retired the side in order in the first, third, eighth, and ninth innings.

Cincinnati had its one moment of glory in the eighth inning. After the Tigers had scored their eighth run on a wild pitch and had runners on first and second, Sullivan came to the plate. The Tigers catcher was a left-handed batter, and the Reds played him to pull with left fielder Jimmy Ripple shading over into the left-center-field alley. Sullivan drove the ball deep into left field near the 340-foot fence, the blow appearing to be at least a two-base hit. Ripple raced to his right and stretched his glove (left) hand to its maximum, snaring the drive while tumbling forward. He rolled over twice and slid on his back with his glove hand reaching upward, demonstrating that he had held onto the ball.

Next to Newsom, Ripple received the most accolades and press coverage. His great catch was called a masterpiece, sensational, and "the greatest play of the series."[2] Bob Murphy, the *Detroit Times* sports editor, noted, "Even the Tigers had to handclap—all save Sullivan, who must have thought things about Ripple that made his ancestors whirl in their graves."[3] Henry McLemore of the Associated Press was so ecstatic that he claimed: "Had Ripple's catch come in the clutch, and not when the game was already won by the Tigers, it would be remembered and talked about for the next century."[4]

Yet easily the bigger story was the heroic performance of the winning pitcher, Bobo "Buck" Newsom. He pitched a brilliant shutout, allowing three harmless singles and letting only one runner reach second, while striking out seven. *Detroit News* sports editor H.G. Salsinger wrote, "Newsom pitched a game that

must be included among all-time classics. … Newsom had a blazing fastball, a quick breaking-curve, and a change of pace. But above everything else he had control. In nine innings only 31 of Newsom's pitches were called balls."[5]

Newsom had a well-established persona; he was frequently called Loud Louie, and was a pop-off who could be abrasive and prone to brag and make bold, self-serving predictions. But not after pitching perhaps his greatest game. He had given it his all in honor of a father he loved who had so recently died. Entering the Tigers clubhouse, he quickly retreated to the trainer's room seeking to pour out his emotions and escape the presence of reporters as tears streamed down his cheeks.[6]

Unable to interview Newsom, the sportswriters sought the impressions of his catcher, Billy Sullivan. "When I asked for the ball down here, I got it there," replied Sullivan. "I don't think he ever pitched a more polished game. … I caught him every game in his 13-game winning streak."[7]

Newsom's teammates and the writers respected his need to be alone, but after a while Bobo moved to his locker and spoke in a solemn manner. "Naturally, I don't feel as good as I might. It was the hardest game I ever pitched and I wanted to win more than I ever did before."[8] After a player said his dad would have been very proud of him, Newsom responded—"I'd give my World Series check for him to have seen it."[9]

Both the players and manager Del Baker were confident they would finish off the Reds and win the World Series. Cincinnati manager McKechnie was equally optimistic, given that he had his two aces, Walters and Derringer, ready to pitch the next two games. He also liked his chances with the other Tigers pitchers. "That big Buck Newsom is out of the way. We won't be seeing any more of him, thank goodness," the manager said.[10]

The die was cast: Bucky Walters hurled a gem to shut out the Tigers, 4-0, in Game Six, which evened the Series again. Newsom did come back for the final game, in Cincinnati, pitching against Paul Derringer. There was no repeat of Game Five. The Reds scored two runs in the seventh off a tired gladiator and won it all, 2-1.

NOTES

1   Charles Ward, "Hank's Homer Clinches Game," *Detroit Free Press*, October 7, 1940, 13.

2   Bob Murphy, "Reds Too Docile," *Detroit Times*, October 7, 1940, 15; *Detroit News*, 17; Charles Ward, *Detroit Free Press*, 16.

3   Murphy, 15.

4   Henry McLemore, "Fancy Diving –Ripple's Catch Rates Wing at Cooperstown," *Detroit Free Press*, October 7, 1940, 13.

5   ⁵H.G. Salsinger, "Umpire," *Detroit News*," October 7, 1940, 17.

6   Sam Greene, "Cheers Still in His Ears, Buck Chokes Back Tears," *Detroit News*, October 7, 1940, 17.

7   Ibid .

8   Ibid.

9   Greene, 18.

10   Lewis Walter, *Detroit Times*, October 7, 1940, 14.

"LISTEN, YOU LUG..."

July 8, 1941: American League 7, National League 5 at Briggs Stadium

By Marc Lancaster

TED WILLIAMS BOUNDED DOWN THE first-base line at Briggs Stadium like the kid he was. He clapped his hands twice as he neared the bag then bounded over it with a joyful skip as he made his way around the bases.

Williams's three-run homer with two outs in the bottom of the ninth had just won the All-Star Game for the American League, and the 22-year-old couldn't imagine that life could get much better.

"I've never been so happy and I've never seen so many happy guys," Williams would write decades later in his autobiography. "… I had hit what remains to this day the most thrilling hit of my life."[1]

Not to mention one of the most memorable hits in All-Star history.

The first midsummer classic held in Detroit will always have a special place in the game's lore because of the way it ended. Ted Williams, in the midst of a season that would see him hit .406, stepping on home plate and sharing a handshake with Joe DiMaggio, who was deep into what would become a 56-game hitting streak.

The rival outfielders had generated all the buzz heading into the game, though it was DiMaggio who commanded most of the headlines. The nine days before the All-Star Game had seen DiMaggio blow past George Sisler's American League record of 41 consecutive games with a hit and Wee Willie Keeler's all-time mark of 45 straight.

He came to Detroit sitting on 48 games and played it cool for inquiring newsmen: "Now the pressure is off. I have my fame. The rest is up to the pitcher who stops me. I'm not worried any more. Sisler's record lasted almost 20 years. By the law of averages mine should too."[2]

DiMaggio, 26, was an All-Star for the sixth time in as many years in the majors and the ever-studious Williams arrived in Detroit prepared to soak in all the knowledge he could from the Yankee great.

Williams bought an 8mm movie camera specifically to bring to the game and used it to film his peers during batting practice, with a focus on the pinstriped No. 5. "I want to study his style," Williams told reporters. "DiMaggio is the greatest hitter I ever saw and probably will see during my career."[3]

As game day approached, National League manager Bill McKechnie of the Reds put his faith in a seasoned pitching staff to hold down an impressive AL lineup. Countering an American League nine that featured six future Hall of Famers (including starting pitcher Bob Feller), McKechnie's seven-man pitching staff had a combined 21 games of All-Star experience under its belt heading into Detroit. Only Claude Passeau of the Cubs from that group was making his first All-Star appearance.

Rain had swept through the area the previous day, but Tuesday, July 8, brought "perfect" weather[4] and had fans streaming toward Michigan and Trumbull for the 1:30 P.M. start. The 1940 American League pennant won by the Tigers waved in the breeze and the ballpark was decked out in patriotic bunting for the occasion.

World War II was nearly two years old at that point, and even though the U.S. remained neutral the signs of what was to come were clear. The hometown team's biggest star, Hank Greenberg, was absent, having been inducted into the Army in May.[5] And proceeds from the game were earmarked for the USO, the first time in the nine-year history of the event that revenues would not be turned over to a fund for retired ballplayers.[6]

As the crowd of 54,674 settled in, Feller took the mound and opened the game by striking out Cubs third baseman Stan Hack. Feller and NL counterpart Whitlow Wyatt of the Dodgers did their part, allowing two baserunners between them in five scoreless innings. It wasn't until they departed that the hitters began to get limbered up. Naturally, Williams played a starring role.

Cecil Travis collected the first AL hit with a one-out double off Paul Derringer in the fourth and DiMaggio moved him to third with a fly ball to the vast reaches of center field. Williams followed with a double to right to put the American Leaguers up 1-0. The NL tied it on a Terry Moore sacrifice fly in the sixth before Lou Boudreau singled in DiMaggio in the bottom of that inning to put the AL back on top.

If the game had ended differently, it would no doubt have been remembered for Arky Vaughan's performance that afternoon. The Pirates shortstop's star turn began in the top of the seventh, when he followed Enos Slaughter's single off Washington's Sid Hudson with a home run into the inviting right-field deck to give the NL a 3-2 lead. Hudson worked himself into and out of a jam after that, escaping the inning with runners on first and third, but all that did was bring Vaughan back to the plate in the eighth. Facing Eddie Smith of the White Sox this time, Vaughan once again visited the upper deck in right to bring home Johnny Mize with a two-run shot that made it 5-2. That round-tripper made Vaughan the first player to hit two home runs in an All-Star Game.[7] He should have been a hero, wrote Gayle Talbot of the Associated Press, but he wound up "just another unfortunate who almost hit the jackpot."[8]

Claude Passeau, the 32-year-old first-time All-Star, was Bill McKechnie's choice to finish the game. Staked to a three-run lead as he came out to start the bottom of the eighth, he got in trouble quickly by allowing a one-out double to DiMaggio. After Passeau got a called third strike on Williams—a decision the slugger would discuss at length with home-plate umpire Babe Pinelli[9]—Ted's Boston teammate Dom DiMaggio rapped a single to center to score his older brother. Boudreau followed with a single and a Pete Reiser error allowed both runners to move up, but Passeau struck out Jimmie Foxx[10] to escape.

Passeau recorded a quick out to open the bottom of the ninth before everything began to unravel for the Mississippian. Ken Keltner collected a pinch-hit infield single and Joe Gordon followed with another single before Cecil Travis walked to load the bases for none other than Joe DiMaggio. After falling into a 0-and-2 hole, DiMaggio topped what appeared to be an easy double-play ball to shortstop Eddie Miller of the Braves. Miller fed to Billy Herman at second to force Travis, but Herman's relay throw pulled Frank McCormick off the bag at first, allowing Keltner to score and keeping the AL alive.

With the game in the balance, McKechnie visited the mound to confer with Passeau, catcher Harry Danning, and the infielders. Rather than choosing to put Williams on base and let Passeau, a right-hander, take his chances with the righty-swinging Dom DiMaggio, the Nationals decided to pitch to Ted. Williams killed time during the conference by sparring with Pinelli over the called third strike his previous time up, but the umpire stuck to his guns, insisting the pitch was a strike at the knees.[11] Williams then took a deep breath and gave himself a "fight talk."

"I said: 'Listen, you lug. He outguessed you last time and you got caught with your bat on your shoulder for a called third strike. You were swinging late when you fouled one off, too. Let's swing and swing a little earlier this time and see if we can connect.'"[12]

Williams worked the count to 2-and-1 and Passeau finally threw him "a fast one, chest high."[13] By the time Williams's bat had completed its trademark arc, the ball was screaming toward the facing of the upper deck in right field as the Detroit crowd roared its approval. Williams was mobbed by his AL teammates as he crossed the plate, with Feller emerging from the clubhouse in street clothes to join the celebration. Once the party moved inside, AL manager Del Baker of the Tigers gave Williams a kiss on the cheek.

There had been talk, then as now, about how much the midsummer exhibition actually meant to the players, but Williams's blow brushed such concerns aside. The next day's *Detroit Evening Times* described a

National League dressing room "plunged into gloom" before columnist Bob Murphy summed up the state of affairs:

"That one pitch destroyed forever the theory accepted in some quarters that there is no spirit in this All-Star game … that there is nothing at stake.

"No college football team ever showed more enthusiasm than the American Leaguers when Williams came trotting through the lengthening shadows toward home plate."[14]

NOTES

1   Ted Williams with John Underwood, *My Turn at Bat* (New York: Simon & Schuster, 1988), 87.

2   Edgar Hayes, "Best National League Hurlers Gun for DiMaggio Today," *Detroit Evening Times*, July 8, 1941.

3   Ben Bradlee Jr., *The Kid: The Immortal Life of Ted Williams* (New York: Little, Brown and Company, 2013), 180.

4   "Early Crowd Hints 58,000 Attendance," *Detroit Evening Times*, July 8, 1941.

5   Greenberg reportedly was in Detroit on leave for the All-Star Game but kept a low profile. Columnist Bob Murphy of the *Detroit Evening Times* wrote in July 8 editions with teasing vagueness about an encounter with the slugger at the Leland Hotel the night before the game, and the July 9 *Detroit Free Press* reported that Greenberg watched the game from "an obscure upper-deck seat where no photographers or reporters were around to make his presence known."

6   *Detroit Evening Times*, July 8, 1941.

7   Vaughan hit only two home runs the rest of the 1941 campaign, giving him six homers for the season in games that counted.

8   Gayle Talbot, "Ted's Big Homer Robs Vaughan of Laurels," *Washington Evening Star*, July 9, 1941.

9   The box score shows Bill Summers of the American League as the home-plate umpire, with Pinelli at third, but J.G. Taylor Spink's *Sporting News* column, July 17, 1941, notes that "the umpires switched midway through the game and the National leaguer, Babe Pinelli, was calling the balls and strikes" at the end.

10   Foxx was the only player selected for the first nine All-Star Games.

11   J.G. Taylor Spink, "That Toe-Tingling Thump by Ted the Terror," *The Sporting News*, July 17, 1941.

12   Ibid.

13   Ibid.

14   Bob Murphy, "Spirit of Players Shown in 1941 All-Star Game," *Detroit Evening News*, July 9, 1941.

"WE WANT GREENBERG!"

July 1, 1945: Detroit Tigers 9, Philadelphia Athletics 5 at Briggs Stadium (First Game of Doubleheader)

By Richard Riis

"WE'LL ALL HAVE THE ANSWER PRETTY soon. Hank Greenberg is coming back. If he can't make it, all the rest of them better cash in their GI pay and open a poolroom somewhere."[1] — Al Simmons

With the surrender of Germany and the Japanese Empire on the verge of collapse, war-weary Americans were eager for a return to peace and life as they had known it before the US entered World War II. The call to military duty had taken a toll no less on the national pastime than on any other occupation or field of endeavor, depriving fans of a phalanx of stars and favorite players and requiring major-league rosters to be filled out with 4-F and minor-league-caliber fill-ins.

Major-league players had returned from military service before. Some, like the Tigers' own Dick Wakefield in 1944, had even played a significant role in their team's fortunes. But no major-league hitter had spent as long away from the game as had the Tigers' slugging hero, Hank Greenberg. Drafted in May 1941 and discharged that December, only to rejoin the Army Air Corps after the attack on Pearl Harbor, Greenberg had spent more than four years in the service. Additionally, unlike many major leaguers who played in armed-services games in the US and overseas while serving in the armed forces, Greenberg had barely played at all — a couple of exhibition games, a 1943 War Bond benefit game at the Polo Grounds and a handful of pickup softball games in China — since his last game with the Tigers, on May 6, 1941.

"There is a question whether Greenberg can regain his former effectiveness as a hitter," wrote Sam Greene of the *Detroit Free Press*. "It will be a debatable question whether a ball player can be divorced from the game for two years or more and come back with anything like his former skill. Greenberg has been away for more than four years. … He will offer the first real test of the theory that they can't come back."[2]

The Sporting News was similarly pessimistic about Greenberg's ability to return to anything approaching his American League MVP form of 1940. "Nearly five seasons have elapsed. Greenberg now is 34 years of age. Quite obviously he is not in possession of the physical qualities which made him the highest salaried ball player of 1941. Perhaps, while in the service, Hank became rusty in the game."[3]

Although Greenberg himself was keen to pick up where he left off, he too hedged his bets. "Yes, I want to return to major league baseball," he had told the *New York Times* in February. "And if I can't return as a player, I want to return as a manager, a coach, or even to a job in a front office."[4]

"But I'd really love to get back and hit my 250th home run," he added. Two home runs against the Yankees in his last game had left Hank stuck at 249 for four years.

On June 14 Greenberg left the Army separation center at Fort Dix, New Jersey, spent a few days visiting family in New York, then flew to Detroit to rejoin the Tigers. Arriving at Briggs Stadium early on June 21, Greenberg took batting practice with Tigers reliever Zeb Eaton, after which he jogged the bases, shagged flies in the outfield, and fielded some balls at first base. There were no plans to play him in that afternoon's game against Cleveland, but the sight of Greenberg in a Tigers uniform brought chants of "We want Greenberg" from the early arrivals so long and loud that Hank was compelled to climb on top of the dugout to acknowledge the jubilant crowd, shaking hands and signing autographs.

When the Tigers left the next day for a road trip, Hank stayed behind. "After ten days or two weeks," said Greenberg, "I'll have a lot better idea than I have now of how much or how little I can help the club. I believe it will be a matter of timing. I know I need plenty of batting practice."[5]

Bill Crouch, a local sandlotter who'd had brief stints with the Dodgers, Phillies, and Cardinals, was hired to serve as Greenberg's personal pitcher for hour upon hour of daily drills at the ballpark. Blisters developed on Hank's hands and the skin peeled off his palms. His throwing arm grew sore and his legs ached. After 10 days of toil he still wasn't sure of his timing at the plate, but with the Tigers struggling to hit .240 as a team and clinging to a slim 1½-game lead over the Yankees, the pressure was mounting to put Greenberg in the lineup. Manager Steve O'Neill gave him a day's reprieve from practice and announced that Greenberg would play in the first game of the Tigers' doubleheader against the Philadelphia Athletics on July 1.

"Hank will help the club if he never gets the bat off his shoulder," stressed Tigers general manager Jack Zeller. "Just having him around will pay off in inspiration to the rest of the fellows."[6]

The largest crowd of the year so far—47,729 in paid attendance plus nearly 1,000 servicemen admitted free—filled Briggs Stadium that Sunday afternoon to see the return of Hank Greenberg. O'Neill sat Jimmy Outlaw, the Tigers' leading hitter at .284, and put Greenberg in left field, batting cleanup.

The stadium erupted with tumultuous applause each time Hank came to bat. His hands raw, his arm

still sore, Greenberg flied out twice to right field and popped up to the catcher in his first three trips to the plate against Athletics starter Jesse Flores. In the seventh inning Hank walked on four straight pitches from reliever Bobo Newsom, then pulled his left hamstring running from first to third on Doc Cramer's single.

In the field Greenberg handled the ball but twice. Once he scooped up a ball hit by Charlie Metro and threw to second base, but there was no play as Metro settled for a single. In the eighth inning Hank, still hobbled by the pulled hamstring, backed against the left-field screen to pull down a long fly, again off the bat of Metro, for his only putout of the game.

Thanks to a six-run outburst in the seventh inning highlighted by Rudy York's three-run homer, the Tigers had pulled themselves out of a 5-2 hole to take an 8-5 lead by the time Greenberg came to bat again in the bottom of the eighth. Leaving aside his 36-ounce bat in favor of Cramer's 34-ounce bat, hoping it would help him get around better on the ball, Hank took three straight balls from left-hander Charlie Gassaway, then watched the reliever's fourth pitch go by for a called strike. On the next delivery, Greenberg whipped Cramer's bat around and connected. As the ball cleared the fence in left-center and settled in the pavilion some 390 feet away, the crowd rose to its feet. To a standing ovation Hank trotted around the bases in an improbable but unforgettable coda to a hero's return to baseball.[7]

That the Tigers took both ends of the doubleheader was far from the story of the day, as "for the big crowd," in the words of one newspaper account, "and for millions interested in a soldier's transition from military life to resumption of a major-league career, one man gripped attention."[8] With a single swing of the bat, Hank Greenberg had silenced any doubt and threw the doors of opportunity open wide for his fellow servicemen returning home.

Hank Greenberg slugs one out

SOURCES

Books

Greenberg, Hank, with Ira Berkow, *The Story of My Life* (New York: Times Books, 1989).

Rosengren, John, *Hank Greenberg: The Hero of Heroes* (New York: New American Library, 2013).

Smith, Burge Cameron, *The 1945 Detroit Tigers: Nine Old Men and One Young Left Arm Win It All* (Jefferson, North Carolina: McFarland, 2010).

Newspapers

Detroit Free Press.

Detroit News.

NOTES

1   Red Smith, "When Hank Came Back," *New York Herald Tribune*, January 30, 1956, 24.

2   Sam Greene, "Greenberg Gives New Flag Punch to Tigers," *The Sporting News*, June 21, 1945, 1.

3   "Returning Servicemen Create Problems," *The Sporting News*, June 21, 1945, 12.

4   Arthur Daley, "Sports of the Times," *New York Times*, February 13, 1945, 28.

5   Sam Greene, "Hank in A-1 Shape—Old Suit a Perfect Fit," *The Sporting News*, June 28, 1945, 6.

6   Sam Greene, "Hank Breaks In Again With a Bang," *The Sporting News*, July 5, 1945, 2.

7   "Tigers Win Two; Hank Homers," *Newsday* (Long Island, New York), July 2, 1945, 13.

8   Sam Greene, "Hank Breaks In Again…," 2.

HUTCHINSON ENDS YANKS' 19-GAME WIN STREAK

July 18, 1947: Detroit Tigers 8, New York Yankees 0 at Briggs Stadium

By Mike Whiteman

MICHIGAN AND TRUMBULL WAS ONE of the more popular destinations in the major leagues in the mid-1940s. The Tigers led all of baseball in attendance in 1944. In 1945 they did even better as they attracted over 30 percent more home rooters than the next team while drawing a Detroit record 1,280,341 spectators. The 1946 season saw the Tigers ranking behind only the New York Yankees in home attendance.

And why not? Detroit had fielded the world champions in 1945 and second-place teams in 1944 and 1946 behind stars like Hank Greenberg, Hal Newhouser, and Dizzy Trout. The Tigers were one of the premier teams in the American League, having fielded a winning team in 11 of the last 13 seasons (1934-1946), and won four pennants and two world championships in that span. Arguably, they were the most successful team in the American League outside of New York.

The Yankees had recently not experienced much in the way of success, however. After winning pennants from 1941 through 1943, they had gone three years without winning the AL race, almost an eternity for the New Yorkers. In 1946 they had finished 17 games behind pennant-winning Boston, their furthest off the flag since 1929.

In 1947, though, the Yankees were playing like a team on a mission, and were threatening to make a mockery of the junior-circuit race. After getting off to a sluggish start, the Yankees hosted Boston May 23-26 and swept the defending champs while outscoring them 40-5 over the four games. In fact, since May 23, Bucky Harris's squad was 45-12, playing .789 ball, and riding a 19-game winning streak. Pundits were calling this squad a team for the ages. Opposing players and managers grudgingly admitted that the Yanks were clearly the class of the league.

A victory this afternoon, July 18, 1947, would give the Yankees 20 wins in a row and with it the American League record for the longest winning streak, which they currently shared with the Hitless Wonders, the 1906 Chicago White Sox. The major-league standard was 26, held by John McGraw's 1916 New York Giants.

The Yankees were entrusting right-handed pitcher Randy Gumpert with the streak. Gumpert was undefeated (3-0) with a 4.08 ERA as a part-time starter thus far in the season. He had his first sustained opportunity in 1946 and took advantage of it, going 11-3 with a 2.31 ERA.

Taking the mound for Detroit was right-hander Fred Hutchinson, a pitcher whose main weapons on the mound were his control, his change of pace, and his heart. Hutch came onto the big-league scene pretty quickly, having made his major-league debut against the Yankees as a 19-year-old. That contest, on May 2, 1939, was memorable: It was the game in which Lou Gehrig had voluntarily ended his 2,130-game playing streak. Hutch was a bit player in the drama of that day, pitching only two-thirds of an inning, but allowing eight runs. After his disaster of a debut, Hutchinson continued to struggle in his first two seasons, working a combined 6-13 record in 1939 and 1940 around minor-league stints. Back in the International League full-time in 1941, Hutchinson spun a 26-7, 2.44 record and seemed poised to get back to Detroit in 1942 — until he joined the Navy after Pearl Harbor. Upon his return in 1946, he immediately became a factor in the Tigers rotation, going 14-11, 3.09 in 1946 and 7-3, 3.63 thus far in 1947. This was his first start since June 19; because of a sore shoulder, he had been limited to occasional relief outings. The visiting Yankees were likely not Hutch's first choice of an opponent in his return to the rotation; he came into the game with a 6.68 ERA in 31 career innings against them.

The contest was scheduled to start at 5:30 P.M. As night baseball was gaining in popularity—about a quarter of American League games were played at night—Detroit was the last AL holdout, not yet having installed lights in Briggs Stadium. In 1943 the Tigers started holding "twilight games." In 1947 seven of them were scheduled from June through August. These games were quite popular with fans, as they allowed workers the opportunity to catch a game after their employment was done for the day. The first such game in 1947, played June 10 against the Philadelphia Athletics, drew 36,143 fans, and the Tigers management was hoping to top 200,000 twilight spectators for 1947. This day's crowd was listed at 28,718—significantly higher than the usual Detroit crowd.

After going down in order in the first inning, the Yanks found themselves in a hole early, as Detroit put two runs on the scoreboard in the bottom of the frame.

Joe DiMaggio, who was hitting .375 with 17 home runs over the past 19 games, led off the second inning with a single. Unfazed, Hutchinson retired first baseman George McQuinn and got third baseman Billy Johnson to ground into a double play to end the inning. The Yankee Clipper was the only baserunner Hutchinson allowed until Snuffy Stirnweiss's bunt single in the seventh inning.

During the streak, the New Yorkers had come from behind to pull out victories six times. Could this be the beginning of another such rally? It would be a daunting task, as the Tigers were up 3-0 and Hutchinson had looked almost untouchable. But Stirnweiss was stranded at first, and the Tigers then scored four runs in the bottom of the seventh, chasing Gumpert. They tacked on another run in the eighth off Yankee right-hander Karl Drews to increase the lead to 8-0.

In tallying their runs, the Tigers had ripped out 18 hits—16 of which were singles! The only extra-base hits were two doubles by Hutchinson, a .316 career hitter entering the 1947 season. The Tigers left 10 runners on base, indicating that the score could have been worse for New York.

In the top of the ninth, Hutchinson set New York down in order, ending the Yankees' winning streak in a mere hour and 43 minutes. He allowed only five balls out of the infield, and Yankees coach John Corriden called Hutchinson's masterpiece "the best game anybody has thrown at us all season."[1] Batterymate Bob Swift was impressed as well, saying that Hutchinson was "almost perfect."[2]

With the end of the streak, the Yanks were 58-27, the Tigers 45-35—10½ games back. Hutchinson certainly looked to be back in form. During the Yankees' 19-game streak, Detroit had gone 14-5, an indicator that they too were capable of reeling off a victory streak. With more than 70 games remaining, could the Tigers make a run at the AL flag?[3]

SOURCES

James, Bill, and Rob Neyer, *The Neyer/James Guide to Pitchers* (New York: Fireside, 2004), 252.

Sporting News

Eals, Clay, "Fred Hutchinson," The Baseball Biography Project, sabr.org/bioproj/person/8584a2d4, accessed October 4, 2014.

Ferkovich, Scott, "Behind Fred Hutchinson, the Tigers Halted the Yankees 19-Game Winning Streak in 1947," Detroit Athletic Co., blog.detroitathletic.com/2014/06/25/behind-fred-hutchinson-tigers-halted-yankees-19-game-winning-streak-1947/, accessed October 20, 2014.

NOTES

1   Sam Greene. "Hats Off—Fred Hutchinson," *The Sporting News*, July 30, 1947.

2   Ibid.

3   The Tigers were not able to mount a run, and on August 21 even fell into fourth place, 15 games behind. The Yankees' lead was never less than 9½ games the rest of the season and they ended up 97-57, 12 games ahead of the second-place Tigers. The Yanks went on to defeat Brooklyn in seven games in the World Series.

58,369 FANS MOST EVER AT THE CORNER

July 20, 1947: Detroit Tigers 12, New York Yankees 11 (11 innings) at Briggs Stadium

By Ruth Sadler

SUNDAY, JULY 20, 1947, WAS A SUNNY day in Detroit after a cool and rainy Saturday. The second-place Tigers were wrapping up a four-game set with the New York Yankees, whom they trailed by 11½ games.

Good weather had been in short supply in Detroit. Tigers management was expecting a crowd of 40,000 for Friday's series opener, fans eager to see if their Tigers could end the Yankees' 19-game winning streak, tied for the longest in American League history. There were many umbrellas among the 28,718 fans who braved dark skies before Friday's twilight start, then rain in the early innings, as Fred Hutchinson pitched a two-hitter to hand the Yankees their first loss since June 29. It was a cool 63 degrees on Saturday, and the rain was lighter, but that only helped push attendance to 31,772 to see a 2-1 loss. Normally, Detroiters could expect highs in the low 80s in July.

The Yankees would be leaving town after the doubleheader, but so would the Tigers—for 15 days. It was the fourth of five Sunday doubleheaders at Briggs Stadium that year, the last before lights were installed. Less-than-ideal weather had been putting a damper on crowds all season, even with two games for the price of one. Despite rain and drizzle, 36,443 saw their first-place team split with the Chicago White Sox in the May 25 doubleheader. But a month later, after the Tigers had gone from first place and eight games over .500 to third place and a .500 record, only 13,292 were willing to deal with a thunderstorm to see the Tigers sweep the last-place St. Louis Browns on June 29 and go two games over. On Sunday, July 13, 40,286 had seen the Tigers sweep the A's in a doubleheader, the biggest crowd of the 11-day homestand and only the second day of the homestand with no rain recorded. Would the sun again bring more fans?

The ballpark's last expansion, during the winter of 1937-38, had raised the official capacity to 56,000, making Briggs Stadium the AL's third largest ballpark behind Yankee Stadium in New York and Municipal Stadium in Cleveland.[1] Once this season, paying customers had more than filled every seat. The season's largest crowd (56,367) had turned out for a Memorial Day doubleheader, on Friday, May 30, to see the then-first-place Tigers split with the last-place Browns. It was a relatively chilly 57 degrees. (The normal high would be in the mid-70s). The second largest crowd was for a single game, on Sunday, June 8, when 55,941 had seen the first-place Tigers beat the Boston Red Sox, 5-0, to pick up a half-game on the Yankees, who split a doubleheader in St. Louis.

Sunday's crowd was going to be buoyed by a group of 150 from Fayette County, Pennsylvania, coming to Detroit by special train.[2] They would be there for Pat Mullin Day, honoring their hometown favorite, Tigers outfielder Pat Mullin, between games with gifts including a gold-studded Elks ring.[3] They were not disappointed: Mullin, who had been a member of the AL All-Star team earlier in the month, homered in both games.

What fans also got was a dry day, with a low of 51 giving way to a high of 74, a big improvement over most days of the homestand, which had been warm (four were above 80) but wet. It must have felt like baseball weather to a lot of people in the Detroit area, because thousands were converging on the corner of Michigan and Trumbull.

What they got (if they were Tigers fans) was a great day of baseball. Hal Newhouser won his 10th with a three-hitter in the opener to win, 4-1. He faced only 28 batters (and threw 89 pitches), and the Yankees left none on base (a mark that has been accomplished many times in both leagues). The Yankees scored in the fifth, when they got two of their hits, triples by Joe DiMaggio and Bill Johnson. Mullin, Eddie Lake, Dick Wakefield, and Hal Wagner drove in runs for Detroit.

The second game was a wild one that Detroit won in 11 innings, 12-11. The Tigers' 5-4 lead evaporated in the sixth when the Yankees batted around to take an 11-5 lead. Mullin's two-run pinch homer in the bottom of the sixth cut the deficit to four. By the bottom of the ninth, according to accounts in the *Detroit News* and *Detroit Free Press*, thousands had left.[4]

Before this exodus, the crowd had been announced as a Briggs Stadium record 58,369. Club officials put the overflow in the outfield, something they hadn't done since the 1930s.[5] The July 30 edition of *The Sporting News* noted that it was the largest Sunday crowd of the season, beating the 58,339 at Yankee Stadium on April 27 for Babe Ruth Day ceremonies.[6]

After that exodus, estimated by the *Detroit News* at 15,000, John McHale led off with a pinch single off Randy Gumpert, the third Yankees pitcher. Eddie Lake followed with a single. Next up was Roy Cullenbine, who had walked four times. He sent Gumpert's pitch into the right-field stands to pull the Tigers within one run (11-10) with none out. Allie Reynolds, the winner of Saturday's game, replaced Gumpert. After Dick Wakefield reached first base, Reynolds gave up a game-tying double to George Kell (his first hit in 13 at-bats).[7] Vic Wertz was walked intentionally, and Hoot Evers sacrificed. Eddie Mayo was walked to fill the bases with one out. Doc Cramer, batting for Bob Swift, fouled out. McHale, who had started the ninth-inning rally, came up again, but he watched a third strike to end the rally.

After rookie Art Houtteman pitched a perfect 11th, Wertz opened the Tigers' half of the inning with a single, but he was forced by Evers. Mayo sent a double to right-center, and Evers scored the winning run with a head-first slide to beat Tommy Henrich's long throw.

The *Detroit News*, an evening paper, ran a panoramic photo across the top of its sports section the next day with a white headline superimposed on the photo: "58,369 — BRIGGS STADIUM RECORD TIGERS WIN! 4-1 AND 12-11"

But the editors didn't squeeze a word of the story on the front page of the first edition. The morning *Free Press* had a two-column headline (in an eight-column paper): "58,369 See Tigers Whip Yanks Twice." The game account was continued in the sports section.

And then?

The record crowd gave a boost to Tigers season attendance, but the numbers were dismal, compared with the record-breaking 1946 season. The *Free Press* noted that at 939,913 after 50 games, the Tigers were 252,547 behind the 1946 attendance at that point, and it blamed the rain.[8] The Tigers finished the season with 1,398,093 paying customers, fourth in the eight-team AL. That ranks 45th of the team's 114 seasons through 2015 and second (to 1946) of those with only day games.

When the ballpark, by then known as Tiger Stadium, closed after the 1999 season, this July 20, 1947, crowd remained the largest ever to pay to see a game at Michigan and Trumbull.

SOURCES

Books

Anderson, William M. *The Glory Years of the Detroit Tigers 1920-1950* (Detroit: Wayne State University Press, 2012), 434.

Bak, Richard. *Cobb Would Have Caught It* (Detroit: Wayne State University Press, 1991), 129.

Newspapers

Salsinger, H.G. "58,369 — Briggs Stadium Record Tigers Win! 4-1 and 12-11," *Detroit News*, July 21, 1947.

Smith, Lyall. "58,369 See Tigers Whip Yanks Twice," *Detroit Free Press*, July 21, 1947.

Smith, Lyall. "Attendance Short of '46 Mark," *Detroit Free Press*, July 22, 1947.

Detroit Free Press, July 21, 1947.

"Tigers Set Home Crowd Mark With 58,369, July 20," *The Sporting News*, July 30, 1947.

Detroit News, July 19, 1947.

Detroit News, July 21, 1947.

Online Sources

Farmersalmanac.com/weather-history.

Wunderground.com.

"Pat Mullin," Fayette County Sports Hall of Fame, fayettecountysportshalloffame.com/2012/mullin.html , accessed December 14, 2014.

Personal Correspondence

Debra Elliott, email correspondence with author, January 23, 2015.

NOTES

1   William M. Anderson. *The Glory Years of the Detroit Tigers 1920–1950* (Detroit: Wayne State University Press, 2012), 434.

2   "Pat Mullin," Fayette County Sports Hall of Fame, fayettecountysportshalloffame.com/2012/mullin.html , accessed December 14, 2014.

3   "Tigers Set Home Crowd Mark with 58,369, July 20," *The Sporting News*, July 30, 1947.

4   "Winning Run in Eleventh That 15,000 of 58,369 Failed to See," *Detroit News*, July 21, 1947; Lyall Smith, "58,369 See Tigers Whip Yanks Twice," *Detroit Free Press*, July 21, 1947.

5   Richard Bak. *Cobb Would Have Caught It* (Detroit: Wayne State University Press, 1991), 129.

6   "Tigers Set Home Crowd Mark."

7   Game accounts are inconsistent as to how Wakefield reached base (or if he even did at all). Both the *Detroit News* and the *Free Press* wrote that he was walked by Reynolds. The *News* said that Mierkowicz ran for Wakefield and later scored the tying run. Baseballreference.com and Retrosheet, which both have a box score but no play-by-play account of the contest, show that Wakefield had no walks in the game, but Mierkowicz had one base on balls in two plate appearances (he struck out in his second at-bat later in the game). *The Sporting News* box score does not even show Mierkowicz running for Wakefield.

8   Lyall Smith, "Attendance Short of '46 Mark," *Detroit Free Press*, July 22, 1947.

"LOOK AT YOUR WONDERFUL LIGHTS HERE..."

June 15, 1948: Detroit Tigers 4, Philadelphia Athletics 1, at Briggs Stadium

By Scott Dominiak

WALTER O. BRIGGS WAS DEFINITELY old school.

As the owner of the Detroit Tigers, he had long believed that the national pastime was meant to be played in the daytime. "Baseball belongs to the sun and the sun to baseball," he argued.[1]

But the national pastime was entering a new era. Ever since May 24, 1935, when Cincinnati's Crosley Field hosted the first major-league contest under the stars, more and more ballparks were erecting light towers.

By the beginning of the 1948 season, the Tigers remained the last bastion of daytime-only baseball in the American League. That changed on June 15, when the Bengals finally played the first night game at Briggs Stadium (That left Wrigley Field in Chicago as the only remaining major-league park without lights.).

Many baseball fans may wonder why it had taken the Tigers so long. The primary reason, of course, was Briggs himself. And even though his son, Walter "Spike" Briggs Jr., who was a member of the front office, encouraged his father to install lights as early as 1936, the elder Briggs resisted.

It should be noted, however, that the senior Briggs had indeed consented to install light towers for the 1942 season, and had even placed an order for the steel. But when the Japanese attack on Pearl Harbor on December 7, 1941, dragged the United States into World War II, Briggs canceled the order and the steel was used for the war effort. Some of those close to Briggs said that he was pleased not to have to go through with the installation.

Three years after the war ended, however, Briggs had a change of heart, and realized that his namesake ballpark would have to enter the modern age. In other cities, night baseball had opened up a whole new customer base. It allowed the workingman to head down to the ballpark after his day at the office (or the factory) was done. Briggs was forced to admit that night baseball made economic sense.

He insisted on the best lighting system available, which included eight 150-foot-high light towers with a total of 1,386 bulbs. The cost was slightly more than $400,000. On May 10, 1948, the press was invited to a test run. Briggs, wheelchair-bound as a result of polio, threw the switch to light up the grand ballpark. To demonstrate how bright it was, groundskeeper Neil Conway sat at second base, reading a newspaper.

Six weeks later, the highly anticipated night arrived at the corner of Michigan and Trumbull. The gates were opened at 6:00. The Tigers, managed by Steve O'Neill, took batting practice from 7:15 to 8:00, while Connie Mack's visiting Philadelphia Athletics did so from 8:00 to 8:30. The evening was chilly, only 59 degrees at game time. "It's a coffee night," said Charlie Jacobs, a concessionaire, "nothing much but coffee. Too cold for anything else."[2]

It had been decided to wait until it was nearly fully dark before turning on the lights, thus allowing them to take full effect. When the switch was flipped at exactly 9:29, the bright bulbs flooded the green field with a dazzling glow, and the crowd of 54,480 let out a collective cry of wonder.

And then the game commenced.

A's shortstop Eddie Joost led off by drawing a base on balls from Detroit native Hal Newhouser. At 27, the left-handed Newhouser already had 138 big-league wins and two Most Valuable Player awards under his belt. He retired the next two A's, and then walked Ferris Fain to move Joost into scoring position. A double by Hank Majeski gave Philadelphia a 1-0 lead.

Newhouser remained shaky in the top of the third as he walked the first two batters. But a double play and a groundout saved the Tigers from further damage.

In the bottom of the third the Tigers tallied two runs on three walks and a single by Hoot Evers. Newhouser, meanwhile, found his groove and allowed only one hit and two walks the rest of the way.

Detroit padded its precarious 2-1 lead in the bottom of the eighth when Dick Wakefield and Pat Mullin each hit a solo home run to close out the scoring at 4-1.

In pitching his eighth complete game of the season, Newhouser gave up only two hits, walked six, and struck out five to lower his ERA to 2.98. It was his seventh consecutive victory. A's starter Joe Coleman, who also went the distance, saw his record drop to 7-3, despite a solid effort.

Detroit won its fifth game in a row to improve to 27-25 and remained in fourth place, seven games out of first. The second-place A's, three games off the pace, fell to 31-21.

From his box seat behind third base, American League President Will Harridge gave his stamp of approval of the scene. "This is the best lighted park of them all," he testified at 10:49 P.M. "It sets a new standard for night baseball."[3]

And what about the 84-year-old Mack, who had managed the A's since 1901 and had played in his first big-league game in 1886, not long after Thomas Edison began toying around with his first incandescent light bulb in his Menlo Park laboratory? "Look at your wonderful lights here at Briggs Stadium," Mack exclaimed. "It makes it just like day in your beautiful park. And what a beautiful park! Briggs Stadium is the finest park in baseball."[4]

Others, however, were more skeptical. Said George Kell, the Tigers' All-Star third baseman, "I'm an afternoon ballplayer. Playing at night seems like a carnival or a sideshow."[5]

One fan in attendance, who had seen his first ballgame at old Bennett Park in the 1907 World Series,

observed, "I think it's much better than a day game. For my money, you can't beat it."[6]

Night games quickly proved to be a success in the Motor City. The Tigers played 14 games under the lights in 1948, with an average attendance of around 45,000, a significant increase over afternoon affairs.

That cool June evening in 1948 wasn't the first time that baseball had been played under artificial lighting at Michigan and Trumbull. On September 24, 1896, when old Bennett Park still stood at the location, the Western League's Tigers played a doubleheader exhibition against the National League's Cincinnati Reds. Makeshift electric lights were originally scheduled to be strung up between games. With dusk approaching, however, and Detroit leading 13-4 after eight innings in the opener, the umpire halted the game in order to allow the lights to be hastily hung.

Details of the game have been lost to time, although one newspaper stated that the event was a financial success, with nearly 1,200 cranks on hand.

It took more than 50 years for another night game to be played at the corner of Michigan and Trumbull.

But it was worth the wait.

SOURCES

Bak, Richard, Charlie Vincent, and the *Free Press* Staff. *The Corner: A Century of Memories at Michigan and Trumbull (Honoring a Detroit Legend)* (New York: Triumph Books, 2000).

Enders, Eric, *Ballparks Then and Now* (San Diego: Thunder Bay Press, 2002).

Whitt, Alan, ed. *They Earned Their Stripes: The Detroit Tigers All-Time Team* (Champaign, Illinois: Sports Publishing, Inc., 2000).

NOTES

1   Richard Bak, *A Place For Summer: A Narrative History of Tiger Stadium* (Detroit: Wayne State University Press, 1998), 215.

2   H.G. Salsinger, "The Umpire," *Detroit News*, June 16, 1948.

3   Salsinger.

4   Leo Macdonnell, "Mostly Night Contests Predicted by Mack," *Detroit Times*, June 16, 1948.

5   F. A. Batchelor Jr., "Tigers Like Night Games," *Detroit Times* June 16, 1948.

6   Riley Murray, "Fans Roar Approval of New Lights," *Detroit Free Press* June 16, 1948.

"A FELLOW DOESN'T HAVE A NIGHT LIKE THAT VERY OFTEN"

June 23, 1950: Detroit Tigers 10, New York Yankees 9 at Briggs Stadium

By Chip Mundy

A RECORD-SETTING HOME-RUN barrage and a thrilling finish at Briggs Stadium left a big impression on even the most time-tested of baseball minds in June of 1950.

Detroit Tigers manager Red Rolfe seemed amazed. "Did you ever see a game like last night's? I never did," he said.[1]

Will Harridge, president of the American League, sat in the press box high above home plate. He simply said, "Never saw anything like it."[2]

Rolfe and Harridge were both correct. What happened on a warm Friday night at Briggs Stadium on June 23, 1950, was something nobody had seen: A record 11 home runs in one major-league game. The previous record of 10 had been accomplished three times; once in 1923, another in 1930, and again in 1947.

Toss aside the home-run record, and it still was an entertaining, back-and-forth game that ended in improbable fashion—a two-run, game-ending, inside-the-park home run to wipe out a one-run deficit and give the Tigers a thrilling 10-9 victory over the defending world champion Yankees.

Lyall Smith, sports editor of the *Detroit Free Press*, wrote that Briggs Stadium "was a madhouse by game's end."[3]

The Yankees led the Tigers 9-8 going into the bottom of the ninth. New York had left-hander Joe Page, its top-notch relief pitcher (he had led the AL in saves with 27 in 1949), on the mound. But the Tigers saddled Page with a blown save and a loss.

Tigers third baseman George Kell popped out to start the ninth before Vic Wertz lined a double to the wall in left-center. That brought Hoot Evers to the plate.

Evers, a right-handed hitter who had not hit more than 10 homers in any of his first four seasons, laced a 1-and-1 pitch to right-center. The ball took a bounce and caromed off the wall at the 415-foot mark. Wertz easily scored the tying run, and as Yankees center fielder Joe DiMaggio chased the ball, Evers raced around the bases. As he approached third, DiMaggio's relay to Yankees rookie second baseman Billy Martin was off-target. Tigers third-base coach Dick Bartell waved Evers home, and Evers scored standing up for his second homer of the game and 12th of the season.

"When he hit that ball in the last of the ninth, every player in our dugout was on his feet," Kell wrote in the *Detroit Free Press*. "We knew it was for extra bases when it left his bat. We were screaming, 'Take three, take three,' hoping that he'd be in a spot to score on a fly ball.

"But when the relay was wide, he kept going, and I'll bet he set a record for going around the bases. I never saw anybody run like that, and every guy on the team was running right with him."

Kell asked Evers about the big hit after the game.

"I just want to sit here for a while and think about it," Evers said. "A fellow doesn't have a night like that very often … maybe once in his life and that's all."[4]

The pregame outlook did not suggest a slugfest, at least not for the Tigers. Yankees manager Casey Stengel had Tigers nemesis Tommy Byrne on the mound. Byrne, a 30-year-old left-hander, came into the game with an 8-1 record and was 17-2 since July of 1949. In 14 career starts against the Tigers, Byrne was 11-2 with a 2.83 ERA and three shutouts.

"We know Byrne and the Yankees are always tough on us, but we're bound to start hitting and getting

Hoot Evers had his best year in 1950

A-No. 1 pitching again, so I am not too worried," Rolfe said.[5]

Rolfe gave the ball to 25-year-old left-hander Ted Gray, a World War II veteran who in five previous starts against New York was 1-1 with a 5.63 ERA. It appeared that, other than being left-handed, the only similarity between the two pitchers was that both were born on New Year's Eve.

It was to be a four-game showdown between the top two teams in the AL. The Tigers had the best record in baseball at 37-18 and tied the 1911 Tigers' franchise mark for the best record after 55 games. The Yankees had the second-best record in baseball at 38-21.

Night baseball was still somewhat of a novelty in Detroit, which in 1948 had become the last American League team to install lights. This was just the fourth night game at Briggs Stadium in 1950 and the 31st overall, and a crowd of 51,400 showed up — the third crowd of more than 50,000 at that point in 1950.

The Yankees scored first as Hank Bauer belted a two-run home run in the top of the first and added a solo shot in the third. After DiMaggio followed with a double, Yankees catcher Yogi Berra smacked a two-run homer to right to give New York a 5-0 lead.

New York second baseman Jerry Coleman sent Gray to the showers with a solo home run in the top of the fourth. Rolfe turned to veteran right-hander Dizzy Trout, a two-time 20-game winner for the Tigers who had started against Washington the night before but lasted just an inning and two-thirds in a 5-2 loss.

This time, Ol' Diz was on his game, both on the mound and at the plate. He belted a one-out grand slam in the bottom of the fourth for his 18th career home run and second career grand slam. It gave him at least one home run in nine consecutive seasons.

But the Tigers weren't done in the fourth. Second baseman Jerry Priddy homered to cut New York's lead to 6-5 and chase Byrne from the game. Right-hander Fred Sanford, who lost 21 games with the St. Louis Browns in 1948, came on in relief for the Yankees, but he failed to retire a batter.

Kell, the 1949 AL batting champion, who came into the game leading the majors with a .371 average, singled and scored on a home run by Wertz — it was the most majestic of the 11 home runs as it bounced off the roof in right field. Evers followed with the first of his two homers to give the Tigers an eight-run inning and a place in the record book.

The four home runs by the Tigers in the fourth inning tied the AL record of most homers by one team in an inning, set by Boston on September 24, 1940.

Trout, who came on in the fourth, retired 11 out of 12 batters to keep Detroit's lead at 8-6 before DiMaggio homered to left to cut the Tigers' lead to one. Although it was the second homer in two days and fourth in the past six for DiMaggio, he clearly was not the same hitter known as the Yankee Clipper.

DiMaggio came to Detroit with an uncharacteristic .250 batting average that had been as low as .239 six days earlier. He was just three days removed from collecting the 2,000th hit of his career, making him the third active player with at least 2,000 hits, joining Luke Appling and Wally Moses.

"I haven't got that feeling that I used to have that I can walk up there and hit any pitcher who ever lived," he said.[6]

Trout's run came to an end in the top of the eighth when Old Reliable Tommy Henrich, pinch-hitting for Coleman, smacked a one-out, two-run homer to give New York a 9-8 lead. It was the 10th home run of the game—tying the major-league record for most combined home runs by two teams in one game—and it ended Trout's night. Rolfe replaced him with Paul Calvert, who gave up two hits before being relieved by Fred Hutchinson. He got out of the inning with no further damage.

Trout, meanwhile, showered and went to his car to listen to the remainder of the game on the radio. Thinking he might be the losing pitcher two days in a row, he opted to listen to broadcaster Harry Heilmann call the final inning on the radio.

The win went to Fred Hutchinson, another pitcher who was a starter the majority of the time but came out of the bullpen for this game. Hutchinson pitched 1⅔ perfect innings in relief, although he was aided by Evers in the top of the ninth. Evers went back to the fence in left and made a leaping catch of a ball hit by DiMaggio that had a chance to leave the stadium.

Hutchinson, however, did not want to overlook the contributions made by Ol' Diz.

"If I had my way, Diz," he said with a slap on the shoulder, "I'd have them give you credit for the game. You deserved it."[7]

NOTES

1   Roscoe McGowen, "Yanks Are Topped by the Tigers, 4-1," *New York Times*, June 25, 1950.

2   Lyall Smith, "Old Diz Lights Fuse, It May Be Flag Blast," *Detroit Free Press*, June 25, 1950.

3   Ibid.

4   George Kell, "Kell Tells," *Detroit Free Press*, June 25, 1950.

5   Associated Press. *Jackson Citizen Patriot*, June 23, 1950.

6   Peter Golenbock. *Dynasty: The New York Yankees 1949-64.* (Englewood Cliffs, New Jersey: Prentice-Hall, Inc., 2010), 37.

7   Kell.

"WE'RE THE BIG GUYS NOW..."

July 10, 1951: National League 8, American League 3 at Briggs Stadium

By Marc Lancaster

RALPH KINER HAD AN IDEA WHAT might be coming as baseball's stars gathered in Detroit, even if the sporting world at large had yet to figure it out.

In the summer of 1951, the American and National Leagues were still perceived as playing a different type of game. The junior circuit, in its 50th year of existence, was all about power. It was Babe Ruth's league, even three years after his death. The senior circuit, through 75 years of history, was still viewed in some quarters as if the Deadball Era remained in full force.

Dueling columns that ran in the *Detroit Free Press* the day of the 1951 All-Star Game bore that out. George Kell of the Tigers lauded the NL's fine pitching staff, to be led by Robin Roberts for the second consecutive year.

Kiner, though, offered up some friendly advice for the public and his opponents: "I just want to give you Detroit fans and you American Leaguers a few tips: You're going to see one of the all-time greats in Stan Musial, a terrific competitor in Jackie Robinson and a fine home-run hitter in Gil Hodges. The National League starting team is loaded with power."[1]

Once the 18th midsummer classic got underway, the Pittsburgh slugger's words would be borne out.

* * *

The idea had been for All-Star week to serve as a jewel in a yearlong celebration of Detroit. Baseball's grand showcase had been ticketed for Shibe Park in Philadelphia that year, but the Motor City's civic leaders and Tigers owner Walter O. Briggs had appealed to baseball officials to make the game a centerpiece of the 250th anniversary of the city's founding.[2] Both leagues' owners agreed to the switch at the 1950 winter meetings.[3]

As game day approached, though, the mood was far from festive. The Tigers limped into the All-Star break in fifth place at 34-38. And their beloved broadcaster and former outfielder, Harry Heilmann, was too sick to carry out his duties as part of the NBC-TV broadcast team appointed by Commissioner A.B. "Happy" Chandler.[4]

Heilmann, 56, had been diagnosed with lung cancer that spring and his health had deteriorated quickly. Still, the baseball world was stunned when word made its way through the streets and hotels of Detroit that Heilmann had finally succumbed at Henry Ford Hospital around 8 A.M. on the eve of the big game. "HARRY HEILMANN IS DEAD" read the banner front-page headline on that afternoon's *Detroit News*, which included a tribute by one of Heilmann's closest friends, longtime *News* sports editor H.G. Salsinger.[5] But the pall cast by the four-time batting champion's passing might have been best summarized by a visiting writer, Burton Hawkins of the *Washington Evening Star*: "He was too early to play in an All-Star game, but in death he dominates this one."[6]

Inside the ballpark the day after Heilmann's death, players from both leagues joined 52,075 fans in a minute of silence requested by public-address announcer Eddie Fitzgerald. Bob Murphy described the scene in the *Detroit Evening Times*: "Inside the sacred walls of a church, on such an occasion, you might have expected to hear a baby cry or a man cough or someone drop the prayer book. But not at Briggs Stadium in the mass testimonial to Harry Heilmann. You couldn't hear a sound."[7]

When the moment had passed, Heilmann's 64-year-old former outfield mate Ty Cobb delivered a ceremonial first pitch from the front row of the stands and it was time to play ball.

* * *

Toeing the mound for the first official pitch was American League starter Ned Garver of the Browns. In typical fashion, St. Louis had managed only 22 wins in the first half, but Garver had recorded 11 of them. His All-Star status moved more than one scribe to observe that this was the first time he had pitched with a real major-league team behind him.

Though Garver's worthiness was universally acknowledged (he would finish second to Yogi Berra in MVP voting that year after winning 20 games on a last-place team), the same could not be said about the rest of Casey Stengel's pitching staff. The American League owners had put in place a rule requiring that its eight-man staff for the game include one hurler from each team — no more, no less.[8] That left Stengel with options such as Bobby Shantz of the A's (7-6, 5.32 ERA) and 40-year-old Connie Marrero of the Senators, while the likes of Bob Feller and Allie Reynolds sat at home.

Garver, at least, was up to the task. He started the AL off by allowing a lone unearned run in three innings of work, as a Nellie Fox error allowed the visitors to push a run across in the opening frame. The Americans got that one back in the second, though, when Berra singled and Ferris Fain brought him all the way around on a triple to right.

But the day began to crumble when Stengel brought in the lone Yankee pitcher, Eddie Lopat, to start the fourth. Stan Musial, the leading vote-getter heading into the game,[9] parked Lopat's first offering in the upper deck in right field and the gates were open for manager Eddie Sawyer's NL sluggers. Lopat was fortunate to retire Jackie Robinson on a deep drive to left-center, but Gil Hodges followed with a single and Bob Elliott of the Braves drove him in with a homer that just cleared the wall in left, putting the NL up 4-1.

The hometown Tigers' two starters, Vic Wertz and George Kell, brought the fans back to life with solo homers off Sal Maglie in the fourth and fifth innings, respectively, while Detroit pitcher Fred Hutchinson shut down the NL in the fifth after replacing Lopat. But that was the end of the positive news for fans of the old English 'D.'

The Dodgers stepped to the forefront the following two innings, as Robinson opened the sixth with a walk and Hodges, who led the majors with 28 homers heading into the game, unloaded on Hutchinson to bump the NL edge up to 6-3. In the seventh, Robinson's bunt single scored Richie Ashburn and the rout was on.

Ashburn also was responsible for two defensive gems in the game, throwing Fain out at home plate in the second inning and later going to the wall in deep right-center in the sixth to rob Wertz of his bid for another homer. Kell, who knew the ballpark better than anyone playing in it that day, called Ashburn's grab "as fine a job of defensive play as you'll ever see. He went back awfully fast and timed his leap perfectly to cut off what could have been a home run."[10]

The final blow to American League pride came in the eighth, when Kiner took Mel Parnell deep to left for his third All-Star home run in as many years. That was also the sixth round-tripper of the game between the two teams, establishing a record that still stood as of the 2014 All-Star Game,– though it has been matched twice, including in 1971, the next time the game came to Detroit.

The National League's power had carried the day and would be the talk of the sport as the second half of the season resumed. The senior circuit had prevailed in the All-Star Game for the second consecutive year but only the sixth time in 18 games overall, and the victors reveled in the new order that had been established.

"It is the National that has the home-run hitters now, not the American," Gil Hodges said afterward. "Yes, sir, times have changed." Added Kiner, happy to be proved right: "We're the big guys now and they are the little boys. I could see that before the game when we lined up for the national anthem. I looked over at the American League bunch and thought: 'Gee, what a bunch of little guys compared to a few years ago.' For the first time our boys looked like the big men."[11]

NOTES

1   Ralph Kiner and George Kell, "All-Stars Look at Their Game," *Detroit Free Press*, July 10, 1951.

2   As part of the 250th birthday festivities, golf's U.S. Open had been held at Oakland Hills Country Club in suburban

Birmingham three weeks earlier. Ben Hogan won by two strokes to repeat as Open champion.

3   "Two-Day Play-Off Period Provided By New American League Ruling," *New York Times*, December 12, 1950.

4   1951 All-Star Game program, 31.

5   *Detroit News*, July 9, 1951.

6   Burton Hawkins, *Washington Evening Star*, July 10, 1951.

7   Bob Murphy, *Detroit Evening Times*, July 11, 1951.

8   Sam Greene, "A.L.'s Defeat Will Scrap Pitcher Rule," *Detroit News*, July 11, 1951.

9   Musial's 1,428,383 votes beat out second basemen Nellie Fox (1,419,428) and Jackie Robinson (1,412,144) for popularity honors.

(*The Sporting News*, July 11, 1951.) Robinson's popularity was the strongest indication of how much the game had changed since Detroit hosted an all-white collection of stars 10 years earlier. He was joined in this game not only by Don Newcombe, Roy Campanella and Larry Doby, but also by Cuba's Minnie Minoso and Connie Marrero and Chico Carrasquel of Venezuela (who was voted the AL starter at shortstop by the fans, edging out Phil Rizzuto).

10 George Kell, "NL Finally Unlooses Power," *Detroit Free Press*, July 11, 1951.

11 "National League Forecasts New Era of Power," Associated Press via *Washington Evening Star*, July 11, 1951.

"I'VE GOT TO GET MARRIED MORE OFTEN"

May 15, 1952: Detroit Tigers 1, Washington Senators 0 at Briggs Stadium

By Gregory H. Wolf

"IF MANAGER RED ROLFE HAD WRITTEN the script, the Tigers could not have arranged a more dramatic finish," wrote the AP's Jack Handy.[1] With two outs in the bottom of the ninth inning in a scoreless game, outfielder Vic Wertz blasted a dramatic home run to give the Detroit Tigers a 1-0 victory over the Washington Senators and preserve Virgil "Fire" Trucks' masterful no-hitter. It was the second and last no-hitter thrown by a Tigers pitcher in their Corktown neighborhood ballpark located at the intersection of Michigan and Trumbull Avenues. George Mullin tossed the first gem, on July 4, 1912, in the inaugural year of Navin Field, against the St. Louis Browns.

Two years removed from a 95-win season and a second-place finish, the Tigers arrived at venerable Briggs Stadium on May 15, 1952, for the rubber match of a three-game set in last place in the AL with a miserable 6-18 record, 10½ games behind the league-leading Cleveland Indians. Skipper Bucky Harris's Senators were one of the early-season surprises in the AL. In second place, just two games off the lead, the Nationals, as they were affectionately called, had won 10 of their last 14 games and were 14-9.

Tigers coach Rick Ferrell, a former backstop who caught more than 1,800 games, but never a no-hitter in his 18-year big-league career, was concerned about Trucks as the 35-year-old right-hander prepared for the game. "He didn't warm up long enough," said Farrell after the game. "He didn't look loose to me at all."[2] Farrell's observations were justified. Trucks was once considered one of the hardest-throwing pitchers in baseball. He struck out 420 batters with the Class D Andalusia (Alabama) Bulldogs in his first year of Organized Baseball (1938), and had compiled a 103-74 record since his debut with the Tigers in 1941. But the affable Alabaman suffered a serious arm injury in 1950, missed almost the entire season, and struggled in 1951 to regain the heater that helped him lead the AL in strikeouts and shutouts in 1949. In his first four starts of 1952, Trucks was pummeled for 30 hits and 16 earned runs in just 15⅔ innings. The Senators sent 28-year-old righty Bob Porterfield to the mound. A midseason acquisition from the Yankees in 1951, the Virginia native sported a career record of 20-20 and was making just his 47th start.

The Thursday afternoon game attracted a sparse crowd of just 2,215 paid customers, but they were joined by what the *Detroit News* called 3,000 "screaming children" on a school outing, perched in the left-field pavilion.[3] They were treated to a classic pitchers' duel and a double-no-hitter through five innings during which both teams had managed just two baserunners; Porterfield had issued his only two walks of the contest, and Trucks nicked Eddie Yost with a curve in the third. An inning earlier, the Senators' Gil Coan scampered to second when Tigers second baseman Jerry Priddy fumbled his sure-out grounder and threw over first baseman Bud Souchock's head.

With two outs in the bottom of the sixth, Tigers third sacker George Kell singled to right for the first hit of the game. Detroit finally managed to get a man in scoring position when Wertz led off the seventh with a double, but he was promptly picked off second base. Trucks hit a "bouncing single" with two outs in the eighth, but was forced out at second when shortstop Johnny Lipon, with just six hits in his previous 37 at-bats, hit a soft grounder.[4]

While the Tigers were looking for chinks in Porterfield's armor, Trucks used a "baffling assortment of fastball and sliders" to keep the Senators off balance.[5] Trucks hit his second batter, Jim Busby, with two outs the sixth. The fleet-footed center fielder who had finished second with 26 steals the previous season, attempted to swipe second. According to the *Detroit News*, Busby was trapped between bases, but Priddy committed his third error of the game, a low throw in the rundown permitting Busby to move into scoring position. Trucks issued his first and only walk in the eighth inning, and then ended the frame by striking out Yost looking on a "hotly disputed" call.[6]

With palpable tension in the air and spectators in the ballpark silent, Trucks set down the first two batters in the ninth inning. Less than three weeks earlier, his teammate, right-hander Art Houtteman, was just one out away from a no-hitter before yielding a hit to Cleveland's Harry Simpson in the Tigers' 13-0 shutout at Briggs Stadium. Trucks stared down the Senators cleanup hitter, Mickey Vernon, and struck him out swinging for his seventh and final punchout

Virgil Trucks had a weird year in '52

of the contest to complete the nine-inning no-hitter, but there was no celebration. Trucks had a feeling of déjà vu. He was in a similar position as a member of the Buffalo Bisons of the International League in 1941, when he had a no-hitter through nine innings, yet lost the game in the 10th inning, 1-0. "I was thinking about that after I struck out Vernon and we had to bat in the ninth," he told Tigers beat writer Watson Spoelstra.[7]

After Kell grounded weakly to shortstop to lead off the bottom of the ninth inning, left fielder Pat Mullin smashed what looked like a home run to deep right-center field, but Busby snared the ball "just five feet short" of the stands.[8] Slugger Vic Wertz, who had led the club in home runs each of the previous three seasons, hoped to repeat his heroics from the day before when he clouted the game-winning home run in the bottom of the eighth inning in the Tigers' 3-2 victory. He took a mighty swing at one of Porterfield's few mistakes of the game, a "knee-high fastball."[9] As the ball soared inside the right-field foul pole, right fielder Jackie Jensen "took one fast look," wrote Lyall Smith of the *Detroit Free Press*, and "started for the dugout."[10] As the lumbering slugger rounded the bases, his teammates mobbed Trucks in the dugout. Wertz' blast was the first game-ending home-run with two outs in the ninth inning to preserve a no-hitter in big-league history.

"Control, that was the story," said Trucks ecstatically.[11] "I could put my fastball where I wanted it," he told the *Detroit News*. "I must have thrown 30 fastballs and I believe I was as fast as I have ever been with this club."[12] Larry Staples of the AP wrote that Trucks "didn't give up a hint of a hit."[13]

The Tigers celebration in the clubhouse after the game belied their last-place standing. An ebullient Trucks, sporting a two-day beard, joked about his lucky baseball shoes. "Mine were pinching my feet, so Art [Houtteman] gave me his shoes right before the game," he told Lyall Smith.[14] Wertz, who had been nursing a heel injury, exclaimed excitedly, "I've got to get married more often."[15] Since marrying Lucille Caleel three days earlier, the Pennsylvania native had smashed game-winning home runs in his first two games back with the club.

While the Tigers suffered through their worst season in franchise history in 1952, Virgil Trucks had one of the most incongruous and surprising seasons imaginable. On May 25 at Briggs Stadium, his next start after the no-hitter, he held the Philadelphia Athletics hitless for the first 6⅓ innings. On August 25 he tossed his second no-hitter of the season, defeating the New York Yankees, 1-0 in the Bronx, striking out eight and walking one. He finished the season with a dismal 5-19 record, yet his wins included two no-hitters, a one-hitter, a two-hitter over 7⅔ innings (the Philadelphia game), and a six-hitter.

NOTES

1   Jack Handy (AP), "Trucks No Run, No Hit Job Tops Shutout Day," *The Fresno* (California) *Bee The Republican*, May 16, 1952, 29.

2   UP, "Wertz' Homer Clinches 1-0 No-Hitter For Trucks," *Traverse City* (Michigan) *Record-Eagle*, May 16, 1952, 12.

3   Watson Spoelstra, "No-Hitter Trucks' Fourth in Four Leagues," *Detroit News*, May 16, 1952, 45.

4   Sam Greene, "140 on Record - Second for Tigers," *Detroit News*, May 16, 1952, 45.

5   UP, "Wertz' Homer Clinches 1-0 No-Hitter For Trucks."

6   Spoelstra.

7   Ibid.

8   Larry Staples (AP), "Virgil Trucks Hurls No-Hitter As Tigers Nip Nats, 1-0," *Oneonta* (New York) *Star*, May 16, 1952, 11.

9   Lloyd Northard (UP), "V (for Virgil and Vic) Spells No-Hit Win for Tigers," *Salt Lake City Tribune*, May 16, 1952, 48.

10   Lyall Smith, "Virgil's Feat Tigers' 1st in 40 Years," *Detroit Free Press*, May 16, 1952, 16.

11   Staples.

12   Spoelstra.

13   Staples.

14   Smith.

15   AP, "Tigers' Trucks Pitches 1-0 No-Hit Game," *Chicago Tribune*, May 16, 1952, C1.

THE TIGERS OUTSLUG THE YANKEES AND TAKE FIRST PLACE

June 17, 1961: Detroit Tigers 12, New York Yankees 10 at Tiger Stadium

By Steve J. Weiss

THE EXPLOSIVE TIGERS-YANKEES matchup that took place at Tiger Stadium on June 17, 1961, was one of the high points of a season that served as a pivotal one for the Tigers in a number of ways. The team surprised baseball by improving from a 71-83 mark the year before, to battling the iconic yet hated Yankees for first place throughout the season. The Tigers finished with a 101-61 record, one of the greatest single-season improvements in baseball history. Up to then, only Detroit's 1934 World Series team had achieved 101 wins or a better winning percentage, and the only Tigers teams to subsequently better the 1961 team's mark were the World Series champions of 1968 and 1984.

The Tigers' new found winning ways in 1961 captured Detroit's sports fervor. Attendance rose at newly named Tiger Stadium to over 1.6 million, a gain of almost a half-million from the season before. Significantly, the season marked the Tigers' move, albeit belatedly, toward incorporating baseball's integration, as rookie second baseman Jake Wood and newly acquired center fielder Billy Bruton assumed the top two spots in the Tigers' batting order, adding much-needed speed and run-scoring ability.

Expectations were not high for the 1961 team. The prior season had been another dismal one, marking a 10-year span beginning in 1951 during which the team finished in the top half of the American League standings only one twice (1957 and 1959). The 1960 team finished in sixth place, and the season had been mostly forgettable except for an unusual trade: In August the Tigers dealt skipper Jimmie Dykes to Cleveland for Indians manager Joe Gordon. After the season the Tigers made some key moves. The club hired veteran manager Bob Scheffing and completed a bold trade, sending veteran second baseman Frank Bolling to Milwaukee in a package that brought them Bruton, a gifted outfielder; catcher Dick Brown; and reliever Terry Fox, all of whom played key roles in the 1961 team's success. The move also opened up second base for Wood, who became the first black player to rise through the Tigers' farm system to become a lineup regular. Indeed, he became an exciting fixture in the leadoff spot, scoring 96 runs and stealing 30 bases.

The slugging provided by Al Kaline, Rocky Colavito, and Norm Cash was a key to the team's success. Kaline finished second in the league to Cash in batting (.324 average, .393 on-base percentage), smacking 41 doubles and scoring 116 runs in the process. Cash hit .361, and with Colavito combined for 86 homers and a lofty 272 RBIs, the latter total greater than was accumulated in their historic 1961 season by the Yankees' Roger Maris and Mickey Mantle, the Yankees' vaunted duo.

In addition to the firepower provided by their newly enhanced lineup, the Tigers were bolstered by stellar performances from a trio of starting pitchers: Frank Lary, Jim Bunning, and Don Mossi. The three stalwarts combined for a 55-27 record and 46 complete games. When needed, they were ably supported by Fox, who came out of the bullpen to sport a 1.41 ERA.

The Tigers raced to a 17-5 start, and finished May at 29-16, 3½ games ahead of the Yankees. But the Yankees' bats started booming in June, leading to a big weekend series in Detroit that found the teams locked in a three-way tie for first place with Cleveland. On Friday, June 16, before a packed house of 51,744 fans, Wood and Bruton combined their speed and clutch hitting to score two key runs and Phil Regan held the

Yankees in check, leading the Tigers to a 4-2 victory. At night's end, the Tigers were tied with the Indians for first place, one game ahead of the Yankees.

This set the stage for the June 17 game, attended by an enthusiastic crowd of 51,509. The pitching match-up pitted Mossi against the Yankees' Bud Daley, who had been acquired days before in a trade with the Kansas City Athletics. Mossi had finished a mediocre 9-8 the prior year, but started 1961 strongly; he entered the big game against the Bronx Bombers with a 7-1 record. The crafty southpaw retired the Yankees 1-2-3 in the first inning, before the Tigers quickly went to work against Daley.

Wood began the uprising with a single to center. Bruton followed with a walk, and Kaline singled, loading the bases. The Tigers then banged across four runs, featuring a two-run single by Cash that sent the crowd into an uproar. After Mossi disposed of the Yankees in the second, the Tigers added three more in the bottom of the inning, as Kaline followed singles by Wood and Bruton with a double that sent Daley to an early shower. Cash then singled in Kaline. When Tigers shortstop Chico Fernandez tagged reliever Rollie Sheldon for a solo shot the following inning, the Tigers entered the fourth with an imposing 8-0 lead.

The Yankee bats awoke, however, in the top of the fourth, as Maris boomed a home run to the upper deck in right, and a succession of hits by the Bombers stunned the crowd, and shrank the Tigers' lead to 8-5. This brought Scheffing to the mound to replace Mossi with Paul Foytack. After Foytack quelled the rally, the Tigers got one back in the bottom of the inning, and added two more in the sixth on yet another single by Bruton, and a two-run shot to deep left by Kaline. The Tigers' star right fielder added to his superior performance when he singled home Wood in the bottom of the eighth, bringing his RBI total for the game to five and expanding the Tigers' lead to 12-5.

In the meantime, Foytack slammed the door on the high-powered Yankees, allowing only a single by Elston Howard over the next four innings. With this strong performance, and a seven-run lead, Scheffing stuck with Foytack in the ninth. Foytack dispatched the first two hitters, Bobby Richardson and Johnny Blanchard, on fly balls, and stood one out away from victory. With the crowd poised to celebrate a second straight win, the roof began to collapse. Clete Boyer began the Yankee rally by driving a Foytack delivery into the left-field stands. Tony Kubek then ripped a single to center, which was followed by a Maris double into the right-field corner. Many expected Scheffing to go to the bullpen as the ever-dangerous Mantle came to the plate, but the Tigers' skipper stuck with Foytack. Alas, Mantle promptly sent a Foytack offering towering over Kaline's head, deep into the upper deck. The crowd became noticeably subdued as suddenly the lead had diminished to 12-9. Scheffing had seen enough, and replaced Foytack with veteran reliever Bill Fischer, who had joined the team in a trade during the previous season and would be gone before this one was over. Elston Howard greeted Fischer by drilling yet another home run, the Yankees' third of the inning, this one streaking beyond Colavito's grasp

Al Kaline and Mickey Mantle

in left field. With that missile, the Tigers' lead had shrunk to 12-10.

Scheffing walked quickly to the mound to summon Fox, who had watched the New Yorkers' barrage while warming up in the bullpen along the left-field foul line. As Fox walked to the mound, head down in focus, the formerly raucous crowd was reduced to an astonished hush. After Fox finished his warm-up tosses, the dangerous Moose Skowron ambled to the plate. Skowron had launched a two-run shot the night before. In the on-deck circle stood veteran slugger Bob Cerv. Both were very capable of continuing the home-run onslaught that had quickly turned a perceived blowout win toward a potentially disheartening defeat.

Fox wound and delivered, and Skowron took a rip, the crack of the bat producing an ominous sound. The ball screamed toward left field, but fortunately for the Tigers, its trajectory was interrupted by the presence of a well-positioned shortstop Chico Fernandez, who caught the line drive, bringing an end to the tension-filled inning, and delivering an important win to the home team. One could all but feel a gigantic exhale throughout the stadium as the Tigers gathered to pat Fox on the back as he headed toward the winners' dugout.

With the news that the Indians had been defeated by Baltimore, the Tigers now stood alone in first place, and were assured of completing this showdown series ahead of the feared Yankees. Indeed, the Tigers went on to hold first place for almost all of June and July, generating much excitement for Detroit's renewed rabid fan base. They still were only 1½ games behind the Yankees entering another huge series, this one on Labor Day weekend in New York. The Bombers swept the three games and never looked back, recording 109 victories. Still, the night of June 17 stood as a hallmark of an electrifying season that proved to be one of the finest in Tigers history.

SOURCES

Detroit Free Press

New York Times

Murphy, Justin. "Baseball's Best Runners-Up: 1961 Detroit Tigers," April 26, 2008, seamheads.com/2008/04/26/baseballs-best-runners-up-1961-detroit-tigers.

Sargent, Jim. "Jake Wood," The Baseball Biography Project, sabr.org/bioproj/person/0801bd7e.

Keko, Don. "The Detroit Tigers Integrate (1958)," examiner.com/article/the-detroit-tigers-integrate-1958m

"IT WAS A LONG, LONG, LONG BALLGAME"

June 24, 1962: New York Yankees 9, Detroit Tigers 7 (22 innings) at Tiger Stadium

By John Milner

WHEN THE FANS AT TIGER STADIUM settled into their seats for a game between the Yankees and Tigers on June 24, 1962, little did they know that history was about to take place at the corner of Michigan and Trumbull Avenues. The two teams, having played a doubleheader the day before, were looking to finish up the series and move on to their next opponents. The matinee contest turned into a grueling seven-hour marathon.

Both clubs were off to fairly slow early-season starts after having accumulated over 100 wins each in 1961. The Tigers' starting pitcher was Frank Lary, coming off a 23-win campaign. Unexpectedly, in the top of the first, the Yankees plated six runs off Lary to jump ahead. The Tigers countered with three in the bottom of the inning, knocking out Yankees starter Bob Turley in the process. Lary ended up being taken out for a pinch-hitter in the second inning after the Yankees added their seventh run, so by the third inning both teams' bullpens were starting what would be a long day.

In the bottom of the third inning, the Bengals scored three runs to tighten the gap. The appearance of a high-scoring game after three innings would be deceptive as the two teams' bullpens settled in and went to work. For the rest of the regulation nine innings, the only mark made by either team was a run scored by Bill Bruton on a single by Rocky Colavito that knotted the score at 7-7 after six innings. Both teams had opportunities but could not capitalize on them prior to extra innings. The Yankees loaded the bases in the fourth and seventh innings, but could muster only groundballs to the pitcher both times. The Tigers were able to get a runner to third base in the fourth inning, but couldn't get him across the plate.

Once the game went to extra innings, both teams had chances to put an end to the affair. In the 10th, Detroit had runners on first and third but couldn't cash in. The 11th frame brought the Tigers maybe their best opportunity to end the game. Colavito's third hit, a triple, led off. The Yankees intentionally walked the next two batters to load the bases with nobody out. Chico Fernandez's line drive found its way into the left fielder's glove for the first out. Dick Brown then attempted a bunt, but the ploy turned into a double play to end the inning with the score still 7-7.

Colavito commented, "The thing that annoyed me was that I led off the 10th inning with a triple off the 415-foot sign in left-center, but we couldn't score. I was so frustrated because we should've won the damned game right then."[1]

In the 15th inning the New Yorkers got a single by Tom Tresh, who then stole second base and advanced to third on a wild pitch, but was ultimately stranded. In the home half, Detroit put two runners on, but was unable to push a run across.

As the bullpens began to dominate for both teams, opportunities to score were few and far between. Standouts for the Tigers were Hank Aguirre, who pitched five-plus innings of scoreless relief, and Terry Fox, who threw eight innings without allowing a run. The Yankees countered with Tex Clevenger throwing six-plus innings with no runs and 23-year-old Jim Bouton, who finished off the game by throwing seven shutout frames.

The Tigers got a runner to third base in the 20th inning, but to no avail.

Finally, Detroit was basically reaching for anybody that could hold a baseball. To start the 22nd inning, the

Tigers brought in Phil Regan, their sixth relief pitcher of the game. He had pitched the day before until he was knocked out after three innings and eight runs.

It didn't take Regan long to put the Tigers' chances of winning in jeopardy. A one-out walk to Roger Maris was followed by a two-run homer by Jack Reed to put the Yankees up 9-7. In the last gasp for the Tigers, they could not muster much of a threat. Colavito, who got his seventh hit, a single, was the only base runner in the 22nd inning off Bouton, who collected the win.

When left fielder Johnny Blanchard caught the final out off the bat of Norm Cash, the game time read 6 hours and 59 minutes, but Joe Falls, the official scorer, listed it as seven hours. "I figured, who will ever remember 6:59 as the longest game in baseball history, so I shouted out the time, 'seven hours.'"[2] The game ended up being the longest by time in major-league history. Before this game the longest had been a 5-hour 20-minute game between the Boston Braves and Brooklyn Dodgers in 1940.

The Tiger Stadium concession stands sold 32,000 hot dogs and 41,000 bottles of beer before closing early under Michigan labor laws. Yogi Berra caught all 316 pitches the Yankees' pitchers threw, while Colavito ended up with seven hits in 10 at-bats. In true Yogi fashion, his responses to questions regarding the game posed by a SABR biographer in 2010 were short and to the point. When asked how he felt after catching 22 innings, Berra's response was "tired."[3] Asked about Reed's home run, he said, "Good timing. Glad he hit it."[4]

The crowd was listed at 35,368 when the game began, and almost half of the faithful were still there to the end. New York was held scoreless for 19 innings in a row from the third inning to the 22nd, but still collected the win.

It turned into a very long weekend for both teams considering that they had played a day-night doubleheader the day before, and then played the last game of the five-game series on Monday afternoon.

The teams used 43 players total in Sunday's game. "I pitched in that game," said Jim Coates. "Hell, all of us pitched in that game. It was a long, long, long ballgame." Rollie Sheldon commented, "There were far more players in the clubhouse than there were in the dugout. We'd consumed all the beer and they had to send out for more."[5] Yankees reliever Luis Arroyo was one of the few not to enter the game but he must have felt as though he had been involved. Arroyo warmed up in the bullpen on 11 different occasions and, by his own estimate, threw nearly 300 pitches.[6]

The hero for the Yankees, Jack Reed, is an interesting story in itself. The 29-year-old journeyman was a third-string outfielder behind Mickey Mantle and Joe Pepitone and didn't get into the game until the 13th inning. "I knew if I ever hit a home run this would be it. It felt good. It was a fastball down and low."[7] The game-winning home run was the only one he hit in the major leagues. Reed said of his home run, "I really thought it would be a double. I didn't look up, but I knew I hit it good. I didn't have the kind of power where I could stand there and watch it. I was one of those guys that had 'warning track power.' By the time I got to second base, the umpire was telling me it was a home run."[8]

SOURCES

Richman, Milton (United Press International). "On This Day in Sports," June 25, 1962.

Jaffe, Chris. "50th Anniversary: Tiger Stadium's Longest Game," hardballtimes.com.

NOTES

1   Detroitathletic.com/blog June 1, 2012.

2   William J. Ryczek, *The Yankees in the Early 1960s* (Jefferson, North Carolina: McFarland & Company, Inc., 2008): 103.

3   Thomas Van Hyning, "Jack Reed," sabr.org/bioproj.

4   Van Hyning.

5   Ryczek, 103.

6   "Benchwarmer Ford Gets Writer's Cramp," *Detroit Free Press,* June 25, 1962.

7   "It Takes a Third-Stringer to Win a Seven Hour Game," *Detroit News,* June 25, 1962.

8   Ryczek, 103.

"I HAD PRETTY GOOD STUFF"

June 15, 1965: Detroit Tigers 6, Boston Red Sox 5 at Tiger Stadium

By Steven Kuehl

ON TUESDAY, JUNE 15, 1965, MAJESTIC Tiger Stadium held 9,624 spectators who witnessed one of the most historic pitching accomplishments in Detroit Tigers history. The pitching matchup pitted Dave Wickersham (1-4) of the Tigers against Earl Wilson (4-4) of the Boston Red Sox. Wickersham, a 19-game winner in 1964, took the hill to start the game, and was nearly shell-shocked by his first-inning knockout. "I never saw anything like it — they didn't hit a single ball hard and I'm out of there in a couple of minutes," he said after the game.[1] Wickersham faced six batters, retired one, gave up four hits, and surrendered three runs before he was replaced by a young hurler, Dennis "Denny" McLain. The new hurler started his outing by striking out two Red Sox, Eddie Bressoud and Bob Tillman, to finish Wickersham's horrendous first inning.

Wilson, on the other hand, had a very strong start, retiring the first six batters he faced. He surrendered only one hit in the first four innings. But in the fifth inning trouble arrived for Wilson; he walked the bases loaded. Wilson then got Bill Freehan to foul out to first base. Then he walked McLain; Willie Horton scored and Wilson's outing came to an end. Arnold Earley replaced Wilson and got out of the tough situation giving up only one more run. Through five innings, the Tigers trailed the Red Sox, 3-2.

While McLain was on the mound, Tigers fans started to see the "K's" fly. McLain struck out the first seven batters he faced. In the fourth inning he gave up his first hit. It took the Red Sox until the sixth inning to finally score a run against McLain, when Bressoud doubled to left field, driving in Tony Conigliaro, who had walked. Bressoud then scored on a single by Lenny Green. This gave the Red Sox their final runs of the game, and they led the Tigers 5-2.

McLain finished his night by giving up two hits in the seventh inning while striking out another two batters, bringing his total up to 14. "I had pretty good stuff," McLain told the mob of reporters jammed around his locker after the game.[2] Don Demeter hit for McLain in the bottom of the seventh inning.

The Red Sox' Earley pitched relatively well until the bottom of the eighth inning, when the Tigers' offense roared again. Dick McAuliffe, leading off, was hit by a pitch. Jerry Lumpe smacked a double to right field, advancing McAuliffe to third. Gates Brown singled to right field, scoring McAuliffe and advancing Lumpe third. Red Sox manager Billy Herman replaced Earley with Dick Radatz, who got Al Kaline, to pop up to second baseman Felix Mantilla. This brought Horton to the plate and he belted a three-run homer, his 14th of the year, into the left-field seats, to give Detroit a 6-5 lead. Radatz finished his night by striking out the last two batters of the inning.

Chuck Dressen, the Tigers skipper, had brought in Fred Gladding in the top of the eighth. He finished the game for the Tigers by retiring six straight batters in the final two innings, striking out four to bring the team's final strikeout total to 18. Horton's home run was the deciding blow.

It was a night to remember, and historians have remembered it. What McLain did was unmatched by some of the greatest pitchers to don the Tigers' uniform. George Mullin? Harry Coveleski? Tommy Bridges? Schoolboy Rowe? Hal Newhouser? Frank Lary? Jim Bunning? None of them did what McLain did that night. The young right-hander put on one of the most dazzling displays of pitching ever seen in Detroit by striking out 14 batters in 6⅔ innings. His seven strikeouts in a row tied the American League record at the time.[3] The consecutive strikeouts remained a Tigers record, and were matched by John Hiller on October 1, 1970, against Cleveland. Doug Fister broke the mark when he struck out nine Kansas City Royals in a row on September 27, 2012. The major-league record as of 2014 belonged to Tom Seaver of the New York Mets, who fanned 10 straight San Diego Padres on April 22, 1970.

McLain's 14th strikeout, in the seventh inning, matched the 14 K's by Bunning against the New York Yankees on June 20, 1958. But they left him one short of the Tigers' record at the time of 15, set by Paul Foytack against the Washington Senators on July 28, 1956. As of 2014 Anibal Sanchez held the one-game record for the Tigers with 17 strikeouts against the Atlanta Braves on April 26, 2013. (The major-league record of 20 is held by Roger Clemens of the Red Sox; Randy Johnson of the Arizona Diamondbacks; and Kerry Wood of the Chicago Cubs. Clemens achieved the feat twice, against the Seattle Mariners on April 29, 1986, and on September 18, 1996, against the Tigers. Johnson fanned 20 Cincinnati Reds on May 8, 2001, and Wood did it against the Houston Astros on May 6, 1998.)

McLain's Tigers record of 14 strikeouts for a reliever has not been matched through 2014. With changes in how bullpens are used, the club record may never be broken. The major-league record for K's in relief belongs to Johnson, who struck out 16 for the Arizona Diamondbacks on July 18, 2001, against the San Diego Padres, after he took over for the starter, Curt Schilling.

With Gladding's four strikeouts included, the game total of 18 strikeouts is a Tigers record for a nine-inning game.

McLain's first major-league season was in 1963, with the Tigers, at the age of 19. He finished his 1965 season with a respectable record of 16-6, 192 strikeouts in 220⅓ innings pitched, and a 2.61 ERA, the second lowest ERA of his 10-year career. His lowest ERA, 1.96, was in 1968, which was his best season in the major leagues; he finished with a record of 31-6. His WAR (wins above replacement value) in 1968 was an amazing 7.4, which means that McLain would have gotten the Tigers 7.4 more wins than a bench pitcher hurling in his place. Finally, he was also named the AL Cy Young Award winner and the AL MVP in 1968.

SOURCES

Fangraphs.com

NOTES

1   Joe Falls, "McLain Murders Bosox—Whiffs 14," *Detroit Free Press*, June 16, 1965.

2   Ibid.

3   Ibid .

"IT WAS VJ DAY ALL OVER AGAIN"

September 14, 1968: Detroit Tigers 5, Oakland Athletics 4, at Tiger Stadium

By Scott Ferkovich

DENNY MCLAIN BEGAN THE MORNING the same as he always did. His wife woke him up around 10:30. Breakfast was two eggs and sausage, and a Pepsi, his favorite drink. A half-hour later, a representative from the Hammond Organ Company showed up at Denny's home, and they discussed business. Denny was a fine player, and had a gig upcoming in Las Vegas. He was also a fine baseball player, and by noon he had to adjourn the meeting, because it was time to head to work. He was a pitcher for the Detroit Tigers, and on September 14, 1968, his record stood at 29 wins and five losses. He was the talk of the sporting world, as he was gunning for his 30th victory that day.

It was something that hadn't been done in 34 years, not since an equally-brash pitcher named Dizzy Dean accomplished the feat for the St. Louis Cardinals. McLain's Tigers were facing the newly-transplanted A's from Oakland. During batting practice, A's catcher Jim Pagliaroni paraded around the infield with a homemade sign on his back, which read, "Chuck Dobson goes for No. 12 today."[1] McLain stepped into the cage and took a few practice cuts. He immediately broke a bat. Teammate Mickey Stanley picked it up and tossed it into the dugout. "Somebody save the bat Denny McLain broke on the day he won 30."[2]

After BP, Denny drank another Pepsi. A gaggle of reporters swarmed around him at all times. He had fun with them. "Yes, I'm going to ask for $100,000, and that's a low figure."[3] He also complained about a recent feature article about him in *Time* magazine. "I didn't like the booze and broads angle."[4] Poor misunderstood Denny. Still, he recognized the import of the moment. "Isn't this something?" he asked. "I mean, isn't this something?"[5] A reporter inquired how he felt. "I feel fine," he replied. "I guess I'll get a little

nervous when I get out there. But I don't feel anything yet."[6] His catcher, Bill Freehan, lent some levity to the proceedings. "This is a pretty loose club."[7]

The Saturday afternoon contest was the main event across the nation, being broadcast on NBC television's "Game of the Week." As *Detroit Free Press* writer Jack Saylor put it, "This was the World Series, Mardi Gras, and the Academy Awards all wrapped up in one."[8] Among the throng of 33,688 at Tiger Stadium was none other than Dizzy Dean himself, sporting a big white cowboy hat and a western-style string tie. "I'll tell ya, I think he's a great pitcher," Dean observed. "He pitches a lot like me ... throws it hard and light although he's not as fast as I was. He kicks up that left leg the same way I did."[9]

The Tigers were well on their way to the American League pennant, so the drama was focused solely on McLain. Oakland, on the other hand, was a middle-of-the-pack club, although they did have some fine young players that helped turn them into a championship club in a few years. One of those players was 22-year-old Reggie Jackson, who had hit 26 home runs thus far in his first full season in the majors. It was Jackson who opened the scoring in the top of the fourth, with a two-run homer into the lower deck in right. He was given a standing ovation by the players in the Oakland dugout.

Detroit's Norm Cash saw Jackson and raised him one, with a three-run dinger in the bottom half of the inning. The old ballpark shook as the crowd came to life. Two teenage girls in the upper deck waved a banner reading, "McLain and Freehan—Our Power-Charged Battery."

Oakland tied the game on a Bert Campaneris single in the fifth, which scored Dave Duncan. In the sixth, the kid Jackson slammed his second home

There never was any like Denny McLain

run of the game, a solo shot into the upper deck in right. All week prior to the game, he'd been hearing Denny this and Denny that, and he was tired of it. He was determined to carry his team to victory on this day. Before the game, when he'd been told what McLain had had for breakfast, Jackson pointed out for the record that he'd had "two eggs over, a Spanish omelette, six pieces of bacon, a glass of milk, hot tea, cereal, and peaches. And a vitamin pill."[10] In the battle of the breakfasts, Jackson was ahead so far.

The score remained A's 4, Tigers 3, heading into the bottom of the ninth. Al Kaline pinch-hit for McLain leading off the frame, so if Denny was going to get his 30th, Detroit would have to mount a game-winning rally right there. Facing Diego Segui, Kaline worked the count to 3-2, and then took a pitch just off the outside corner. Ball four. The tying run was on base. Dick McAuliffe, unable to lay down a bunt, finally popped up to third for the first out. Mickey Stanley singled, sending Kaline to third. That brought up Jim Northrup, who sent a dribbler to first baseman Danny Cater. Kaline raced home to try to tie the game. Cater's throw to catcher Duncan was wild, and Kaline scored.

Northrup was safe on first, while Stanley took third on the play.

"They told me when I got to third," Kaline said later, "that I should go in if the ball wasn't hit too hard in the infield. So when Northrup's ball was just a trickler, I took off. I made up my mind that if the ball was there already I would grab the catcher with my hands and try to knock it loose from him. I was going to give it my best shot. I saw Duncan go up for the ball just before I hit him. He spun me around but I saw the ball go by him and crawled over to the plate and touched it with my hand to make sure."[11]

Up to the plate stepped Willie Horton. The outfielders were extra shallow for a play at the plate. On a 2-2 pitch, Horton hit a liner over the head of left-fielder Jim Gosger, who probably would have caught it had he been playing at normal depth. Stanley danced across the plate with the winning run, and, in the words of *Free Press* columnist Joe Falls, "It was VJ day all over again."[12]

As the Tigers celebrated on the field and in the clubhouse, and as the fans, refusing to leave, screamed themselves hoarse, the person in the ballpark who was the most disappointed was Reggie Jackson. "All for nothing," he fumed, referring to his two home runs. He had also cut off a runner at home plate with a rifle throw, and made a fine leaping catch in the outfield. "Oh, I hated to lose this game. Why did it have to be us that he beat for that 30th one?"[13] Meanwhile, the man of the hour came out of the dugout for a curtain call. "Look at this, willya?" McLain yelled, awed by the whole scene. "Look at those people! I can't believe it!"[14]

In the locker room after the game, a reporter asked Horton if he'd had a plan up there at the plate. "Plan?" Horton retorted. "I didn't have any plans. I just decided that I was going to hit the ball and run like hell."[15]

Dizzy Dean was delighted at the outcome. "I got a great thrill out of it," he said. "And to win it in the ninth inning like that ... It's one of the greatest games I ever saw."[16]

After the game, while holding court with reporters in front of his locker, McLain was asked if he had told his teammates anything in the dugout in the final inning. "I didn't say anything. But when [Kaline] got on, I knew we had a chance."[17] The Tiger rally was "fantastic. What else can you call it?"[18]

His line score looked very good: Nine innings, six hits, four runs (earned). Ten strikeouts, one walk. And even though it had not been an easy victory by any means, McLain noted, "There was no way I could get tired today."[19]

And how was he going to celebrate his 30th win? "Drink more Pepsi," McLain said, smiling. "A whole lot of Pepsi."[20]

NOTES

1   Joe Falls, "Step-By-Step to History," *Detroit Free Press*, September 15, 1968.

2   Ibid.

3   Ibid.

4   Ibid.

5   Ibid.

6   Ibid.

7   Jack Saylor, "Amazing How He Stands It," *Detroit Free Press*, September 15, 1968.

8   Ibid.

9   Jack Saylor, "Nobody Happier Than Diz," *Detroit Free Press*, September 15, 1968.

10   Larry Middlemas, "A's Slugger Fumes," *Detroit News*, September 15, 1968.

11   George Cantor, "Just Hit It And Run Like Hell," *Detroit Free Press*, September 15, 1968.

12   Falls.

13   Middlemas.

14   Joe Falls. "Golden 30 Stuns Even Denny," *Detroit Free Press*, September 15, 1968.

15   Cantor.

16   Saylor, "Nobody Happier Than Diz."

17   Falls, "Step-By-Step to History."

18   Watson Spoelstra, "Tiger Rally Gives McLain No. 30" *Detroit News*, September 15, 1968.

19   Pete Waldmeir, "Denny Wraps It Up In Style During And After The Game," *Detroit News*, September 15, 1968.

20   Ibid.

AN UNLIKELY HERO WINS THE PENNANT

September 17, 1968: Detroit Tigers 2, New York Yankees 1 at Tiger Stadium

By Jeff Samoray

IN THE AFTERMATH OF THE 1967 Detroit riots, Detroiters desperately needed something positive to take their minds off their torn city. Many sought solace in the Detroit Tigers, who emerged that summer as bona-fide pennant contenders.

An entire generation of Tigers fans had witnessed mostly mediocre baseball since the team last won the pennant in 1945. But in 1967, the team was entrenched in a four-team fight for first place. Detroit stayed in the race until the last day of the season, suffering a gut-wrenching loss to finish just one game out of first.

In 1968, the rejuvenated Tigers leapt from the gate with a 9-1 start. On May 10, they moved into first place for good. The team held off its biggest challengers, the Baltimore Orioles, by taking two of three from them in a late-August series.

Euphoria built steadily as the Tigers marched toward the pennant. The team specialized in comeback victories, winning 40 from the seventh inning on and 30 in their final at-bat.

By September 17, the Tigers' magic number stood at one. That night, Detroit would play the second game in a three-game series with the New York Yankees at Tiger Stadium. Fans still felt a rush of excitement three days after Denny McLain's historic 30th victory. A different Tigers pitcher emerged as a hero on the 17th. But the stellar performance came from the staff's least likely hurler.

Joe Sparma, a 26-year-old right-hander, was in his fifth season with the Tigers and without a defined role. Throughout his career, he showed flashes of brilliance but often struggled with his command. His blazing fastball and hard overhand curve were dominating—when he could find the strike zone. Tigers coaches felt Sparma lacked the focus needed to take his game to the next level.

"The Tigers loved Sparma's arm," said George Cantor, Tigers beat writer for the *Detroit Free Press* from 1966 to 1969. "He threw hard and was hard to hit. But he was always fighting to control his pitches. The coaches were frustrated with Joe, but I'm sure he was frustrated with himself, too."[1]

Sparma didn't help himself by chain-smoking, struggling to control his weight, and feuding with Tigers manager Mayo Smith. Sparma performed poorly in the season's first half, going 7-8 with a 4.01 ERA in 20 starts. Smith removed him from the regular starting rotation after he allowed three runs and five hits in an inning-plus against Oakland on July 17.

"I can't start him and he's too wild to pitch relief," Smith said. "What am I supposed to do—take him out and shoot him?"[2]

Sparma didn't accept his relief role willingly and became morose. The lack of communication with Smith made their relationship tense. Things boiled over on August 14 in Cleveland when Sparma received a spot start. He wasn't sharp, allowing three singles and three walks through 3⅓ innings. The Tigers led 1-0, but Smith removed Sparma in the fourth with two on and one out. Upon reaching the dugout, Sparma threw his glove in disgust and headed into the clubhouse. He felt Smith wasn't treating him fairly, and aired his complaints to *Detroit Free Press* columnist Joe Falls after the game.

"I may be through with this team now," Sparma said. "I don't know if I can pitch for that man anymore."[3] The quotes appeared in Falls' next column.

Fans reacted very negatively to the piece, perhaps fearing a clubhouse squabble might derail the team's postseason chances. Sparma and Smith met briefly to iron out their differences, but their relationship remained frosty.

In his next two starts—the first on eight days' rest and the second 10 days afterwards—Sparma failed to make it into the sixth inning. He remained in Smith's doghouse, wandered aimlessly in the clubhouse and went 14 days without pitching. Some speculated the Tigers would make Sparma available in the 1969 expansion draft.

Then, with the club on the threshold of winning the pennant, Smith gave Sparma a last-minute surprise start.

Right-hander Earl Wilson was slated to start the September 17 game against the Yankees. But he felt shoulder soreness while warming up. Smith asked Pat Dobson to pitch, but he declined, saying he preferred to stick to his bullpen assignment. Smith then turned to Sparma.

"Just go in and throw hard as long as you can," Smith told Sparma.[4]

With five minutes to spare and no time to dwell on the pressure situation he was suddenly thrown into, Sparma quickly composed himself. More than 46,000 fans packed Tiger Stadium, hoping to see Wilson pitch the team to the pennant. They booed loudly when Sparma's name was announced in the starting lineup.

"No, I wasn't mad," Sparma said after the game. "Fifty thousand people booing me and I didn't care. I was just so glad to get a chance to pitch again."[5]

Sparma, who hadn't won a game since July 25, pitched the greatest game of his career. He allowed two singles in the first, but the Tigers erased the threat with a double play. Afterward, he was practically untouchable. Sparma pitched with conviction, remained consistently ahead in the count, and set down 19 of the next 21 batters.

As each inning passed, excitement built in the ballpark, as did fan support for Sparma. He gave the Tigers a 1-0 lead in the fifth inning with a single to

center. The fans responded by giving him a standing ovation during his next at-bat in the eighth.

Anticipation rose to a fever pitch as Sparma strode to the mound holding a 1-0 lead in the ninth. But Jake Gibbs singled with two outs to drive in Dick Howser with the tying run. Sparma struck out Mickey Mantle for the third out.

Meanwhile, news reached the Tigers dugout that Baltimore had lost its game against the Red Sox. That result automatically made Detroit the American League champions. But Tigers officials didn't place the score on the scoreboard, fearing the fans would storm the field and force Detroit to forfeit. Likewise, the Tigers broadcasters withheld news of the Baltimore loss.

"We knew that Boston had beaten Baltimore and we were in," Tigers catcher Bill Freehan said. "But we still wanted to win it ourselves."[6]

Following their customary last-licks fashion, the Tigers did just that in the bottom of the ninth. After the Yankees retired the first two batters, pinch-hitter Al Kaline walked.[7] Freehan then singled to left, moving Kaline to third. The Yankees brought in right-hander Lindy McDaniel to try to end the threat. Detroit countered with pinch-hitter Gates Brown, who walked. With the bases loaded, Don Wert, struggling with a .198 average and 37 RBIs, came to the plate. Fans crowded closer to the lower-deck box seats, anticipating a clutch hit. Sparma watched from the on-deck circle. After working a 2-and-2 count, Wert slapped a slider into right field. Kaline scored from third, giving the Tigers a 2-1 victory, Sparma his ninth win and Detroit its eighth American League pennant.

The winning hit ignited a wild celebration that would never be forgotten by those who witnessed it. Before Kaline could touch the plate, thousands of fans poured onto the field and swarmed around the new league champions. In the locker room, the Tigers whooped with joy, spraying champagne and covering one another in shaving cream. They also dunked teammates and innocent bystanders in the team whirlpool. No one was safe. Reporters, broadcasters, even Tigers general manager Jim Campbell and owner John Fetzer were dunked—suits and all.

During the chaos, Sparma spoke emotionally with reporters.

"I knew I was a competitor," he said with tears in his eyes. "And I think Mayo knew it. I just had to prove it again.[8] I didn't have time to get nervous. All I could think of was all the trouble I've been in this year and how much pain it has caused my wife and my family. [The game] was beautiful, not for me, but for Connie. She's put up with an awful lot from me.[9]

Inside the park, the team staged a field-level fireworks display with slogans like "SOCK IT TO EM TIGERS." Detroiters, finally given something to celebrate, blasted their car horns, hugged strangers and tossed confetti from hotel windows.

And Joe Sparma, the man who had felt "humiliated" by his manager only a month beforehand,[10] could rest easy for at least one night, his name etched forever in Detroit sports history.

SOURCES

In addition to the sources cited in the notes, the author also consulted:

"1968 Detroit Tigers win the pennant part 1 of 3," YouTube video. Uploaded by Frank Albin. youtube.com/watch?v=p8PJpCkuU9s.

WJR-AM. Tape-recorded radio broadcast of New York Yankees at Detroit Tigers, September 17, 1968.

NOTES

1 Jeff Samoray telephone interview with George Cantor, July 8, 2007.

2 George Cantor. *The Tigers of '68: Baseball's Last Real Champions* (Dallas: Taylor Publishing Company, 1997), 95.

3 Joe Falls. " 'Humiliated' Sparma Blasts Mayo," *Detroit Free Press*, August 16, 1968.

4 Larry Middlemas. "Fans, Tigers alike celebrate with vengeance," *Detroit News*, September 18, 1968.

5 Ibid.

6 Ibid.

7 After coming off the disabled list on July 1, manager Mayo Smith mostly used Kaline as a reserve player until after the Tigers clinched the pennant.

8 Ibid.

9 Pete Waldmeir. "In the midst of a hullabaloo, Sparma is an island of emotion," *Detroit News*, September 18, 1968.

10 Joe Falls. " 'Humiliated' Sparma Blasts Mayo," *Detroit Free Press*, August 16, 1968.

JOSE FELICIANO LIGHTS TIGERS' FIRE

October 7, 1968: Detroit Tigers 5, St. Louis Cardinals 3 at Tiger Stadium (Game Five of the World Series)

By Scott Ferkovich

THE ST. LOUIS CARDINALS COULD almost taste it. Up three games to one against the Detroit Tigers in the 1968 World Series, manager Red Schoendienst's team needed only one more victory to bring home their second consecutive championship. Except for Detroit's Game Two victory, the Redbirds had dominated the Tigers, outscoring them 21-4. In battles between aces in Games One and Four, Bob Gibson had been in a league of his own, striking out a combined 27 batters, while 31-game-winner Denny McLain had looked very ordinary in suffering two losses. St. Louis speedster Lou Brock was Detroit's thorn in the flesh, batting .500 thus far, with seven stolen bases.

Despite the dark clouds over the Tigers' World Series chances, it was sunny skies and temperatures in the mid-50s for Game Five in the Motor City, a perfect day for October baseball. A crowd of 53,634 shoehorned its way into Tiger Stadium.

A little-known singer from Puerto Rico named Jose Feliciano was scheduled to sing "The Star-Spangled Banner." He had recently cracked the Billboard charts with his cover version of the Doors' "Light My Fire." Feliciano, who was legally blind, had been invited to sing by Tigers radio broadcaster Ernie Harwell, who was also a songwriter.

Accompanying himself on the guitar, Feliciano performed an altogether new interpretation of the patriotic tune. It was unlike the stodgy, military-sounding renditions of the song that Americans were so accustomed to hearing. It was more like a heartfelt folk song than a battle hymn. It met with scattered applause, and more than a few boos. Immediately, the switchboards at NBC lit up with callers complaining that Feliciano's version was unpatriotic, a desecration. This was during the height of the Vietnam War.

Harwell noted afterward: "I picked him because he's one of the outstanding singers in America today. I feel a fellow has a right to sing any way he can sing it. I imagine there's some criticism about it, but a fellow has to sing it the way he feels it."[1] It was a watershed cultural moment. After Feliciano, it gradually became acceptable for popular singers and artists to perform their own interpretations of the song at sporting events.

In the short term, however, Feliciano's performance had a curious effect on the game. Tiger starter Mickey Lolich, the winner in Game Two, had been warming up in the bullpen. There was a slight chill in the air, and he had just begun to get loose, when he stopped because Feliciano had begun singing. "As you know," he remembered years later, "Jose sang his version of the National Anthem, which by today's standards would be fantastic. But in those days it was a little bit different. And, it was sort of a long version. And, when he got done, I basically, almost had to start re-warming up again. And I hadn't even gotten around to throwing a breaking ball. And when I went out to pitch the first inning, I hadn't even thrown a curve ball yet."[2] Like all pitchers, Lolich was a creature of habit, and indeed, he was not sharp in the first inning, giving up three runs, two on a home run by Orlando Cepeda.

The Tigers managed only one hit in the first three innings, and the Tiger Stadium throng was eerily silent. Then, in the bottom of the fourth, Mickey Stanley led off with a triple. One out later, he scored on a sacrifice fly by Norm Cash. Willie Horton tripled, and then came a key play in the game. Jim Northrup hit a grounder to second baseman Julian Javier. It would have been the third out, but the ball took a bad hop and bounded over Javier's head into right field, scoring Horton. Detroit had suddenly drawn to within one run. It was a ballgame again.

St. Louis, however, threatened to erase the Tiger momentum in the very next inning. After a strikeout by pitcher Nelson Briles, Tiger killer Lou Brock came up to the plate. He already had a double and a single in the game and had scored a run. This time, he doubled again. The next batter, Julian Javier, drove a single into left field. Brock raced around third, headed for home. A charging Willie Horton fielded the ball and quickly gunned a throw to catcher Bill Freehan. Brock and the ball arrived at the same time, but inexplicably, Brock chose not to slide. Umpire Doug Harvey initially waved the "safe" sign, before quickly reversing his decision and calling Brock out. Freehan's brilliant block of the plate had effectively prevented Brock's left foot from touching home. As the catcher remembered it, "I said to the umpire, 'Look at that, there are spike marks on the ground.' They were about 2½ inches away from the plate."[3] The television replay appeared to show that Harvey's call was correct.

"I signaled him to slide," said Curt Flood, the on-deck hitter. "But Lou has his own way of doing things."[4] He also noted, however, that "Freehan was straddling the plate, with one foot in each batter's box, but Lou got his foot in between."[5]

Brock was convinced the umpire had made a bad call. "I don't feel that I touched (the plate), I KNOW I did."[6] After the game, Freehan said, "(Harvey) said if he'd have slid he would have been safe. I don't know. I say his foot came short of the plate coming at my left foot. The big indication was the footmark short of the plate and sort of twisted around as if the foot pivoted. The only reason I tagged him a second time was a reflex action. Brock was coming back to the plate."[7] But the questions remain to this day: Should Brock have slid, or not? Did he ever touch home plate? And did Harvey make the right call?

But those debates would come later. For now, Brock was out. Instead of being up 4-2, St. Louis still clung to a one-run lead. It was the key play of the game — indeed, of the entire Series. It gave the Tigers new life. Brock, their biggest nemesis, had just been taken down a notch. "That play turned us inside out," Freehan said later. "There was an immediate effect on our bench. We've been coming from behind all year.

... They kept saying on the bench, "Mickey hold 'em with three runs and we'll get 'em now.'"[8]

And that is exactly what Detroit did. In the bottom of the seventh, Mr. Tiger himself, Al Kaline, who had waited 16 long years for this World Series moment, came up with the bases loaded and one out. He delivered, drilling a single into right-center, driving in two, and putting the Tigers on top. As he stood on first base, the hometown crowd gave him a long, loud standing ovation. One more run scored in the inning, and the Tigers had a 5-3 lead.

That was all the scoring for the afternoon. Lolich pitched brilliantly, and although he bent a little in the ninth, with the Cardinals putting runners on first and second with one out, he didn't break. He struck out Roger Maris for out number two. Then, it was Brock, tapping a ground ball back to Lolich, who tossed to Cash at first for the final out. The Tigers had lived to see another day in this 1968 World Series.

It was the 41st time that year that the Tigers had come from behind to win from the seventh inning on. *Detroit Free Press* Tigers beat writer George Cantor wrote, "If the Cards hadn't paid much attention to the way Detroit won the pennant this year, (this game) could serve as a quick lesson."[9] Fittingly, it was the beloved Kaline who got the big hit. "You sort of get goose pimples when you see him do so well," noted Freehan.[10]

NOTES

1   Barbara Stanton, "Fans Irate Over Desecrated Anthem," *The Sporting News*, October 19, 1968, 13.

2   Allendale101, "Jose Feliciano (2013) Sings at Comerica Park," YouTube video, 6:53. Uploaded January 16, 2014.

3   Jerry Green, "Did He Touch The Plate? - Two Versions," *Detroit News*, October 8, 1968.

4   Larry Middlemas, "Did He Touch The Plate? — Two Versions," *Detroit News*, October 8, 1968.

5   Ibid.

6   Jack Saylor, "I Know I Touched Plate,' Brock Says," *Detroit Free Press*, October 8, 1968.

7   Green, op. cit.

8   Wells Twombly, "'Brock Play Lifted Us'—Freehan" *Detroit Free Press*, October 8, 1968.

9 George Cantor, "Tigers Come Back From Dead, 5-3," *Detroit Free Press*, October 8, 1968.

10 George Puscas, "Tigers Roar Back With Kaline, Lolich," *Detroit Free Press*, October 8, 1968.

"HE CRUSHED IT"

July 13, 1971: American League 6, National League 4, at Tiger Stadium

By Scott Ferkovich

BY THE END OF THE 1960S, IT SEEMED that the Major League Baseball All-Star Game had turned into an annual exhibition of National League dominance. The senior circuit had won 11 of 13 games during the decade (two games were played in 1960, 1961 and 1962; one game was tied when it was called because of rain). The first All-Star Game of the 1970s proved to be more of the same. Indeed, the final lingering image from Cincinnati's Riverfront Stadium was Pete Rose barreling over catcher Ray Fosse to score the winning run. It was an era in which the games were fiercely contested battles for pride and supremacy, played between two leagues that despised each other. The 42nd version of the midsummer classic took place July 13, 1971, at Detroit's venerable Tiger Stadium. It was a night that the American League finally got some revenge.

It was an All-Star Game in the truest sense of the word. The National League squad featured 12 future Hall of Famers: Willie Mays, Hank Aaron, Willie Stargell, Willie McCovey, Johnny Bench, Ron Santo, Lou Brock, Roberto Clemente, Steve Carlton, Ferguson Jenkins, Juan Marichal and Tom Seaver. (Pete Rose also played in the contest; in 1989 he was found to have bet on baseball games, and was made permanently ineligible for induction.) Among the American League stars were nine future Hall of Famers: Rod Carew, Carl Yastrzemski, Frank Robinson, Brooks Robinson, Luis Aparicio, Harmon Killebrew, Reggie Jackson, Al Kaline and Jim Palmer.

Both skippers, Sparky Anderson and Earl Weaver, are Hall of Fame managers. One of the National League coaches, Danny Murtaugh, is also enshrined in Cooperstown, as a manager. Joe Torre, the 30-year-old St. Louis Cardinals third baseman who was having an MVP season in 1971, later gained entrance to the Hall for his great career as a manager, primarily with the New York Yankees.

Doug Harvey, the third-base umpire, also has a plaque in Cooperstown. The second-base umpire for the game was Jake O'Donnell. This was only his third year of umpiring in the big leagues, and he retired after the end of the season. He later went on to a long career as an NBA referee, and became the only player to officiate in both a Major League Baseball All-Star Game and an NBA All-Star Game.

Perhaps the most talked-about All-Star was the starting pitcher for the American League, Vida Blue. The 21-year-old fireballer from Louisiana had become the best pitcher in all of baseball. His phenomenal first half with the Oakland A's included a record of 17 wins against only 3 defeats, 188 strikeouts in 184 innings, and an ERA of 1.42. The National League hurler was 26-year-old Dock Ellis, who had fashioned a 14-3 record for the Pittsburgh Pirates, with an ERA of 2.11.

During the pregame player introductions, the biggest cheers from the crowd of 53,559 were given to the hometown Detroit representatives: Norm Cash, Bill Freehan, Mickey Lolich and Kaline (as well as Tigers manager Billy Martin, who was selected as one of the coaches for the game).

It was a hot night, and a 25-mph wind was blowing out to right field, so despite the fine starting pitchers, the game promised to have more than a few long balls. This was, after all, Tiger Stadium, a hitter's paradise. By game's end, there were six home runs hit by six different players, all of whom made it to the Hall of Fame: Johnny Bench, Hank Aaron (his first in 58 career All-Star at-bats), Reggie Jackson, Frank Robinson, Harmon Killebrew and Roberto Clemente. In fact, home runs accounted for all the scoring in the contest. The six clouts by six different players tied an

All-Star Game record matched by the 1951 classic, also at Tiger Stadium (then known as Briggs Stadium). Frank Robinson's blast was noteworthy, as it made him the first player to hit a home run for both leagues in All-Star competition. Clemente's round-tripper was his final at-bat in a midsummer classic.

But it was Reggie Jackson's home run that stole the spotlight on this night, and remains one of the most enduring moments in All-Star Game history. It came in the bottom of the third, with the American League trailing 3-0. Luis Aparicio was on first base after having led off with a single, only the second hit for the junior circuit. Reggie Jackson of the A's was sent to pinch-hit for Blue. This was the 25-year-old's second All-Star Game appearance, having gone 0-for-2 in the 1969 competition. Jackson swung at Ellis' offering and sent a high, soaring rocket into deep right field that would have left the park had it not hit a light tower and fallen back onto the playing field.

Tigers broadcaster Ernie Harwell called it the hardest-hit ball he'd ever seen. Longtime Detroit baseball columnist Joe Falls wrote, "Who will ever forget Reggie Jackson's drive? I saw it when he connected, and right away I thought it was going out of the park. I lost it when it got up into the sky, and was disappointed when I saw it falling back to the field after striking the base of the light tower. You can't hit a ball much harder than Reggie Jackson hit it."[1] Kaline, who had seen his share of shots at Tiger Stadium, observed, "It was the hardest hit ball I've ever seen in my life, here or anywhere else."[2] Senators slugger Frank Howard, also known for his titanic blasts, was in awe: "I think it would have gone 600 feet. ... He crushed it."[3]

Jackson himself agreed. "I think this would have to be the longest one I've ever hit," he noted after the game.

The final score was American League 6, National League 4, played in a brisk two hours and five minutes. Vida Blue, while unspectacular (giving up three earned runs in three innings), picked up the win. Frank Robinson was named the game's Most Valuable Player.

Kaline went 1-for-2 in front of the hometown folks. He singled to center in the sixth and scored on Killebrew's home run. Cash and Freehan went a combined 0-for-5. Lolich pitched the final two innings for the save, giving up only Clemente's round-tripper.

NOTES

1   Joe Falls, "A Lucky Night for Baseball," *The Sporting News*, July 31, 1971.

2   Lowell Reidenbaugh, "Everyone Except Reggie Electrified By His Clout," *The Sporting News*, July 31, 1971.

3   Ibid.

LOLICH FANS 15 AS TIGERS TAKE OVER FIRST PLACE

October 2, 1972: Detroit Tigers 4, Boston Red Sox 1 at Tiger Stadium

By Doug Lehman

THE 1972 SEASON WAS MARRED BY A season-opening strike. When agreement was reached, it was decided to play out the schedule as it had been, even if that meant some teams would play a game or two more than others. That resulted in the Detroit Tigers playing one more game than the Boston Red Sox.

For Detroit the most important game of the season took place on October 2, 1972, at Tiger Stadium. The Red Sox came to town for the final series of the season holding a half-game lead over the Tigers. Detroit had just swept a three-game home series from the Milwaukee Brewers to set up the crucial series. Tigers manager Billy Martin sent left-hander Mickey Lolich (21-14) to the mound to face John Curtis (11-7), Red Sox manager Eddie Kasko's choice to attempt to tame the Tigers. This was not a must-win game for Detroit, but it was as close to it as could be. If the Tigers lost to the Red Sox on that October night, they would be 1½ games behind with two games to play and no margin for error.

Lolich was coming off a 12-inning, complete-game 3-2 loss to the New York Yankees four nights earlier. The start against the Red Sox would be his last of the regular season. He had already pitched more than 300 innings during the strike-shortened season and the question was whether he had anything left in the tank. He did.

In the top of the first he struck out two Red Sox and the Tigers were looking forward to getting their licks in on John Curtis. With one out, Al Kaline hit a "drive into the lower deck in left" off Curtis for his 10th home run of the year, giving Lolich a 1-0 lead.[1]

In the second inning Lolich forced Carlton Fisk to ground out to shortstop and then struck out Dwight Evans and Doug Griffin, giving him four strikeouts after two innings. The Tigers threatened in the bottom of the inning when center fielder Mickey Stanley reached second on a single and a wild pitch. But Eddie Brinkman grounded out to Luis Aparicio at shortstop to end the frame.

The top of the third started with Curtis striking out, but then the Red Sox bats seemed to come to life against the lefty Lolich. Singles by Tommy Harper and Aparicio put runners at the corners. Carl Yastrzemski doubled to center field, scoring Harper. Now things got interesting. Aparicio seemed a sure bet to score the go-ahead run, but as he rounded third, he slipped and fell. Picking himself up, he retreated to third base. Meanwhile, Yastrzemski had been hustling around the bases and was standing at third base when Luis returned to the bag. "Then, Yastrzemski half-heartedly started back toward second, but before he retreated more than a few feet, Rodriguez tagged him out,"[2] the play going from the center fielder to the shortstop to the catcher to third baseman Rodriguez. Reggie Smith was called out on strikes (Lolich's sixth strikeout of the game) and Aparicio was stranded at third. The Red Sox had lost their best chance to break the game open and the score was tied, 1-1, after 2½ innings. Aparicio was not certain what happened and said after the game, "I dunno why, but I hit the bag wrong at third and I kinda slipped, but I didn't fall down. Then I hit grass and I fell."[3]

Neither team could generate any offense for the next few innings. Lolich continued to strike out the Red Sox: Fisk, Griffin, Curtis, and Yastrzemski struck out in the fourth and fifth. Lolich was in double digits in strikeouts with 10 after five innings.

The fifth and sixth innings were critical for both teams. Leading off the fifth, Tigers third baseman Aurelio Rodriguez "cracked the 1-1 tie with a shot over the 365-foot sign," giving Detroit a 2-1 lead.[4] After Stanley struck out, Eddie Brinkman singled to left field, but was forced out at second on Lolich's bunt attempt. The inning ended when Tony Taylor grounded out third to first, but the Tigers had the lead. The question in everyone's mind was, "Could Lolich hold on?"

As Lolich took the mound in the sixth, he knew he had the lead and all he had to do was keep getting the Red Sox batters to make outs. The inning went smoothly with a Petrocelli strikeout, a Fisk fly out to right, and Doug Griffin striking out. Lolich now had 12 strikeouts. In the bottom of the sixth, the Tigers drove Curtis from the mound after Kaline scored the Tigers' third run on a single to center by Rodriguez. The insurance run gave the Tigers a 3-1 lead with Lolich in control.

Lolich continued his mastery of the Red Sox in the seventh by striking out Harper, getting Aparicio to pop up to first, and striking out Yastrzemski. Tigers fans were beginning to believe—and Lolich did not disappoint them in the eighth inning, although he did not record a strikeout. Reggie Smith led off with a walk and Petrocelli flied out to right field. With Smith at first base, Red Sox catcher Carlton Fisk ground into an around-the-horn double play, quelling the rally.

The Tigers struck again in the bottom of the eighth inning. Kaline singled to left field. Catcher Duke Sims laid down a sacrifice bunt that was misplayed by catcher Fisk, allowing Kaline to move to third base. With Sims at first and Kaline at third, Red Sox manager Kasko brought in lefty Bob Veale to face Norm Cash. Cash struck out, but Jim Northrup reached on a fielder's choice with Kaline thrown out at home plate. Sims moved to second on the play. Kasko went to the bullpen again, bringing in Bob Bolin to face the hot Rodriguez. The Tigers third baseman made Kasko pay for the decision as he singled to left, bringing in Duke Sims for the Tigers' fourth run.

Mickey Lolich was a bulldog on the mound

Northrup moved to second, but the rally ended when Mickey Stanley forced Rodriguez at second base.

The Tigers now held a 4-1 lead with Lolich coming back out to the mound for the top of the ninth. He got into a bit of a jam by walking the leadoff hitter, Evans, who moved to second when Griffin grounded out. Because there was no designated hitter in the American League yet, the Red Sox pinch-hit Andy Kosco for Bolin. Lolich hit Kosco, putting two Red Sox on base. Lolich dug deep to get his 15th strikeout in Harper and then ended the game when Aparicio flied out to Northrup in left field. Lolich's 15 strikeouts were one less than the team record of 16, which he'd accomplished twice in 1969.

Tigers manager Billy Martin praised Rodriguez after the game, saying, "After watching Rodriguez for two years in Detroit, I put him right there with [Brooks] Robinson. They are the two best third basemen I've ever seen."[5]

The 51,518 in attendance at Tiger Stadium, the second largest crowd of the season, went home happy, but still had to hold their breath for at least one more game. They now led the Red Sox by a half-game with two games to play. Detroit would need to win at least one of those games to win the division.

Mickey Lolich proved again, as he had in 1968 and 1971, that he was the Tigers' ace. When the team needed someone to step up, he did. Lolich said after the game, "This is probably the best I've pitched this year. I had some pretty good stuff."[6] With Detroit winning the American League East by one-half game we will never know if those "missing games" played a factor in the Tigers' championship.

SOURCES

Sporting News

NOTES

1 Joe Falls, "Tigers Win … Can Sew It Up Tonight," *Detroit Free Press*, October 3, 1972.

2 Murray Chass, "Tigers Win, 4-1; Take East Lead," *New York Times*, October 3, 1972.

3 Charlie Vincent, "'I Hit Grass and I Fell,' Looie Moans," *Detroit Free Press*, October 3, 1972.

4 Falls, "Tigers Win," *Detroit Free Press*, October 3, 1972.

5 Watson Spoelstra, "Answers to Tiger questions: Aurelio is praised," *Detroit Free Press*, October 3, 1972.

6 Curt Sylvester, "'Best I've Pitched This Year'— Lolich," *Detroit Free Press*, October 3, 1972.

NORTHRUP'S WALLOP WINS IT

October 11, 1972: Detroit Tigers 4, Oakland A's 3 (10 innings) at Tiger Stadium (Game 4 of the American League Championship Series)

By Raymond Buzenski

AFTER WINNING THE 1968 WORLD Series, the Detroit Tigers seemed poised to be successful for years to come. They were a group of young players who had developed together since the early ''60s, led by veteran Al Kaline. They had overcome daunting adversity: From the 1967 Detroit Riots and the loss of the pennant on the final day of the season, to the 40 victories when behind or tied after seven in 1968, culminating in the world championship after being down three games to one. However, after the Tigers finished second in 1969 and fell to fourth in 1970, the run seemed over.

The front office wasn't ready to concede. First, All-Star—but twice suspended—Denny McLain and two others were traded to Washington for pitcher Joe Coleman, third baseman Aurelio Rodriguez, and shortstop Eddie Brinkman. Then, fiery Billy Martin was hired as manager, replacing Mayo Smith. The team rebounded to a second-place 91-71 record in 1971, behind Mickey Lolich's 25 victories.

The high expectations for the 1972 season were delayed by a strike called during spring training. When the season finally began it was decided that the lost games would not be made up, resulting in an unbalanced schedule. The Tigers and the Orioles shared the AL East lead for the first half, with the Tigers leading by a game at the All-Star break. After a slow start in the second half, the Tigers claimed two players off waivers who played significant roles in the stretch drive. First, catcher Duke Sims was obtained from the Dodgers, where he'd hit .192 in 51 games. In the final two months of 1972, he hit .316 with 19 RBIs in 38 games for Detroit. The day after Sims was acquired, left-handed pitcher Woodie Fryman was

claimed from the Phillies. Fryman, a former All-Star with Philadelphia, had been struggling at 4-10 with a 4.36 ERA. He went 10-3 for the Tigers the rest of the season, including the pennant-clinching victory over the Red Sox, giving Detroit a controversial half-game division win.

The Tigers' opponent in the best-of-five ALCS was the Oakland A's, winners of 93 games during the regular season. The series opened on the West Coast, with Lolich pitching against Jim "Catfish" Hunter. Game One went 11 innings, with the Tigers losing 3-2, despite a Kaline homer that gave them a lead in the top of the inning. The A's rolled in Game Two, winning 5-0 behind John "Blue Moon" Odom. In the eighth inning a play occurred that changed the direction of the series. Lerrin LaGrow, a 6-foot-5 right-hander, threw his first offering to the A's Bert Campaneris low and inside, striking the shortstop on the ankle. Campaneris, believing Billy Martin had ordered a knockdown, jumped up and flung his bat at LaGrow, the war club helicoptering just over his head. After a bench-clearing 15-minute delay, both pitcher and batter were ejected. The next day American League President Joe Cronin fined Campaneris $500 and suspended him for the remainder of the ALCS, as well as the first seven games of the 1973 season (although he was allowed to play in the 1972 World Series against Cincinnati).

The Tigers returned to Detroit needing to win the remaining three games to make the World Series, but felt good about their chances. Bill Freehan summed it up: "There are a lot of guys on this club who remember 1968 and we've been down a couple times this year and people were ready to count us out. I think we all felt 'why quit now,' that there was no use giving up."[1] When Martin was asked what he told the team in the pregame meeting, he replied, "I didn't say anything earthshaking, just that our backs were to the wall, that we'd come a long way and there was no reason to quit."[2] The Tigers' Game Three starter was Joe Coleman, a 19-game winner. He was able to keep the A's off-balance with a wicked forkball, striking out 14 batters in a complete-game victory.

Game Four was a repeat matchup of Lolich versus Hunter. The day was cool and overcast, with a threat of rain throughout the day. Neither team was able to take batting practice, as the field remained covered until just before game time. The A's threatened in each of the first three innings, but were kept off the scoreboard by strong defensive plays by Kaline and Rodriguez. The Tigers also had runners in scoring position in the first and second but failed to cash in. In the bottom of the third, shortstop Dick McAuliffe opened by lifting a low, inside offering into the overhang in right, giving Detroit a 1-0 lead.

Over the middle innings, both pitchers found their grooves, with Lolich retiring 11 in a row at one point and Hunter surrendering only a Norm Cash single in the sixth. In the top of the seventh Mike Epstein ripped a one-out line drive off the facing of the second deck in right, tying the game at 1-1. Later in the frame, backup catcher Dave Duncan walked pinch-hitting for second baseman Dick Green but did not score.

During most of the season, Williams rotated many players at second while Green missed most of the year with back problems, at times playing three or more players at the position. The loss of Campaneris shortened Williams's bench, especially since he had already pinch-hit for shortstop Dal Maxvill in the sixth. Williams decided to keep Duncan in the game as catcher and moved Gene Tenace to second, a position he had played only a few times. The Tigers went 1-2-3 in the seventh.

After Lolich quickly retired the A's in the eighth, McAuliffe started the bottom of the inning with a walk. After a Kaline sacrifice, McAuliffe advanced to third on an infield single. Rollie Fingers was brought in to relieve Hunter. Martin attempted a suicide squeeze, but Freehan was unable to make contact and McAuliffe was caught in a rundown, ending the scoring opportunity.

The A's could only work a two-out walk off Lolich in the ninth. Vida Blue, the previous year's Cy Young Award winner, was brought in to pitch to the Tigers. After he struck out the first two batters, Tony Taylor hit his second double of the game into the right-field corner. After Rodriguez was intentionally walked, Martin lifted Lolich for pinch-hitter Willie Horton, who ended the inning with a fly to center. After nine, the score was 1-1.

In the 10th, pinch-hitter Gonzalo Marquez singled between first and second. Manny Alou then drove the first pitch to the base of the 365-foot sign in left-center. Jim Northrup retrieved the ball and made a strong relay to McAuliffe, who then fired a strike to Freehan at the plate ahead of Marquez. However, in the ensuing collision, Freehan was unable to hold onto the ball, allowing the runner to score and Alou to move to third. Ted Kubiak followed with a soft single to right, giving the A's a 3-1 lead.

With the Tigers down to their last three outs, McAuliffe opened the bottom of the 10th with a line single to right off new pitcher Bob Locker. Kaline followed with a single to left. Right-hander Joe Horlen relieved Locker, and Gates Brown, the Tigers' prolific left-handed-hitting pinch-hitter of the '60s, hit for Stanley. After a wild pitch moved runners up a base, Brown received a four-pitch walk. Freehan then hit a groundball to third baseman Sal Bando, who elected to go for the double play instead of the lead runner at home. However, Tenace, playing out of position, dropped the throw at second and was unable to retrieve it before being taken out by Brown's hard slide. McAuliffe scored and the bases remained loaded with no outs. Norm Cash now faced left-handed reliever Dave Hamilton. After quickly getting behind in the count, Cash fouled off a number of pitches before walking on a 3-and-2 pitch, forcing Kaline home with the tying run. Jim Northrup followed and, on the second pitch, lifted a long single to the fringe of the warning track in right over a drawn-in outfield, scoring Brown and completing the three-run comeback. The crowd of 37,615 erupted, storming the field as if the Tigers had won the pennant rather than forcing a fifth game.

The feeling in the Tigers' clubhouse was one of destiny. Kaline reported, "These guys keep pumping each other on the bench. I don't know what happened—it all came off so fast. But here we are right where we want to be."[3] Northrup followed: "The guys on this club don't let themselves get down. This is where more experience pays off. We've been through it before."[4] However, the next day would end the season for the team. The Tigers lost 2-1 on two close plays at the plate, and Oakland went on to win the first of three consecutive World Series titles.

The Tigers' front office maintained high hopes, but 1972 was the last hurrah for the aging ballclub. Lolich had a subpar year in 1973 and Fryman's record flipped to 6-13. Martin and GM Jim Campbell fought throughout the year about the needs of the club before Martin was fired before season's end. The Tigers fell to third in 1973 and sixth in 1974, bottoming out with 102 losses in 1975. But for one more game on October 11, 1972, the magic of the 1968 World Champions was felt at Tiger Stadium.

SOURCES

Masters, Todd. *The 1972 Detroit Tigers: Billy Martin and the Half-Game Champs* (Jefferson, North Carolina: McFarland & Company, 2010).

Pattison, Mark, and David Raglin. *Sock It to 'Em Tigers: The Incredible Story of the 1968 Detroit Tigers* (Hanover, Massachusetts: Maple Street Press, 2008).

Wendell, Tim. *Summer of '68: The Season That Changed Baseball and America, Forever* (Boston: Da Capo Press, 2012).

Detroit Free Press.

Major League Broadcast, Game Four ACLS; announcers: Monte Moore, Ned Morton, Jimmy Piersall.

NOTES

1   Jack Berry, "Tigers' Do-or-Die Effort Played to Many Empty Seats," *Detroit News*, October 11, 1972.

2   Ibid.

3   Watson Spoelstra, "Northrup Finds Old Magic," *Detroit News*, October 12, 1972.

4   Ibid.

RYAN TOSSES NO-HITTER; CASH WIELDS TABLE LEG

July 15, 1973: California Angels 6, Detroit Tigers 0 at Tiger Stadium

By Gregory H. Wolf

AS DETROIT TIGERS FIRST BASEMAN Norm Cash prepared to dig in against California Angels right-hander Nolan Ryan, who was just one out away from a no-hitter, he looked at home-plate umpire Ron Luciano and asked with all seriousness, "Aren't you going to check my bat?"[1] Known for his unusual humor, Cash had sauntered to the batter's box in the tense situation wielding a table leg. When Luciano, unamused by the prank, calmly informed the slugger he couldn't use the ersatz bat, Cash supposedly replied, "Why not, I won't hit him anyway."[2] Cash was right: he popped up and Ryan recorded his second no-hitter in two months. Ryan's 17-strikeout performance, wrote Angels beat reporter Ron Rapoport, "left friend and foe groping for superlatives."[3] Jim Hawkins of the *Detroit Free Press* called it "one of the most impressive one-man shows in baseball history."[4]

When Detroit and California headed to Tiger Stadium on Sunday, July 15, 1973, to play the final contest of a four-game series, they appeared to be going in opposite directions. Manager Billy Martin's Tigers had pennant aspirations. They had captured the AL East crown the previous year, and were playing their best ball of the season. A five-game winning streak pushed them into fourth place, at 48-42, but only 1½ games behind the division-leading New York Yankees. As for the Angels, skipper Bobby Winkles had gotten the team off to a promising start and briefly occupied first place, but the club had lost its previous four games and 11 of the last 17 games to fall to fourth place at 45-43.

The pitching matchup was a contrast in styles. The Tigers' 37-year-old righty, Jim Perry, faced off against the 26-year-old Ryan. While Perry relied on pinpoint control and ball movement, Ryan overpowered the opposition. Perry, a 15-year veteran and a former Cy Young Award winner with a record of 189-147, was winding his career down. Ryan, who had battled control problems since his debut with the New York Mets in 1966, emerged as baseball's most feared strikeout artist the previous season, his first with the Angels. Expectations in 1973 were high for Ryan, coming off a league-leading 329 strikeouts and nine shutouts. On May 15 Ryan joined Bo Belinsky and Clyde Wright as the only Angels hurlers to toss no-hitters by blanking the Kansas City Royals and fanning 12, but had since then won just five of 13 decisions. "I don't feel like I've done as much for the club as I could be doing," a modest Ryan told the *Los Angeles Times*, pointing to his disappointing 10-11 record and ignoring his 203 punchouts in 180 innings.[5]

On a beautiful summer afternoon, with temperatures in the mid-70s, Tiger Stadium was filled with a large crowd of 41,411 spectators on Cap Day to witness one of the most dominant pitching performances in baseball history. Ryan's first pitch to leadoff batter Jim Northrup was a knee-buckling curveball that ricocheted off catcher Art Kusnyer's shin guard and hit Luciano's right knee. After Northrup flied out, the "Ryan Express" went into overdrive. The 6-foot-2 Texan registered 12 of the next 13 outs by strikeout and also walked three before light-hitting Ed Brinkman grounded to short to end the fifth inning. "I've never seen anyone throw that good before," said Dick McAuliffe, who whiffed in each of his three plate appearances.[6]

The weak-hitting Angels, who ranked 11th of 12 teams in runs scored and batting average and last in slugging percentage that season, scored the game's first run in the third inning. After consecutive one-out singles by Kusnyer and Sandy Alomar, Vada Pinson hit a sacrifice fly to right field to give the Angels the lead. Through the top of the sixth, Perry kept the pressure on Ryan by limiting California to just four hits.

Northrup led off the sixth inning with the Tigers' one "reasonably hard-hit ball," but center fielder Ken Berry traced its arc and snared it in front of the warning track for an easy out.[7] A tough-nosed competitor, Ryan looked for any psychological edge in his battle with hitters. When Cash came to bat in the sixth, Ryan asked Luciano to examine his bat for cork filler. A quick worker on the mound, Ryan kept rolling while his heater and curveball inspired awe. "The curve was really outstanding," said Kusnyer, a little-used backup catcher who was a game-time replacement for the injured Jeff Torborg. "It was really going down. You could tell the hitters were chopping down on the ball."[8] According to Tigers reliever Ed Farmer, Billy Martin ordered his players on the bench to pay $5 early in the game and pull a number out of a hat predicting how many strikeouts Ryan would have.[9] In the seventh, Ryan struck out the side for the third time in the game, and pushed his strikeout total to 16, just three shy of the major-league record of 19 (in a nine-inning game) set by Steve Carlton (1969) and Tom Seaver (1970).

The Angels blew the game open in the eighth inning when Winston Llenas, Bob Oliver, and Al Gallagher each connected for two-out singles off relievers Bob Miller and Farmer to give the Angels a commanding 6-0 lead. But the offensive fireworks had an unintended effect on Ryan. "My arm stiffened up," he said after the game about the long delay. "I was kind of anxious to get going. I knew personally that I didn't have the same stuff. They were hitting my pitches."[10]

In an attempt to jinx Ryan, Martin remained on the dugout steps for the final two innings, reminding the pitcher of his no-hitter. Ryan ignored the taunts and sent down the final six batters in order, but whiffed just one. The final two outs were arguably the most dramatic of the game. Gates Brown hit a line drive to the shortstop, Rudy Meoli. "If it was not right at somebody, it was a hit," wrote Rapoport.[11] In fact, Ryan thought it was a hit, reported Jim Hawkins, but Meoli had shaded Brown slightly to the right and caught the ball on his toes about a foot above his head.[12] After Cash's escapade with the table, he popped up to Meoli in shallow left field. "Ryan didn't require any super plays," wrote Dick Miller in *The Sporting News*, to preserve his gem.[13]

Both squads seemed genuinely impressed with Ryan's dominant performance. Frank Robinson, the Angels' prized offseason acquisition, offered some historical perspective: "I've never seen anyone throw harder and that includes Sandy Koufax."[14] Ryan threw so hard that Kusnyer's left hand was dangerously swollen and had turned purple. "It's a bone bruise," said the catcher proudly in the clubhouse after the game.[15]

"I was more excited about this one," responded Ryan when asked to compare his two no-hitters. "You

Nolan Ryan could bring the heat

know what the pressure is and you know you don't want to lose it." He threw 126 pitches (86 for strikes) and completed the game in 2 hours and 21 minutes. As of 2014, Ryan, Johnny Vander Meer (1938), Allie Reynolds (1951), Virgil Trucks (1952), and Roy Halladay (2010) are the only big-league hurlers to toss two no-hitters in the same season (although Halladay's second no-no was in the National League Division Series). Ryan's gem was also the last no-hitter thrown in Tiger Stadium.

Nolan Ryan went on to throw seven no-hitters and win 324 games in his 27-year Hall of Fame career, yet this game has entered baseball lore because of Norm Cash's practical joke. When Cash came to the plate in the ninth inning, Tigers announcer Ernie Harwell described the bat erroneously as a piano leg.[16] Initially, Cash's escapade did not attract much media attention, and many contemporary game reports, such as in the *Detroit Free Press*, did not mention it. But over time, the story gathered traction as Ryan's stature grew. Whether involving a piano leg or table leg, the anecdote came to epitomize the impossible task of hitting a pitch. Cash's antics moved into the realm of pop culture in 1992 when Carl, a cartoon character in *The Simpsons*, went to the plate with a piano leg in a special episode entitled "Homer at the Bat."

NOTES

1   Ron Rapoport, "Encore! Ryan Hurls Second No-Hitter," *Los Angeles Times*, July 16, 1973, III, 2.

2   Ibid.

3   Ibid.

4   Jim Hawkins, "Ryan No-Hits Tigers . . . Strikes Out 17 To Boot," *Detroit Free Press*, July 16, 1973, 1-D

5   " . . . Feels He Hasn't Done Enough For Angels," *Los Angeles Times*, July 16, 1973, III, 2.

6   Rapoport.

7   Ibid.

8   Ibid.

9   Rob Goldman, *Nolan Ryan: The Making of a Pitcher* (Chicago: Triumph Books, 2014).

10 Rapoport

11 Ibid.

12 Hawkins.

13 Dick Miller, "Ryan's Smoke Sends Tigers Into No-Hit Blind," *The Sporting News*, July 28, 1973, 15.

14 Ibid.

15 Miller.

16 "Bat tales: our favorite stories of all-time," *Detroit Free Press*, March 30, 2008. freep.com/article/20080330/SPORTS02/80330021/Bat-tales-Our-favorite-stories-all-time.

LAGROW KNUCKLES UNDER TO WOOD IN CLASSIC PITCHERS' DUEL

May 7, 1974: Chicago White Sox 1, Detroit Tigers 0 at Tiger Stadium

By Will Bennett

ON AN UNSEASONABLY CHILLY Tuesday night in early May, a small crowd gathered at Tiger Stadium to watch the Detroit Tigers take on the visiting Chicago White Sox. The 7,327 who braved the cold—there were chill warnings in effect for later that night—were in for a treat: arguably the greatest pitching duel Tiger Stadium would ever see.

Detroit sent out Lerrin LaGrow, a young right-hander in his first season as a starter. LaGrow had shown a few flashes of brilliance but was still a largely unknown commodity, more famous for provoking Bert Campaneris to throw his bat at him during the 1972 playoffs than for his pitching.

The Phoenix native was chosen in the sixth round of the 1969 draft out of Arizona State, where he had just won the College World Series, and made his major-league debut in 1970. LaGrow bounced between the minors and the majors for the next four seasons before finally landing a spot in the Tigers rotation in 1974. Though he was known as a fastball pitcher, LaGrow was hardly a prototypical power arm, striking out a meager 2.38 batters per nine innings entering the game.

Despite his low strikeout rate, LaGrow had been successful so far as a starter, allowing 12 runs in 34 innings. One of his biggest problems was run support. After a 10-inning complete-game loss to the Minnesota Twins on April 23, LaGrow groused, "That's not the last 1-0 game I'm going to lose this season."[1]

Starting for the White Sox was Wilbur Wood, a knuckleballing ace whose path to major-league stardom had been a circuitous one. The Cambridge, Massachusetts, native had been signed out of high school in 1960 by the Boston Red Sox. Working primarily out of the bullpen, Wood struggled to make much of an impact with the major-league club before eventually landing in Pittsburgh in 1964.

Wood's career took off following the 1966 season, after the left-hander was traded to the Chicago White Sox. In Chicago, knuckleball specialist Hoyt Wilhelm took Wood under his wing and persuaded Wood, who had previously dabbled with a knuckleball, to feature it as his primary pitch.

Wood quickly became the team's go-to reliever. In 1968 the knuckleballer set a major-league record with 88 appearances (which was broken the following year by Cincinnati's Wayne Granger). In 1971 Wood made the transition to a starting role and quickly became a star, finishing third in the Cy Young Award voting in '71, second in '72, and fifth in '73.

However, Wood was struggling to find his form early in the 1974 season. He had given up 10 home runs in only 51⅔ innings on his way to a 3-5 record. But thanks to White Sox owner John Allyn's offseason purchase of an $8,000 video system that allowed players to watch replays of game footage, Wood was able to diagnose the problem that was plaguing him. "I saw that my stride was much too long and it was causing my ball to break lazy," he commented.[2] With his shortened stride, the knuckleballer hoped to recapture the form that had made him one of the most valuable pitchers in the league over the past few seasons.

The two pitchers were polar opposites: one a young, right-handed fastball pitcher, and the other a veteran left-handed knuckleballer. But on that night, they were every bit each other's equal, going pitch for pitch in a hotly contested battle.

The cold weather seemingly tipped the scales in LaGrow's favor. White Sox manager Chuck Tanner gave star first baseman Dick Allen, who was nursing a hand injury, the night off because he didn't want to risk further damage by letting the slugger play in the cold. Without Allen to contend with, LaGrow breezed through the White Sox order without breaking a sweat, spreading two hits over the first three innings. But Wood was even sharper. Shortening his stride was making a world of difference for the knuckleballer, who was perfect the first time through the lineup.

Tensions that had been running high as both teams struggled to score came to a head in the top of the seventh inning. After Ken Henderson singled for the White Sox, LaGrow attempted to pick him off. Henderson thought Mickey Stanley's tag was a little too forceful and the two got into a shoving match, causing both benches to clear. Cooler heads quickly prevailed, and the two teams avoided escalating the situation. LaGrow erased Henderson on a 6-4-3 double play to end the inning, and the scoring threat was defused as well.

The two pitchers cruised through the next two frames to send the game into extra innings in a scoreless tie. LaGrow had allowed just four hits and a walk while striking out four. Wood, although he was no longer perfect, was still dominant, allowing only one hit and two walks with eight punchouts.

The Tigers finally threatened in the bottom of the 10th. After Al Kaline walked with one out, to break a string of nine consecutive batters retired by Wood, Willie Horton threaded a groundball under third baseman Bill Melton's glove. It was only the Tigers' second hit of the night. The next batter, Jerry Moses, walked on a controversial ball-four call to load the bases. The usually calm Wilbur Wood was furious and stepped off the mound to argue with home-plate umpire Merle Anthony. Chuck Tanner, who happened to be Anthony's roommate when they played together for the Northern League's Eau Claire Bears in 1948, went out to back up his pitcher. "When I saw Wood complain, which he never does, I knew it was a strike and I knew I had to go out there," Tanner said.[3] He was automatically ejected for arguing balls and strikes.

With the bases loaded—and the extra pressure of having to keep his sometimes difficult-to-catch knuck-

leball from the backstop—Wood got Jim Northrup on a soft popup to second base for the second out. Aurelio Rodriguez then grounded back to Wood to end the Tigers' only major threat of the game and send the game into the 11th still scoreless.

Showing no signs of slowing down, LaGrow went out for the 11th. He had allowed just one hit since the fourth inning. But White Sox catcher Ed Herrmann led off the inning determined to break the scoreless tie himself. "I went up there the last two times trying to hit one out," he said later.[4] Herrmann worked his way to a full count before finally getting his pitch, which he drilled into the right-field bleachers for his second homer in as many games.

"I didn't want to walk him and I didn't want to throw my second-best pitch. So I threw my fastball and it was up," LaGrow said after the game.[5] That would stand as his only mistake of the game. LaGrow retired the side and put the fate of the game on the shoulders of his offense, which had managed only two hits to that point.

Any hope of a comeback was soon dashed. Facing Ed Brinkman and then the top of the order for the fifth time, Wood put the Tigers down one-two-three in a drama-free bottom of the 11th to seal the victory.

Both pitchers went the distance in a fierce pitchers' duel, and unfortunately for Tigers fans who had stuck around through the cold, LaGrow's prophecy that he would lose another 1-0 game had come true.

Looking back on the game through a sabermetric lens confirms what everyone in the crowd knew to be true: This was one of the greatest combined pitching performances The Corner had ever hosted. According to one metric, Bill James's Game Score (GSc), it's believed to be *the* greatest. GSc serves as a shorthand for a pitcher's effectiveness in a single game, factoring in innings, runs allowed, hits, walks, and strikeouts. In a nine-inning game, the maximum GSc is 114 (for a 27-strikeout perfect game), with a Quality Start roughly equating to a GSc of 50. LaGrow's 11-inning performance earned a GSc of 86, while Wood's masterful shutout earned a 99. Their combined total of 185 represents the highest Game Score on record at Tiger Stadium. With an unlikely pair, an unproven youngster in Lerrin LaGrow and a struggling ace in Wilbur Wood, each pitching the game of his life, it's almost unfair that only one could go home the victor.

SOURCES

Holtzman, Jerome. "Chisox Owner Allyn Gets Assist in Wood Comeback," *The Sporting News,* May 25, 1974.

Ferkovich, Scott. "The best-pitched game at Tiger Stadium featured two pitchers you'll never guess," Detroit Athletic Co., blog. detroitathletic.com/2014/08/22/best-pitched-game-tiger-stadium-featured-two-pitchers-youll-never-guess/, accessed May 1, 2015.

Wolf, Gregory H. "Wilbur Wood," The Baseball Biography Project, sabr.org/bioproj/person/ac0fe9f8, accessed May 1, 2015.

NOTES

1   Jim Kaplan, "The Week (May 5-May 11)," *Sports Illustrated,* May 20, 1974.

2   George Langford, "Sox nip Tigers 1-0 in 11 on Hermann homer," *Chicago Tribune,* May 8, 1974.

3   Ibid.

4   Ibid.

5   Larry Paladino, Associated Press, "Tiger Notes Quotes," in the *Owosso* (Michigan) *Argus-Press,* May 8, 1974.

THE BIRD IS THE WORD

June 28, 1976: Detroit Tigers 5, New York Yankees 1 at Tiger Stadium

By Scott Ferkovich

BASEBALL FANS THROUGHOUT THE country in 1976 had been hearing the scattered chatter, ever since mid-May. Talk of something new and exciting happening in Detroit. Some rookie pitcher with long hair. Didn't they say he talked to the baseball? Got on his knees before each inning and groomed the mound? Stomped around the field like a hyperactive kid? Kind of a flake? He certainly hadn't been pitching like one. He'd started eight games, winning seven of them. Of his seven complete games, two were 11-inning affairs. His only loss was a complete-game six-hitter in which he'd given up only two runs, while the Tigers had been shut out. His ERA was hovering in the low 2's. "I don't think even Walter Johnson even started this fast," said his manager, Ralph Houk.[1]

And he was drawing crowds. Big crowds. The year before, the Tigers had lost 102 games, an awful team with no identity, which had given their fans no reason to want to come out to Tiger Stadium. But suddenly here was this gregarious 21-year-old kid, who came out of nowhere to mow down hitters and wow the fans, who were packing the ballpark. He was from Worcester, Massachusetts, and his name was Mark Fidrych. But they called him The Bird because his curly golden locks made him look like Big Bird, one of the signature Muppet characters from "Sesame Street." And June 28, 1976 was the night that greatness was thrust upon him, as the rest of the nation finally found out what all the fuss was about.

Here were the Tigers, an otherwise ordinary team, facing the Yankees, who had been making mincemeat of the rest of the American League. New York was in first place by a wide margin, with stars like Thurman Munson, Chris Chambliss, Graig Nettles and Mickey Rivers. New York's manager was Billy Martin, who had guided Detroit to a division title just a few years before. The ABC television network was featuring the game on "Monday Night Baseball," to be broadcast coast to coast (except in Detroit itself, where the game was blacked out). Tiger Stadium was rocking from the get-go, with 47,855 Birdwatchers. Thousands, according to various estimates, were turned away when the box office ran out of tickets. Things hadn't been this exciting at the corner of Michigan and Trumbull since the Tigers won the World Series in 1968. "My phone started ringing at eight in the morning and didn't stop all day," noted Detroit's Bill Freehan, who had starred on that '68 team, and was now in his final year. "Everyone wanted tickets to see The Bird pitch."[2]

Reporters wanting to learn more about Fidrych peppered him with questions before the game. Surely he must feel some sense of awe to face the Yankees? Had he ever heard of Mickey Mantle? "Sure," he said, "he was a ballplayer, but now he's retired." What about Roger Maris? "No," chirped The Bird, "never heard of him." OK, maybe that's going back a ways, but what about the 1968 Tigers? He must have heard of them, since he would have been 12 years old at the time. "I was only 11, but I never heard of them, either. I was too busy working trying to make a living. Carry groceries, carry golf clubs — anything to make a buck. I had to go out once in a while, you know."[3]

Game time neared. The fans stood up and cheered as Fidrych bolted out of the dugout and headed for the bullpen for his pregame warm-up. Once the contest started, the Bengals jumped out in front in the first inning on a two-run homer by Rusty Staub. That was all they needed in a 5-1 win. In yet another complete game, Fidrych clowned the Yankees, scattering seven hits with zero walks, the only New York tally being a home run by Elrod Hendricks. The radar gun had him

The Bird threw 24 complete games in 29 starts in '76

clocked as high as 93 miles an hour, both in the first inning and in the ninth. Working quickly, he talked to the ball (or to himself) the whole time. But it was his excellent control, hard slider, and fearlessness that gave the Yanks fits all evening. The game lasted only an hour and 51 minutes. The Bird was now 8-1. All the while, he was, in the words of *Detroit Free Press* writer Charlie Vincent, "a perpetual motion machine on the mound."[4]

Near the end, Bob Uecker, one of the announcers on the ABC broadcast, raved, "I gotta tell you. ... I've seen a lot of ball games played, and I've caught a few. I don't think I've ever seen a pitcher this keyed up, in the ninth inning of a ball game, or all through the ball game. You'd think this guy'd be running out of gas by now ...but he is just starting to heat it up."[5] Not to be outdone, his broadcast partner, Bob Prince, marveled, "He's giving me duck bumps and I've watched over 8,000 ballgames!"[6] The crowd kept chanting "Let's Go Mark!" Elrod Hendricks grounded out to end the game, but the drama was just beginning. Also in the ABC booth was Warner Wolf. As Fidrych dashed

off the mound to hug backstop Bruce Kimm — who caught all of Fidrych's starts that season — as well as other teammates, Wolf cried, "And the Tigers act like Fidrych has just won the seventh game of the World Series!"[7] Prince added, "He is some kind of unbelievable!"[8] The Bird hopped around, shaking hands with teammates, with the umpires, with anybody in his path, much to Wolf's utter amazement. "Young Mark Fidrych, thanking his teammates! Look at that, he's thanking his teammates! He's thanking the umpires ... everybody ... the ground crew!"[9] Then The Bird ducked into the dugout and disappeared down the runway.

But nobody left. Nobody went home. The fans stood chanting "We want Mark! We want Mark!" "He's gotta come back," Wolf declared. "Come on, Mark! Nobody has left the ballpark!"[10] The clubhouse attendant had to go back and find Fidrych to tell him to get himself back out there. Finally, after about two minutes, a dazed Bird popped back up out of the dugout, doffing his cap with a boyish grin. Tiger Stadium erupted again. He reached over the top of the dugout, shaking fans' hands (including those of a policeman). Overcome with emotion, Fidrych covered his head in his arms, and tried to escape into the dugout, but his teammates urged him back onto the field.

Bob Uecker corralled Fidrych in front of the Detroit dugout for an interview. "Mark," he noted, "I've never seen anything like this in my life, and I know it's a very emotional moment for you."[11] "Hell, yeah," said Fidrych.[12] The Bird's youthful innocence was on full display, as he claimed that "everything is just so new to me." He referred to Hendricks, who had hit the home run, as "that one guy." "Damn," he said at one point, "I couldn't ask for anything more!" Uecker asked him what he was doing when he was grooming the mound. "I want to dig my own hole," The Bird clarified. The camera got a close-up of Fidrych's oversized feet as he stood there, sans shoes, in stirrups and dirty stockings. "I never played before this many people before. In the minor leagues, sometimes they had 2,000 people there. And when the place is packed, you want to do good."[13] The national television audience ate up The Bird. On a warm June night in Detroit, his legend had been born.

His teammates were enthusiastic in their praise of the rookie. "The best part about this game," said Freehan, "was that with all of its ballyhoo, Fidrych didn't disappoint them. Lots of times in these situations the game turns into a dud. ... It takes a lot of courage, ability, and concentration to do what he did."[14]

"Every person can see the enthusiasm in Mark," gushed Staub. "He brings out exuberance and an inner youth in everybody. It's contagious."[15]

"[Denny] McLain didn't draw that many people," said John Hiller, a teammate of McLain's on the 1968 championship squad. "I even watched the game. I don't usually do that."[16]

"It was fun as hell," noted Mickey Stanley, another '68 hero. "It was like a World Series game."[17]

The Yankees won the American League pennant in 1976. The Tigers finished fifth. Mark Fidrych numbered 19 wins, led the AL in complete games with 24, and ERA at 2.34. After the season, he became the first baseball player ever to get his picture on the cover of *Rolling Stone* magazine. But arm problems cut short his career seemingly before it had even started. At age 26, his time in the big leagues was finished. But the memories lasted forever. "One word doesn't describe it," Fidrych said of that exciting summer of '76. "It was the ultimate."[18]

NOTES

1 Jim Hawkins, "Go, Bird, Go! Fidrych Kills NY, 5-1," *Detroit Free Press*, June 29, 1976.

2 Dan Ewald, "The Bird Pulls His Superman Act," *Detroit News*, June 29, 1976.

3 Joe Falls, "The Bird Makes It Look Like Old Days," *Detroit Free Press*, June 29, 1976.

4 Charlie Vincent, "Bird: The People Really Get Me Up," *Detroit Free Press*, June 29, 1976.

5 Bourke457, "Fidrych Fame: The Bird Beats the Yankees," YouTube Video, 4:40. Uploaded January 15, 2014. https://www.youtube.com/watch?v=sMSD03BX5Ds

6 Ibid.

7 Ibid.

8 Ibid.

9 Ibid.

10 Ibid.

11 Bourke457, "Fidrych Yankee Interview," YouTube Video, 4:49. Uploaded January 15, 2014. https://www.youtube.com/watch?v=hbCdwCRqBGI

12 Ibid.

13 Cyndi Meagher, "A Nation Sees Detroit's Finest," *Detroit News*, June 29, 1976.

14 Ewald.

15 Ibid.

16 Ibid.

17 Ibid.

18 UPI, "Mark Fidrych Retires to End Two-Year Comeback Bid," *Bangor Daily News*, June 30, 1983.

THE BERGMAN GAME

June 4, 1984: Detroit Tigers 6, Toronto Blue Jays 3 at Tiger Stadium

By Maxwell Kates

ASK A TIGERS FAN OF RECENT VINTAGE to associate "Blue Jays" and "extra innings" and the memories will not be positive. On August 10, 2014, Detroit squandered a 5-0 victory, eventually losing when Jose Bautista sliced a game-winning single in the 19th inning. Thirty years before, the Tigers and Blue Jays faced off in an equally riveting overtime contest. In both cases, the victory went to the home team.

No longer the perennial doormats of the American League East, the 1984 Blue Jays under manager Bobby Cox won 26 of their first 40 games. Yet, since the Tigers opened with 35-5, Toronto was already 8 games back. Through a series of shrewd blockbuster trades, Toronto general manager Pat Gillick had assembled a team anchored by veterans Dave Collins, Damaso Garcia, and Alfredo Griffin. Meanwhile, the farm system began to harvest stars Lloyd Moseby and Dave Stieb while original Jay and Detroit native Ernie Whitt worked behind the plate.

All were in the starting lineup on June 4 to open a four-game series in Detroit with Alan Trammell, Lou Whitaker, Kirk Gibson, and Larry Herndon. A crowd of 26,733 converged on Tiger Stadium while millions more watched at home. Dubbed "the Showdown in Motown," the game was broadcast by Howard Cosell, Al Michaels, and Earl Weaver on ABC Monday Night Baseball.

Manager Sparky Anderson sent Juan Berenguer to start for the Tigers. The Panamanian right-hander, a well-travelled veteran, faced many former teammates, including ex-Kansas City Royals Rance Mulliniks and Willie Aikens. The Tigers were slumping while the Blue Jays suddenly forgot how to lose. As pitching coach Roger Craig pointed out, if Toronto swept, Detroit's lead would be reduced to half a game:

"I think it's important to remember that Toronto came to Tiger Stadium with 15 wins in its previous 19 games while we had lost six of our previous nine," Craig recalled after the season. "… No matter how well we played, they were still on our heels. In the recesses of my mind I [feared] they could catch us."[1]

The Blue Jays drew first blood when Willie Upshaw homered to lead off the second inning. Upshaw was on second base in the sixth when George Bell struck Berenguer for a second home run; 3-0 Blue Jays. Berenguer was living up to his unflattering nickname of "El Gasolino," yielding eight hits and two walks in 6⅔ innings, while also striking out seven. After speedy Damaso Garcia doubled, Anderson yanked Berenguer. He replaced him with reliever Willie Hernandez, who got out of the inning without any further damage.

Meanwhile, Dave Stieb was cruising for the Blue Jays. He entered the game with a record of 7-1, and would soon start his second consecutive All-Star Game. He had given up only three hits through six, but his luck was about to change.

"The seventh was the real key that night," Tigers' first baseman Dave Bergman told reporter Eli Zaret years later. "Our ballclub was so strong that our order that night had John Grubb hitting sixth, Chet Lemon seventh, me eighth, and Howard Johnson ninth. Stieb plunked Lemon, who was on first with one out."[2] After Bergman rapped a single, the "Showdown in Motown" began to resemble *Blazing Saddles'* Battle of Rock Ridge when Johnson tied the game with a home run. Before the inning was over, reliever Dennis Lamp was brought in to pitch. Neither team scored in the eighth or ninth as the game went to extra innings.

Hernandez pitched three solid innings before he was replaced by Aurelio "Senor Smoke" Lopez in the 10th. Rookie portsider Jimmy Key pitched the bottom half of the inning. Lance Parrish led off with a base hit for the possible go-ahead run. After Darrell Evans sacrificed to advance Parrish, Key was relieved by right-hander and occasional anthem singer Roy Lee Jackson. Rusty Kuntz grounded to the mound for the second out before Jackson walked Lemon.

Enter Dave Bergman.

Like many of his opponents that game, Bergman had developed as a player in the Yankees' farm system. Born in 1953 in Evanston, Illinois, Bergman broke in with New York in 1975. In eight major-league seasons, including stops in Houston and San Francisco, Bergman had developed a reputation that "if you threw me a slider down and in, you better get it in because I can golf it out of the ballpark."[3] What followed was in Roger Craig's estimation "one of the greatest pitcher-batter confrontations I have ever witnessed. This was baseball in its simplest and purest form," he elaborated, "Jackson, the pitcher, against Bergman, the hitter; first place team against second place team; tenth inning of a tied game; two outs and two runners on base."[4]

Bergman remembered telling himself as he strode to the plate to "go up there and slash and have a good time." He added, "little did I know."[5]

Down in the count 0-and-2, Bergman fouled off pitch after pitch before looking at balls one and two. He fouled pitch number eight before extending the count full, passing on a low fastball. Three more foul balls followed. By now, the at-bat was seven minutes old. Jackson's 13th pitch to Bergman was "a slider six inches off the ground" but that was the one he liked.[6] Down went Jackson as that ball landed in the upper deck. The Tigers and their fans could once again believe in miracles.

"There comes a time in every season when a hitter puts all his mechanics together," Bergman told writer George Cantor many years later. "That night was it for me."[7] It was Bergman's first home run in a Detroit uniform. Sparky Anderson called it "the greatest at-bat in my life."[8] The final score: Tigers 6, Blue Jays 3, won on pitching, defense, and three-run homers. Roger Craig recalled the postgame commotion:

"There were between fifty and sixty reporters in our clubhouse, which is one of the smallest in the league, and four television mini-cameras converged on Bergman's locker. We had beaten the club that was gaining on us."[9] Ironically, Bergman's monumental plate appearance almost never happened due to a groin pull late in the game. As he remembered, "I told Pio DiSalvo, our fabulous trainer, that he had to do something because I'm not coming out of this game. … It was probably about the eighth inning that he took me out of the clubhouse and wrapped me up." He continued, "If Pio's not the trainer, I may be out of that game before I could deliver the biggest hit of my career."[10]

Toronto finished the 1984 season with a record of 89-73, second best in the American League but 15 games behind the eventual world champion Tigers. The Blue Jays excelled in their rotation, but their bullpen was their demise. In the years to follow, with Tom Henke and later Duane Ward established as their closers, the Blue Jays won five of the next nine division titles, along with the World Series in both 1992 and 1993. Although the Tigers returned to the World Series twice after 1984, they have been unable (as of 2014) to claim baseball's ultimate prize.

Bergman hit six more homers in 1984, including another three-run extra-inning tiebreaker against the Blue Jays on September 7. He remained with the Tigers until 1992, when he retired to enter the investment industry. Bergman lost his battle with cancer in early 2015. In his own words, the home run off Jackson cemented his legacy as a player:

"Fans don't remember the ground balls I've booted or the times I struck out with the bases loaded. But that game … proves again that it's better to be lucky than good. I had a blue collar, lunch bucket kind of career but that at-bat has lived with me ever since."[11] Perhaps the best compliment Bergman received was from a former minor-league manager of his, Bobby Cox:

"The next day," Bergman recalled, "I was talking with guys near the cage and, as a sign of recognition that I got him the night before, he threw one at my back. Then he smiled and said, "Nice job last night.'"[12]

SOURCES

"Roy Lee Jackson." The Fleer Corporation, 1984, 158.

Usereau, Alain. *The Expos in Their Prime: The Short Lived Glory of Montreal's Team, 1977-1984* (Jefferson, North Carolina: McFarland & Company, Inc., 2013).

Zweig, Eric. *Toronto Blue Jays Official 25th Anniversary Commemorative Book* (Toronto: Dan Diamond and Associates, Inc., 2001).

Acknowledgements

David Eisenstadt, Gary Fink, Michael Frank, Keith Friedman, Francis Kinlaw, Marilyn Klar, Steve Lauer, Craig Lukshin, Andy McCue, Jeffrey Miller, T. Kent Morgan, and Larry Thompson.

NOTES

1   Roger Craig and Vern Plagenhoef, *Inside Pitch: Roger Craig's '84 Tiger Journal*, (Grand Rapids, Michigan: William B. Eerdsmans Publishing Company, 1984), 85.

2   Eli Zaret, *'84: The Last of the Great Tigers—Untold Stories from an Amazing Season* (South Boardman, Michigan: Crofton Creek Press, 2004), 90.

3   Ibid.

4   Craig, 85.

5   Zaret, 91.

6   Ibid.

7   Jerry Nechal, "Dave Bergman" in *Detroit Tigers 1984: What A Start! What A Finish!*, Mark Pattison and David Raglin, eds, (Phoenix: Society for American Baseball Research Inc., 2012), 52.

8   Sparky Anderson and Dan Ewald, *Bless You Boys: Diary of the Detroit Tigers Season* (Chicago: Contemporary Books, 1984), 84.

9   Craig, 85.

10   Zaret, 91.

11   Ibid.

12   Ibid.

SLURVES, YACKADOOS, AND AN AMERICAN LEAGUE PENNANT

October 5, 1984: Detroit Tigers 1, Kansas City Royals 0 at Tiger Stadium (Game 3 of the American League Championship Series)

By Susan A. Lantz

IT WAS A BEAUTIFUL DAY FOR BASEBALL, with the temperature in the mid-60s. Sunshine would have made it perfect, but despite the clouds and overcast, a great crowd of 52,168 showed up at Tiger Stadium on the afternoon of Friday, October 5, 1984, for Game Three of the American League Championship Series.

Fans in Detroit did not care that the local economy had tanked and many people were out of work. They didn't care that the NHL's Red Wings still seemed like the Dead Things, the NBA's Pistons were not yet the Bad Boys, or that the NFL's Lions were following their usual un-lion-like pattern. The Tigers had started the season with a roar, going 35-5, and led the division from wire to wire, the first team to do so since the 1955 Brooklyn Dodgers. The Tigers had won 104 regular-season games, the most in the team's history. They were a tonic for a town that badly needed one, a reason for people in Detroit to feel good.

For the most part, no one was too concerned that the Major League Umpires Association had gone on strike before the start of the postseason, forcing the American League to use a substitute crew for this ALCS. Detroit was a union town, and probably more fans than not supported the umpires—as long as the crew working the game got it right. Retired umpire Bill Deegan had worked home plate for the first two games and would again today, while his two most experienced assistants would again be at first and second base (Jon Bible and Randy Christal, respectively). Different fill-in umpires, none of whom had worked the previous games in the series, were assigned to the umpiring positions at third and the outfield.

Detroit had won the first two games of the Series in Kansas City. The first contest, on Tuesday, was a comfortable 8-1 win, pitched by Jack Morris and Willie Hernandez. The next night had been more of a nail-biter. Dan Petry held the Royals to two runs through seven innings, but Hernandez gave up a run in the eighth that tied the game (it was only his second blown save of 1984; he had gone 32-33 in save situations in his Cy Young and MVP award-winning season). Aurelio Lopez kept the Royals scoreless through three more innings, and the Tigers scored two runs courtesy of a Johnny Grubb double in the top of the 11th to win 5-3.

The Tigers' pitching staff could not boast any 20-game winners, but five pitchers had won at least 10 regular-season games: Morris (19), Petry (18), Milt Wilcox (a career-high 17), Juan Berenguer (11), and Lopez (10). The bullpen was about as good as it got with Lopez (who also saved 14) and Hernandez. The pitching staff had an ERA of 3.49 and a WHIP (walks and hits per inning pitched) of 1.262, which were both the lowest in the American League. Their pitchers had given up fewer hits and fewer runs than another other team in the league, and topped the circuit in saves.

During the regular season the Tigers had scored 829 runs and allowed their opponents only 643 runs—the first team to lead the AL in both categories since the 1971 Baltimore Orioles. In addition, Detroit hit 187 home runs, the most in all of baseball. It was a balanced attack: No one had driven in 100 runs (Lance Parrish drove in 98, Kirk Gibson 91); and no one had scored 100 runs. Only one player, Alan Trammell, had hit over .300 (he hit .314), but five other players (with at least 300 at-bats) had hit .280 or better. Eight players had hit at least 12 home runs. The Tigers' batting average was only fourth best in the league, but they led the league in on-base percentage and were second in slugging. They were second in the league in walks, too, and led in the league in intentional walks. Every player except backup catcher Dwight Lowry and utilityman Mike Laga had stolen at least one base, including 35-year-old Johnny Grubb and 37-year-old Darrell Evans (Kirk Gibson led the team with 29).

But now it was October baseball, and regular-season numbers didn't matter. Still, the Tigers could hit and score runs, and that's what the fans had come to see.

Before the game was over, Detroit would manage only three hits, as would the Royals. But it was Wilcox, the 34-year-old Hawaiian-born right-hander, who would win the game that gave the Tigers the pennant.

He'd won 17 of the 33 regular-season games he'd started and lost only eight, finishing with an ERA of 4.00. He'd gone 9-2 since July 19. Opposing Wilcox for Kansas City was Charlie Leibrandt, who sported an 11-7 record in his 23 regular-season starts, with a 3.63 ERA.

The game's lone run came in the bottom of the second inning. Detroit's Barbaro Garbey beat out a single on a groundball to second baseman Frank White. Chet Lemon then hit one to third baseman George Brett, who threw to White to force Garbey. Evans, the 16-year veteran seeking his first World Series appearance, singled to center, with Lemon taking third.

Next up was Marty Castillo. At age 27, and with only 201 career games in the majors under his belt, Castillo mostly rode the pine for manager Sparky Anderson in 1984. The California native could catch or play third base, and had a cannon for an arm. But he batted only .234 during the regular season, and was known more for his practical jokes than for his ability to hit a baseball.

With a runner on third and one out, Castillo hit a groundball to Onix Concepcion at short, who scooped it up and threw to White at second for the force. White gunned the ball down to Steve Balboni, the first baseman, for what would have been an inning-ending double play. But Castillo, who wasn't blessed

with great foot speed, chugged it down the line and beat the relay. Lemon scored, and the Tigers had an early lead.

Lou Whitaker came to the plate next, and on a 2-and-1 pitch, Castillo stole second, and then advanced to third on catcher Don Slaught's throwing error. Whitaker attempted to bunt Castillo home, but grounded out, first baseman to the pitcher.

That was all the scoring in the game. Leibrandt was strong, but Wilcox was better, throwing eight innings while giving up only two hits and two walks, to go with eight strikeouts. Hernandez picked up the save.

The Tigers were going to the World Series for the first time since 1968.

The game was a vindication for Detroit. All season long, the players had had to deal with the pressures and expectations that went with a 35-5 start. What if they were to collapse in the end? The critics and naysayers ignored the fact that every other team had the opportunity to get off to a comparable start. But all season long, the Tigers played consistent baseball, winning 104 regular-season games.

The victory was a signature moment for Sparky Anderson in his managerial career. After he was fired in Cincinnati, his detractors had claimed that anyone could have managed the Big Red Machine and won. But Anderson skippered Detroit to the pennant in 1984 with far fewer big-name stars. "They questioned me after Cincinnati," he said, "but no one will ever question me again. That's the most gratifying thought I can think of. Ever since I was fired, I've wanted to prove it was wrong."[1]

It was a red-letter day for Castillo, who appeared in only 70 games for the 1984 Tigers, but is remembered for his clutch postseason production. Not only did he knock in the winning run in this pennant-clinching game, he later hit a home run that gave the Tigers a lead they would not relinquish in Game Three of the World Series. Castillo set personal—but modest—highs in almost every major offensive category while serving as a defensive substitute at both catcher (36 games) and third base (33 games).

It was a game of redemption for Wilcox. As a rookie with Cincinnati in 1970, he pitched three strong innings of relief to win the pennant-clinching Game Three of the National League Championship Series. But he subsequently lost Game Two of that year's World Series, giving up three hits and two runs in relief while retiring only one batter. (The Reds lost the Series to Baltimore in five games.) A model of consistency in his previous seven seasons with the Tigers, Wilcox pitched through pain for most of the year, using his repertoire of "slurves" and "yackadoos."

"I stayed healthy enough to never miss a start, but I had a feeling this was possibly my last year. I had seven cortisone shots (in 1984)," he said.[2] He kept a lot of the symptoms from the trainers and his teammates. "There was often a question whether Milt was able to pitch on a given night, but he always went out there," Darrell Evans said. "We weren't aware of what he was going through at the time. The guy's a warrior and you have to have enough of these guys and that's why it's so hard to win."[3]

Wilcox showed that he had what it took to help win a pennant—this time, in the American League.

NOTES

1 Tom Gage, "Anderson Gets His Vindication," *The Sporting News*, October 1, 1984: 28.

2 Mark Pattison and Dave Raglin, *Detroit Tigers 1984: What a Start, What a Finish!* (Phoenix: Society for American Baseball Research, 2012), 166.

3 Ibid.

GIBBY COOKS THE GOOSE

October 14, 1984: Detroit Tigers 8, San Diego Padres 4 at Tiger Stadium (Game Five of the World Series)

By Susan A. Lantz

IT WAS NOT AN IDEAL DAY FOR BASEBALL, with temperatures in the mid-60s and a 30 percent chance of rain. Despite the foggy conditions, 51,901 Tigers fans flocked to the corner of Michigan and Trumbull in great numbers on October 14, 1984.

It was Game Five of the World Series, the Tigers vs. the San Diego Padres, and Detroit was primed to celebrate a championship.

The team was a tonic for a town that badly needed one. With a 35-5 start to the season, and wire-to-wire domination of the American League, the Tigers had given the city a reason to feel good, in spite of the bottomed-out economy and high unemployment.

The Tigers had won the first game of the Series in San Diego, 3-2, with Jack Morris pitching a complete game. They had lost the following night, 5-3, when Dan Petry gave up five runs in 4⅓ innings. When the Series moved to Detroit, the Tigers won the third game, 5-2, thanks to strong pitching by Milt Wilcox, Bill Scherrer, and ace reliever Willie Hernandez. Jack Morris went the distance again in Game Four for the win.

The Tigers wanted a win in this Game Five. They didn't want to go back to a raucous Jack Murphy Stadium in San Diego for a possible Game Six or Seven. If the Tigers were going to win the World Series, they (and their fans) wanted it done in Detroit.

Petry was on the mound again for the Tigers. He'd gone 18-8 in his 35 regular-season starts, with seven complete games, two shutouts, and an ERA of 3.24. He'd gotten no decision in the second game of the American League Championship Series, but had taken the loss in Game Two of the World Series. The Padres countered with lefty Mark Thurmond, who had a 14-8 record in 29 regular-season starts, with an ERA of 2.97. He'd pitched the second game of the National League Championship Series and lost, 4-2, to the Chicago Cubs. In Game One of the World Series, he'd given up three runs in five innings and took the loss.

San Diego didn't score off Petry in the first. The Tigers, however, started off with a bang, with second baseman Lou Whitaker hitting a line-drive single to right. Shortstop Alan Trammell hit a grounder to Garry Templeton, his San Diego counterpart, forcing Whitaker at second. Right fielder Kirk Gibson then blasted Thurmond's first pitch into the right-field upper deck. Detroit tacked on a third run thanks to three straight singles by Lance Parrish, Larry Herndon, and Chet Lemon.

Padres manager Dick Williams pulled Thurmond and put in 24-year-old Andy Hawkins, who had a record of 8-9 in 22 starts and 14 relief appearances. At 4.68, he had the highest ERA of all the Padres starters, but he'd taken over in Game Two of the Series when starter Ed Whitson had not been able to get out of the first inning, and Hawkins had got the win. He got out of this inning without further damage. The Padres were relieved, while Tiger fans were thrilled; they loved to watch their boys hit.

San Diego got on the board in the third, when a single by Steve Garvey plated Bobby Brown, making it 3-1. The Tigers did not score in their half of the frame.

The Padres struck again in the top of the fourth. Petry began to lose command, and a walk, a double, and a single eventually tied the score, 3-3. Detroit manager Sparky Anderson pulled Petry and put in Scherrer, who had a 1.89 ERA in 18 regular-season games after joining the team in late August. Tony Gwynn flied out to right on Scherrer's first pitch.

And so things remained until the home half of the fifth. Gibson led off by slashing a sharp grounder to third. Graig Nettles dove for the ball, but it banged off his glove into left field, and Gibson had himself a

Kirk Gibson's home run brought down the house

single. Parrish hit a high drive to left that looked as though it had a chance to leave the yard, but Carmelo Martinez hauled it in at the warning track. Hustling all the way, Gibson advanced to second. Herndon then walked on four pitches. Craig Lefferts replaced Hawkins on the mound. Lemon also walked, loading the bases.

Left-handed-hitting Johnny Grubb was scheduled to bat against the southpaw Lefferts. But Anderson, playing the percentages, sent in an unlikely pinch-hitter, Rusty Kuntz. Mostly riding the pine in 1984, he'd hit .286, but had become something of a folk hero in Detroit owing to his underdog status.

Kuntz hit a fly to shallow right field. The ball should have been right fielder Gwynn's play to make, but he had his arms spread indicating he had lost the ball in the lights. Backtracking second baseman Alan Wiggins was forced to make the catch. Gibson took everyone by surprise by tagging up and scoring on the weak-armed Wiggins, giving the Tigers the lead 4-3.

"If Gwynn catches that ball, I'm still going," Gibson insisted later, "but there probably would have been a severe collision at the plate. Instead, I scored easily."[1]

It was gutsy run for the money on Gibson's part, and the key play of the game. "I'm an aggressive player. It was 3-3. What are you going to do? Play scared?"[2]

Neither team managed another baserunner until the bottom of the seventh, when Parrish greeted new pitcher Rich "Goose" Gossage with a home run over the left-field wall to pad Detroit's lead to 5-3.

Willie Hernandez, Detroit's sensational reliever, took the mound to start the eighth. He retired two batters on four pitches, then Kurt Bevacqua sent his first pitch over the wall in deep left, bringing the Padres back to within a run, 5-4.

The close game was blown open in the bottom of the eighth, however, when Gibson hit a three-run home run deep into the right-field bleachers, scoring Marty Castillo and Lou Whitaker and giving the Tigers an 8-4 lead. Before the homer, Padres manager Dick Williams had conferred with Gossage on the mound. Williams had apparently wanted to walk the left-handed-hitting Gibson to load the bases, preferring the righty-righty matchup of Gossage and Parrish. But Gossage talked his manager out of it, figuring he could get Gibson out.

"I didn't expect to be walked," Gibson said. "I looked over to the dugout and Sparky was holding up four fingers and saying, 'They're gonna put you on.' And I looked back at him and shook my head and held up 10 fingers and said, 'I'll bet you 10 bucks I'm gonna hit it out.' Sparky still owes me the 10 bucks. I'm not worried, though. He'll pay."[3]

Gibson's blast brought a roar from the crowd that could reportedly be heard for blocks. The most memorable image from the World Series was Gibson jumping up and down with his arms above his head in triumph after he circled the bases. Reliever Aurelio Lopez threw strikes on 21 of his 25 pitches and struck out four of the seven batters he faced, picking up his second win of the Series. When Hernandez earned his third save by getting Gwynn to fly out to Herndon for the final out, the Tigers were World Series champions for the first time since 1968.

"I guess this is what fairy tales are made of," Gibson gushed in the post-game celebration in the Tiger clubhouse.[4]

Trammell was named the Series MVP. "We're the champions. We get the ring. This is what it's all about," he exclaimed.[5]

"This team is so good, it can go as far as it wants," said a jubilant Sparky Anderson.[6]

Wrote Martin F. Kohn in the next day's *Detroit Free Press*: "For Detroit, for Michigan, for the Midwest, for everybody who has been with the Tigers in spirit, the victory was a moment to cherish in a season to savor."[7]

Columnist Tom Gage summed it up succinctly: "And the enchanted team lived happily ever after. Thus ends the Tigers' storybook season."[8]

NOTES

1 Tom Gage, "Tiger Magic: It's Real," *Detroit News*, October 15, 1984.

2 Jerry Green, "Hard Work Wins it For a Rough Town," *Detroit News*, October 15, 1984.

3 Dave Nightengale, "The 'Real' Kirk Gibson Ends the Padres' Misery," *The Sporting News*, October 22, 1984.

4 Jay Mariotti, "Gibson Homer Marks the Climax of Fabulous Season," *Detroit News*, October 15, 1984.

5 "Quotable," *Detroit News*, October 15, 1984.

6 Mariotti.

7 Martin F. Kohn, "Gr-r-reat! Fans Go Wild Over Tigers," *Detroit Free Press*, October 15, 1984.

8 Gage.

TANANA BEATS TORONTO TO CLINCH DIVISION TITLE

October 4, 1987: Detroit Tigers 1, Toronto Blue Jays 0, at Tiger Stadium

By David Raglin

SUNDAY, OCTOBER 4, 1987, WAS THE culmination of the Showdown Series between the Detroit Tigers and the Toronto Blue Jays, the likes of which, given the wild card format, will not be seen in the regular season again.

The Tigers started the 1987 season 11-19, in sixth place in the American League Eastern Division, 9½ games behind the Milwaukee Brewers, who had started 13-0. Coming on the heels of a 9-20 spring training during which they looked terrible, it seemed that the door had closed on the team that amazed the baseball world in 1984 with its 35-5 start and its first World Series title since 1968. Despite the slow start to their season, a 10-2 stretch brought the Tigers' record to .500, and on August 19 they climbed over the Blue Jays into first place for the first time. From mid-August the Tigers and the Jays traded the division lead back and forth, and on September 23 Toronto was in first by half a game. The regular season would conclude with the two contenders facing off seven times in the final week and a half in what has become known as the Showdown Series—four games in Toronto, then a break while they played other clubs, and finishing with three games at Tiger Stadium.

It looked as though the series in Detroit might not mean anything. Toronto won the first three games at Exhibition Stadium, all by one run (4-3, 3-2, and 10-9). The Jays were leading in the fourth game 1-0 in the ninth, with ace closer Tom Henke on the mound, three outs from going up 4½ games, when Kirk Gibson led off the ninth with a homer to tie it up. The teams traded runs in the 11th before Gibson singled in the winning run in the 13th.

The Tigers were still alive, but barely, as Toronto was still up by 2½ games. Unfortunately for the Blue Jays, however, down the stretch Toronto suffered two key injuries. In the first game of the Showdown Series, MVP candidate Tony Fernandez broke his elbow landing on a piece of wood at the edge of the second-base cutout after being upended by Bill Madlock trying to break up a double play. Next, Detroit native Ernie Whitt broke some ribs trying to break up a double play against the Brewers on September 29. Toronto was swept at home by Milwaukee in that series, while Detroit split against Baltimore to set up the final weekend—Toronto up by one game with three to go. The Tigers won the first two games, so going into Game 162, they were up by one game. A Detroit win would give the Tigers the division by two games. A Toronto win would set up a one-game playoff on Monday at Tiger Stadium, since the Tigers had won a coin flip.

The Blue Jays made some changes to their regular lineup for this final game of the regular season. George Bell had been the number 4 hitter all season, but manager Jimy Williams moved him into the 3 spot for this game, and moved Jesse Barfield from his usual 6 slot up to number 5. With Whitt injured, Williams had September call-up Greg Myers catch the first two games of the series, but he went with veteran Charlie Moore in the final game. Cecil Fielder played first instead of Willie Upshaw. Manny Lee was at short for the injured Fernandez, as he had been ever since the injury, and with lefty Frank Tanana on the mound for Detroit, Garth Iorg played third instead of platoon partner Rance Mulliniks.

The Tigers' lineup was their usual one against a lefty starter, in this game Jimmy Key. Mike Heath caught instead of Matt Nokes, and Larry Herndon was in right field in place of Scott Lusader. The only exception to the usual lineup was Jim Morrison at third in place of Tom Brookens, who had awoken at 2:30 A.M. with vomiting and diarrhea and gone to Henry Ford Hospital. Brookens made it to the park for the game and put on his uniform, but never left the clubhouse.

The game did not look like a 1-0 classic early on. Tanana started Nelson Liriano 0-2 but walked him. Lloyd Moseby struck out for the first out on a fastball at the knees. George Bell stung the ball for a single to left, sending Liriano to second and giving Toronto two on with one out. All day, Tanana was unable to get his curveball over for strikes. However, Tanana got Juan Beniquez to strike out on a changeup and Barfield to hit a soft one-hopper to second for the third out.

The Tigers also got their first man on base, Lou Whitaker, on a solid single to right field, although it was apparent as Whitaker ran to first that his bad ankle was bothering him. After that promising start, Bill Madlock, a midseason acquisition from the Dodgers, hit a sharp grounder to third, producing an Iorg-Liriano-Fielder around-the-horn double play. Kirk Gibson popped to Lee at short to end the first inning.

After a scoreless 1-2-3 top of the second, Alan Trammell led off the bottom of the second for Detroit. Amid chants of "MVP," Trammell tried to get on with a bunt to the left side of the infield but hit it a bit hard to third baseman Iorg, who was playing in and threw Trammell out easily. Larry Herndon then hit a 2-and-1 pitch that looked as though it would land in left fielder Bell's glove at the edge of the warning track, but it caught the wind and Bell could not back up in time to make a leap for the ball. It landed in the second row of the left-field seats and the Tigers led 1-0. It was the only fly ball to the outfield Key would allow all day.

Tanana was in danger of giving up that lead in the next two innings. The third started with a single by Charlie Moore, as Tanana had still not gotten a curveball over the plate. Nelson Liriano swung through

a changeup for the first out but with Lloyd Moseby up, a bouncing curveball got past catcher Mike Heath, sending Moore to second. Moseby eventually struck out, and after the Tigers intentionally walked George Bell, Beniquez hit a one-hopper to short for a fielder's choice to end the inning.

In the fourth with one out, Cecil Fielder hit a solid liner just past Jim Morrison for a single. The next hitter was Manny Lee, and Jimy Williams put on the hit-and-run. However, Williams noticed that Lee had missed the sign and he took off the hit-and-run. Fielder missed the change and was thrown out at second. Lee then hit a triple to right field that bounded off the wall past right fielder Larry Herndon and would have tied the game but for the earlier snafu on the basepaths. Garth Iorg hit a can of corn to Chet Lemon in center to strand Lee at third.

The Tigers left two men on in the fourth and the Jays left two on in the seventh and one in the eighth, but the score stayed 1-0 entering the top of the ninth. Before the bottom of the eighth and the top of the ninth, police lined up to keep fans off the field in case the Tigers won the game.

Frank Tanana pitched the game of his life

Fielder led off the top of the ninth. After starting off 1-and-2, he worked the count full before swinging through a Tanana fastball for the first out. Manny Lee was next, and he hit a one-hopper to defensive replacement Jim Walewander at third. Walewander held the ball a bit long, and his subsequent rushed throw to first was in the dirt, but first baseman Darrell Evans scooped the ball for the second out. With two out and nobody on, Garth Iorg swung at the first pitch and hit a tapper between the mound and first base. Tanana dashed over, grabbed the ball, turned 270 degrees clockwise and underhanded the ball to Evans. The toss was right on the mark, and the Tigers had won the division.

As the Tigers celebrated to the left of first base, Lou Whitaker grabbed second base out of the ground. He would give it to double-play partner Alan Trammell with the following inscription "To Alan Trammell, MVP, 1987. Congratulations, Louis Rodman Whitaker." (The writers, however, voted the award to George Bell.) The police presence worked as few fans ran on the field.

The Showdown Series was an incredible seven games. All seven games were decided by one run, three were walk-offs, and in all but the last game, the team that scored first lost the game. The Tigers' 98-64 record was the best in baseball, but after these exhausting games, the Tigers ran out of gas against the Minnesota Twins in the playoffs, losing four games to one.

SOURCES

WDIV TV (Detroit) broadcast of the game

Detroit Free Press

Pattison, Mark, and Dave Raglin. *Detroit Tigers Lists and More: Runs, Hits, and Eras* (Detroit: Wayne State University Press, 2002).

LOCAL KID SHERIDAN MAKES GOOD WITH HOMER

October 10, 1987: Detroit Tigers 7, Minnesota Twins 6 at Tiger Stadium
(Game 3 of the American League Championship Series)

By Jeff Samoray

BEFORE GAME ONE OF THE 1987 American League Championship Series between the Detroit Tigers and Minnesota Twins, Tigers manager Sparky Anderson made a statement about Pat Sheridan. Although the Tigers outfielder ended the season 5-for-68 and spent most of the last three weeks on the bench during a tight race for first place, Anderson had a hunch.

"It wouldn't surprise me if Pat won a few ballgames and is the hero," Anderson said. "World Series and playoffs have produced some strange heroes."[1]

Potential heroes and proven veterans filled the Tigers' roster, which is one reason why Detroit was heavily favored to win the ALCS. The team played at a .659 clip after stumbling out of the gate with an 11-19 record, and finished with more wins (98) than any other team in the majors. Stacked with left-handed power, the team hit 225 home runs, then the second highest single-season total in major-league history. Detroit also had 20 players with postseason experience (12 played for the 1984 World Series champions).

In contrast, the Twins played one game under .500 after the All-Star break and lost their last five regular-season games after clinching their division. Minnesota had the worst road record (29-52) of any division or pennant winner in major-league history. With their 85-77 record, the Twins would have finished fifth in the American League East, 13 games behind Detroit. Minnesota beat Detroit four times in 12 meetings that season. The Twins had just six players with postseason experience.

But no team that season could match Minnesota's exceptional home-field advantage. The Twins led the majors with a 56-25 home record (Detroit was second at 54-27) and capitalized on it in the first two games of the best-of-seven ALCS, played at the raucous Hubert H. Humphrey Metrodome in Minneapolis. More than 50,000 fans packed the stadium for each game, generating ear-piercing decibel levels and enthusiastically waving their "homer hankies"—a new promotional giveaway that has since become nearly ubiquitous at postseason baseball games.

Detroit blew a late lead in Game One and lost 8-5, then endured a 6-3 thumping in Game Two. Tigers fans hoped the team's fortunes would turn once they returned home.

The series moved to Detroit's Tiger Stadium for Game Three on Saturday, October 10. The weather was cold, gray and brisk with a game-time temperature of 49 degrees and winds of 10 to 15 miles per hour. The Twins started right-hander Les Straker, a 28-year-old rookie who won eight games that season after spending 10 years in the minor leagues. The Tigers countered with Walt Terrell, a veteran right-hander who was 13-2 with a 2.47 ERA in home games that season.

Terrell, who was pitching on eight days' rest, struggled early to find a groove and often fell behind in the count. Still, he allowed just one walk, no hits and no runs in his first two innings.

The Twins blew a chance to put runners at first and third with no outs in the third. Tom Brunansky walked, then attempted to steal as Steve Lombardozzi lifted a pop fly to short right. Brunansky reached second base but retreated quickly toward first, thinking the ball had been caught. The ball actually fell safely, and Sheridan threw to Lou Whitaker to complete an easy force out at second. Terrell retired the next two batters and the game remained scoreless.

The Tigers broke the game open in the bottom of the third. A double by Sheridan, single by Whitaker, and a walk to Darrell Evans loaded the bases with no outs. Kirk Gibson hit into a fielder's choice at second to drive Sheridan home with the game's first run. After Gibson stole second base, the Twins drew their infield in with cleanup hitter Alan Trammell at the plate. On a 1-and-1 count, Sparky Anderson noted a slight movement by Straker while he peered at the catcher's signals from the rubber. As Anderson bolted from the dugout pointing toward the mound, home-plate umpire Drew Coble called a balk, scoring Whitaker and advancing Gibson to third. Anderson's actions may have prompted the umpire's call, but Straker also had a reputation for balking, having committed five that season. Trammell singled to center on the next pitch, scoring Gibson with the Tigers' third run. After retiring Matt Nokes on a popup and walking Chet Lemon, Straker was lifted by Twins manager Tom Kelly, having thrown 69 pitches in 2⅔ innings. Reliever Dan Schatzeder faced pinch-hitter Larry Herndon, who hit a two-RBI double to left, giving Detroit a 5-0 lead. Tom Brookens, the ninth Tiger to bat that inning, flied out to end the frame.

Greg Gagne got the Twins' first hit and run to start the fourth with a home run to left. The Twins scored another after a one-out walk to Kent Hrbek and consecutive singles by Gary Gaetti and Randy Bush. Terrell retired the next two batters to keep the score 5-2.

The Twins continued to chip away at the Tigers' lead in the sixth. Terrell walked Randy Bush with two outs, then Brunansky homered to left, making the score 5-4.

Minnesota opened the seventh with back-to-back singles by Sal Butera and Dan Gladden, putting runners at the corners and prompting Anderson to insert rookie reliever Mike Henneman. Gagne hit a grounder to third baseman Brookens, whose throw home nabbed pinch-runner Mark Davidson. After Kirby Puckett's foul fly advanced Gladden to third and Gagne to second, Detroit walked Hrbek intentionally to load the bases and bring Gaetti to the plate. The move backfired, as he singled to right, driving in two runs and giving the Twins a 6-5 lead. A fly out ended the Twins' threat, but the Tigers' lead had evaporated.

Schatzeder and subsequent reliever Juan Berenguer (both former Tigers) had held Detroit scoreless for 4⅓ innings after its five-run outburst. Only two Tigers had reached scoring position after the third inning. Had the Twins maintained their lead through the final six outs, they would have achieved the biggest comeback in LCS history and taken a commanding 3-0 series lead.

To start the eighth, Kelly inserted hard-throwing right-hander Jeff Reardon, the team's closer and saves leader (31).

"We were pretty tight in the dugout [at that point]," Trammell said after the game. "It kind of felt like life or death."[2]

After a first-pitch single by Herndon, Anderson inserted pitcher Jack Morris to pinch-run. The move was unusual in the designated-hitter era when pitchers seldom bat. But Morris had served as a pinch-runner twice that season and was said to be among the team's fastest runners. As it turned out, he didn't need to break a sweat. Brookens popped out to first on a bunt attempt. Then Sheridan, a left-handed hitter who had recently been encouraged by his coaches to avoid pulling the ball,[3] lined a first-pitch fastball into the upper deck in right, giving Detroit a 7-6 lead.

The explosive home run unleashed a burst of electricity in the ballpark. As Sheridan and Morris rounded the bases, thousands of ecstatic fans tossed "Go Get 'Em Tigers" giveaway placards onto the field. Reardon stood in stunned disbelief as the cards littered the field. Sheridan emerged from the dugout for a rousing curtain call. The game was delayed for several minutes while the grounds crew scrambled to gather up the placards. The 49,730 in attendance continued roaring when play resumed. The inning ended with a groundout, walk and foul out.

Henneman retired the Twins in order in the ninth and raised his arms in triumph after striking out Gaetti to earn the win. Reardon took the loss.

Sheridan, who hadn't hit a home run since August 20, spoke humbly with reporters about his game-winning hit.

"I'm from Detroit, so it's certainly a dream where you hope you can get in that situation and come through," said Sheridan, who grew up in Wayne, Michigan and played baseball at Eastern Michigan University in nearby Ypsilanti. "I sucked it in, tried to keep working hard, and here I am today. … I've never been in the limelight and I probably wouldn't be very good at it. I'm glad I helped the team win, but I wouldn't consider myself a hero."[4]

Chet Lemon thought Sheridan's blast might shift momentum toward the Tigers.

"[Sheridan] lifted us right off that ground with that one," Lemon said. "And it could very well be the turning point for us. … I don't think it could have happened to a better guy. He's been struggling, but overall he's done a lot of good things for us. If we had to pick one guy overall to hit that home run, we'd have picked Patrick."[5]

As the cheers faded, so did the Tigers' hopes of winning the ALCS. Minnesota defeated Detroit 5-3 and 9-5 in Games Four and Five, respectively.

The Twins, who had played poorly away from the Metrodome all season, took two of three on the road to earn their first World Series appearance since 1965.

Detroit wouldn't return to the postseason until 2006, seven seasons after leaving Tiger Stadium. Sheridan's game-winning homer marked the Tigers' last postseason victory at the corner of Michigan and Trumbull.

SOURCES

In addition to the sources cited in the notes, the author also consulted:

NBC Television Network. Recorded broadcasts of games One, Two and Three of the 1987 American League Championship Series.

NOTES

1 "Sheridan a hero in '85, too," *Detroit Free Press*, October 11, 1987.

2 Mitch Albom, "That's the Way!" *Detroit Free Press*, October 11, 1987.

3 Tom Gage, "Sheridan's shot shocks Twins 7-6," *Detroit News*, October 11, 1987.

4 Joe LaPointe, "Pat on the back," *Detroit Free Press*, October 11, 1987.

5 "Tigers mini-quiz," *Detroit News*, October 11, 1987.

"IT'S AN OUTRIGHT CRIME TO LOSE THAT GAME"

May 28, 1995: Chicago White Sox 14, Detroit Tigers 12 at Tiger Stadium

By Jerry Nechal

AS THE SMALL SUNDAY-AFTERNOON crowd of 10,813 settled into their Tiger Stadium seats, it's doubtful anyone realized they were about to witness a special moment in baseball history. The previous day's game between the Detroit Tigers and the Chicago White Sox was a 1-0 pitchers' duel. Since the turn of the century, more than 130,000 major-league games had been played. Never before had two teams combined for more than 11 home runs in a game. But on May 28, 1995, that record, as well as five others, would be tied or broken. "It was wild," said Sox manager Gene Lamont. "It was more than wild. I don't know the word for it."[1]

Several forces aligned themselves to make it all happen. These included the stadium, the lineups, and the weather. Tiger Stadium had always been a hitters' park and was ranked by some as the most homer-friendly in the big leagues.[2] The pitching staffs of both teams ranked toward the worst of the league in ERA and home runs allowed that year. The starting lineups on both sides included several players with established home-run power; the most notable were Frank "Big Hurt" Thomas for the White Sox and Cecil "Big Daddy" Fielder for the Tigers.

The weather, however, was the chief culprit. It had rained in the late morning and fog was reported at game time.[3] During the game a 16-mph wind, with gusts up to 22 mph, was blowing out to left field. Likewise, as the contest progressed, temperatures rose with the damp conditions even as the barometer fell. Such a mix reduces air density, which allows batted balls to travel farther.[4]

The players were in agreement on the conditions. "It was the jet stream today," said Detroit second baseman Lou Whitaker. "Or something out there was streaming. Actually, it was more like screaming."[5] Chicago catcher Ron Karcovice declared, "Anything you hit good up in the air today was gone."[6]

For the fans, the 3-hour 46-minute contest was far from a boring, one-sided slugfest. There were three ties, three lead changes and scoring in eight of the nine innings. The outcome remained in balance until the final at-bat.

Things started well for the Tigers. In the bottom half of the first inning they began the home run deluge off Chicago starter James Baldwin, racing to a 4-0 lead. Chad Curtis led off with a 415-foot home run to left-center. After a walk to Lou Whitaker and a single by Alan Trammell, cleanup hitter Cecil Fielder came to bat. Sensing the conditions and what might be in store, Chicago center fielder Mike Devereaux retreated to a fielding position well over 400 feet from home plate. Detroit publicity director Dan Ewald commented, "I never saw anyone play as deep in my life."[7] Fielder was equal to the challenge, launching a 463-foot blast over Devereaux' head into the lower center-field bleachers. After one inning, the Tigers were up 4-0.

The White Sox responded with one run in the second. After two hits, Karcovice's sacrifice fly provided Chicago's first score. In the bottom half of the inning, it was deja vu for the Tigers. Curtis led off again and hit another 400-plus-foot homer to left-center. After a single by Whitaker and Trammell's strikeout, Fielder also repeated his first at-bat with a second 400-foot round-tripper. That was it for rookie pitcher Baldwin. Reliever Kirk McCaskill escaped the inning without further scoring, but the Tigers now led, 7-1.

Detroit starter David Wells had entered the game with a 2.81 ERA. With a six-run lead, things looked good for the home team; but on this day no lead was safe. In the top of the third the White Sox quickly put two runners aboard on an error and a walk. Thomas doubled in one run. Two more scored on a groundout and a sacrifice fly. Chicago was back in it now, trailing by just three runs. The Tigers retaliated in their half of the inning. Chad Curtis again came to the plate after one out. This time, McCaskill kept Curtis in the park, holding him to a double. One out later, Curtis scored on a single by Trammell. The score was 8-4, Detroit.

In the fourth Wells came in for a surprise against the bottom third of the order. Aided by the wind, Ron Karkovice, Ray Durham, and Craig Grebeck swatted consecutive home runs to left field. For Durham it was his first in the big leagues. For the astonished Grebeck, it was his only homer of the season. After the game he remarked, "I don't ever think home run. I can't hit home runs."[8] Wells departed and reliever John Doherty retired the next three hitters.

Detroit did not sit still in the bottom of the inning. Leadoff hitter Kirk Gibson celebrated his 38th birthday with a 410-foot homer to deep right-center. Again the Tigers only scored one as Chicago inched closer, 7-9.

The fifth inning was quiet in terms of home runs, but the White Sox crept even closer. They scored twice on a groundout and a sacrifice fly to finally tie the game, while the Bengals, for the third straight inning, managed only one run, on an RBI single by Whitaker. But Detroit was back on top, 10-9.

The two teams traded home runs in the sixth. Frank Thomas smoked a line drive into the right-field stands to tie it up again. Gibson responded with his second home run, this one traveling 429 feet. Later in the inning the Tigers failed to score with the bases loaded, as Lou Whitaker flied out. Detroit still led by a run at 11-10.

In the seventh Chicago tied it yet again, this time on Karkovice's long homer to left-center. Detroit again loaded the bases with two outs, but could not capitalize. For the first time in the game, the Tigers were held to a scoreless inning. The score was now tied at 11-11.

Sweet Lou was a five-time All-Star

The eighth inning proved to be pivotal. Pitcher Buddy Groom, who had entered the game in the seventh, was on the mound again for Detroit. The White Sox loaded the bases on a double by Tim Raines, an intentional walk to Thomas and another walk to John Kruk. Robin Ventura popped out. Mike Henneman, the Tigers closer, replaced Groom. Raines scored on a groundout to third. Durham then lofted a fly ball to left-center. The wind blew the ball away from center fielder Curtis; a routine fly became a double and two runs scored. A remorseful Curtis later told reporters, "I should have caught that ball."[9]

The Tigers batted in the bottom of the eighth trailing for the first time. With two outs Whitaker answered with a wind-assisted home run to right. As he rounded the bases, "Thus Spoke Zarathustra," the theme song from *2001: A Space Odyssey*, the home-team home-run anthem, played on the stadium speakers for the seventh time that day. The music matched the moment in that four records had just been broken. The combined 12 home runs by both teams set a major-league record. Whitaker's blast was the 10th solo home run, another record; the seventh homer by a Tiger, a club record (since broken); and finally, extra-base hit number 21, an American League record.

These records were of little consequence at the moment, as Detroit still trailed by two runs. The White Sox brought in their closer, Roberto Hernandez. The next two batters reached base –Trammell on an error and Fielder, hit by a pitch. Gibson came to the plate looking for his third homer. He had hit the game-winner against Hernandez on Friday night. This time Kirk flied out to end the inning. "I missed the pitch this time, I just missed it," he said later.[10] The Tigers were now on the short end of the score, at 12-14.

Chicago failed to score in the top of the ninth inning. As the Tigers came to bat, the crowd stirred. Today anything was possible. Travis Fryman singled to open the frame and bring the tying run to the plate. However, the next three batters went quietly on two strikeouts and a popout to end the game. The ninth inning was the first in the game in which no scoring took place.

In spite of all their homers and the early lead, the Tigers lost, 14-12. They left 15 runners on base and went only 3-for-14 with runners in scoring position. The loss was agonizing. In his last year of managing, an unhappy Sparky Anderson moaned, "It's silly to give up runs like that. … I don't think that's a record to be cherished."[11] The always competitive Gibson lamented, "It's an outright crime to lose that game."[12] In the other locker room the White Sox were elated. "Crazy game," said Frank Thomas, "…(W)e showed we can come back and play winning baseball."[13] All said and done, it was a game for the ages.

SOURCES

Publications

Knight, Keith, and Alex Schuster. "A Study of Home Runs in the Major Leagues," Department of Statistics University of Toronto, May 1992.

Websites

projectprospect.com/article/2012/08/28/home-run-weather-analysis.

wunderground.com/history/airport/KDET/1995/5/28/DailyHistory.html?req_city=NA&req_state=NA&req_statename=NA.

wxedge.com/articles/20120422how_does_the_weather_affect_baseball

Other

Jerry Nechal telephone interview with Mal Sillars, consulting meteorologist, October 9, 2014.

NOTES

1   "Tigers, Sox: It's homerific," *San Francisco Examiner,* May 29, 1995, D5.

2   Keith Knight and Alex Schuster, "A Study of Home Runs in the Major Leagues," Department of Statistics University Of Toronto, May 1992.

3   Weather History for Detroit MI," *Weather Underground,* October 29, 2014, wunderground.com/history/airport/KDET/1995/5/28/DailyHistory.html?req_city=NA&req_state=NA&req_statename=NA.

4   Richard Sparago, "How Does Weather Affect Baseball?," *WXedge.com,* April 22, 2012, wxedge.com/articles/20120422how_does_the_weather_affect_baseball.

5   "Tigers, Sox: It's Homerific," *San Francisco Examiner*, May 29, 1995, D5.

6   Associated Press, "This Is the Ultimate Home Run-Run Derby. White Sox, Tigers Hit a Record, 12," *Los Angeles Daily News*, May 29, 1995, S3.

7   Joe Falls, "Memorable homers come to mind, naturally, during historic day for long-ball hitting," *Detroit News*, May 29, 1995, 2B.

8   Paul Sullivan, "Sox Survive Record 12-HR Tilt," *Chicago Tribune*, May 29, 1995, 1.

9   Tom Gage, "Whirlwind Game Befuddles Curtis," *Detroit News*, May 29, 1995, 5B.

10 Tom Gage, "Bats Boom During Entire game, but It's a Bust in the End for Detroit," *Detroit News*, May 29, 1995, 5B.

11 Paul Sullivan, "Sox Survive."

12 Tom Gage, "Bats Boom," *Detroit News*, May 29, 1995, 1B.

13 Paul Sullivan, "Sox Survive."

18 PITCHERS USED; 3 RECORDS SET

September 14, 1998: Chicago White Sox 17, Detroit Tigers 16 at Tiger Stadium

By Steven Kuehl

IN SEPTEMBER BASEBALL FANS ARE typically focused on playoff races. The 1998 season gave fans some extra excitement, a home-run contest. It pitted Mark McGwire of the St. Louis Cardinals against Sammy Sosa of the Chicago Cubs. Each slugger entered their contests on Monday, September 14, 1998, with 62 homers, making them the current record-holders by having passed Roger Maris's record of 61. In a rare occurrence, they finished their games that day with the same number.

Luckily for baseball fans, excitement came the way of a very unlikely source, the Detroit Tigers and the Chicago White Sox. The Tigers entered the game with a record of 57-92, and the White Sox had a record of 70-78. With the White Sox in second place in the American League Central Division, 11½ games behind the Cleveland Indians, and the Tigers in last place, 25 games back, this game held no meaning in the hunt for October.

Before the game, White Sox manager Jerry Manuel sat in the visitors' dugout and took a minute to reflect. "Baseball is funny," he said. "Tonight we have the two youngest teams in the American League facing each other. You really don't know what you're going to get."[1]

What came next was what McGwire and Sosa had produced for weeks: a spectacular back-and-forth slugfest. A 5-hour, 12 minute contest that went 12 innings and produced 33 runs, 41 hits (with six home runs), four stolen bases, and five errors.

Larry Parrish, the Tigers' interim manager after the team fired Buddy Bell on September 1, sent Justin Thompson to the mound. Thompson (10-14) came into the game with a personal five-game losing streak. Thompson had a history of arm problems, and had had elbow surgery the year before. White Sox manager Manuel sent out 23-year-old rookie John Snyder (6-2).

The game started with the White Sox' Ray Durham reaching on an error by left fielder Bobby Higginson. Nonetheless, Thompson made it through the inning unscored upon, even with Durham stealing third base after a groundout by Craig Wilson moved him to second. Snyder started the game with an uneventful 1-2-3 inning.

The fireworks started in the second inning when the White Sox tallied five runs, including a two-run home run by shortstop Wilson, who was playing in only his sixth game. The Tigers clawed back in their half of the inning on a Joe Randa double that scored one run.

Randa had come into the game only hours after learning he had been named the American League player of the week for hitting .476 with two homers and two doubles on the Tigers' trip to Chicago and Boston. "I've felt all along that if I had stayed in the lineup, these are the kinds of things that would have happened." Randa said.[2]

Thompson settled down with a 1-2-3 third, and the Tigers clawed back even more against Snyder in the home half of the inning. Juan Encarnacion hit a three-run shot to left-center, cutting the score to 5-4 in favor of the White Sox.

Thompson saw his outing come to an end in the fifth inning after he gave up three straight hits, good for another run and a 6-4 lead. He was replaced by A.J. Sager.

The Tigers scored again in the bottom of the fifth to again draw within one. They took their first lead of the game one inning later, on a two-run home run by Randa. A single by Brian Hunter tacked on one more tally before the inning was over, and it was 8-6 Tigers.

The teams combined for eight runs in the seventh. Before the White Sox were done, they'd scored six times off three Tigers pitchers, Matt Anderson, Marino

Santana, and Dean Crow. The Tigers chipped away at the White Sox' 12-8 lead in the bottom of the inning by scoring two runs.

That was the way it stayed until the bottom of the ninth, when the Tigers tied the game at 12-12 on a double by Tony Clark and a single by Bobby Higginson. Parrish hoped that Higginson's single would pass a slump-escaping feeling through his bones, allowing him to come on strong for the rest of the season. The Tigers managed to load the bases with one out, but Frank Catalonatto and Brian Hunter were unable to come through with the winner.

The White Sox rallied for three runs in the top of the 10th to take what would normally look like a comfortable lead. But the Tigers answered back in their half, on an RBI single by Easley and a two-run clout by Higginson, his 23rd of the season.

Finally, at a few minutes past midnight, the White Sox' Durham and Wilson began the 12th with homers off Doug Bochtler. "I hit it as hard as I could," Durham said. "I was almost too tired to run the bases."[3] After blowing leads of 6-4, 12-10, and 15-12, the White Sox bullpen mercifully came through at the end. Scott Eyre, who had come on to pitch a scoreless 11th, gave up a run before fanning Higginson to end the game. "Everyone was ready for it to end," Eyre said.[4] Chicago emerged with perhaps the first 17-16 win at Tiger Stadium since Bobby Layne quarterbacked the Detroit Lions.[5]

"Great comebacks by both sides," Parrish said after the 41-hit extravaganza. "Both offenses never quit."[6] The Tigers and White Sox had combined for 77 runs in their four games thus far in September—and only once in those four games had the score stayed unchanged for at least two full innings.

The game saw two batters with five hits (Belle and Encarnacion), two White Sox with five RBIs (Albert Belle and Wilson), and three Tigers with four RBIs (Encarnacion, Higginson, and Randa). Belle came to the plate an astonishing eight times, with five other batters seeing action seven times. Belle's five hits were a career high.

With all of the focus on McGwire and Sosa in 1998, players like Belle and Ken Griffey Jr. of the Seattle Mariners flew under the radar. Griffey led the AL in home runs (56), with Belle second at 49. Belle's five RBIs shot him over the 1,000-career-RBI plateau and brought him to within one RBI of the White Sox' season record of 138 set by Zeke Bonura in 1936. Belle went on to crush the old record, finishing the season with 152 RBIs. Already in 1998 Belle had established the club season records for home runs with 45 (he would finish the year with 49) and total bases with 365 (falling one short of 400 by season's end). He had a career-high WAR (wins above replacement) of 7.1 in 1998.

The 17 White Sox runs were the most allowed by the Tigers in an extra-inning ballgame. Detroit also established a club record for runs scored in an extra-inning game. Not since the Philadelphia Phillies beat the Chicago Cubs 23-22 at Wrigley Field on May 17, 1979, had a losing team scored so many runs in a contest.

Thanks to all the hitting, the extra innings and the September roster expansions, the Tigers set a team record by using 10 pitchers, and the two teams tied a major-league record for most pitchers in an extra-inning game, 18.

The latter record has been broken a few times. As of 2015 it was 21, used by the Tampa Bay Rays and Baltimore Orioles on September 20, 2013. Since 1914, there have been seven instances where a single team used 11 pitchers in a game. The Tigers club record of 10 still held in 2015.

The White Sox immediately went on a 9-4 run to finish the season at 80-82, while the Tigers won 8 of their next 12, good for a final record of 65-97 in the AL Central. Parrish said, "We're relaxed and finally having some fun." Tigers pitcher Doug Brocail agreed, saying, "I don't know how many people know this, but there's a lot of new life in this clubhouse now. How it happened, I don't care. But we've got it."[7]

NOTES

1   Teddy Greenstein, "Sox 17, Tigers 16/41-hit Marathon Ugly, Then Surreal," *Chicago Tribune*, September 15, 1998.

2   John Lowe, "Sox slug Tigers, 17-16," *Detroit Free Press*, September 15, 1998.

3   Greenstein.

4 Ibid.

5 John Lowe, "Sox slug Tigers, 17-16," *Detroit Free Press*, September 15, 1998.

6 Lowe.

7 "Club in no hurry to push Parrish for its manager," *The Sporting News*, September 28, 1998, 70.

TEARS AND CHEERS: THE FINAL GAME AT MICHIGAN AND TRUMBULL

September 27, 1999: Detroit Tigers 8, Kansas City Royals 2 at Tiger Stadium

By Gregory H. Wolf

"TONIGHT WE MUST SAY GOOD-BYE. SO long old friend. We will miss you."[1] With his voice breaking, legendary radio announcer Ernie Harwell uttered those somber words to mark the end of a storied era on Monday, September 27, 1999, as the Detroit Tigers played their final game at Tiger Stadium, the venerable 87-year-old ballpark at the intersection of Michigan and Trumbull Avenues. In an emotionally charged atmosphere, the Tigers defeated the Kansas City Royals, 8-2, to conclude a day filled with nostalgic celebrations.[2]

"The Tiger Stadium experience is about so much more than winning and losing," said Hall of Famer Al Kaline. "It is a bond that all people of Detroit share."[3] "Mr. Tiger" knew his history. For the previous 103 years the Tigers had played ball on "The Corner" in the Corktown neighborhood of the Motor City, first as a member of the Western League and then as a charter member of the American League, beginning in 1901. On April 20, 1912, Navin Field, a concrete and steel structure that seated about 23,000, opened its doors, replacing 15-year-old Bennett Park, an outdated wooden-framed park. Expanded to 53,000 and renamed Briggs Stadium in 1938 and later Tiger Stadium in 1961, the ballpark witnessed the rise of Detroit as one of the wealthiest cities in the US and also its decline. It was the home of six pennant winners, four World Series champions, and countless heroes.

Fans began arriving at the stadium before noon hoping to catch a glimpse of a private reception in Tiger Plaza for former players from the last seven decades. "This was the best place ever to play baseball," said Darrell Evans, member of the 1984 champions. "The people were right on top of you."[4] Perhaps he was thinking of the right-field "porch," which hung over the field and robbed many outfielders of easy fly balls.

George Kell, a five-time All-Star with the Tigers in the late 1940s and early 1950s, took a less nostalgic approach. "I do love this old ballpark," he said. "But there's just not enough revenue to compete with the Yankees, Atlanta, Texas, and Baltimore. You've got to have box seats, luxury boxes, and a bigger concourse to get the people in and out, the parking."[5] As early as the 1940s, explained Bill McGraw of the *Detroit Free Press*, the city had planned the demise of Tiger Stadium in a failed bid to land the Olympics.[6] In the 1970s taxpayers opposed the sale of bonds to finance a new stadium that led to the city taking it over in 1977. "It's obvious the damn thing is falling down," said then Mayor Coleman Young.[7] Even after millions of dollars in renovations, it was clear by the early 1990s that a new stadium was necessary.

The official pregame ceremony began about 3:15 P.M. when Harwell introduced team owner Mike Ilitch, Detroit Mayor Dennis Archer, Michigan Governor Joe Engler, and Baseball Commissioner Bud Selig. Each received a hefty round of boos as they addressed the fans from a microphone behind home plate. The mood changed when the 64-year-old Kaline, described by Harwell as embodying "the spirit of the Tigers," took center stage.[8] "[Tiger Stadium] looked like an impressive battleship, a fortress at Michigan and Trumbull," said Kaline, recalling his impression upon seeing the stadium as an 18-year-old rookie in 1953. "[It had a] peacefulness that seemed almost magical. I again find myself humbled and somewhat overwhelmed by the events unfolding in front of us. There is just too much history to put into words. Tiger

Stadium's strength lies not in dazzling architecture or creature comforts, but rather in character, charm, and history."9

On a sunny, 84-degree autumnal day, the over-flowing crowed of 43,356 was treated to a few more surprises. Billy Rogell, the 94-year-old former infielder for the Tigers (1930-1939), threw out the ceremonial first pitch. Minutes before the start of the game, Kaline and Hall of Famer, George Brett, both dressed in base-ball uniforms as honorary captains of their respective teams, took the lineup cards to home plate.

As Detroit's starting nine took the field in their famous home white uniforms, spectators noticed something different. Not only were there no names on the jerseys, the starters wore the numbers of the all-time Tiger team selected by fans. Right fielder Karim Garcia (a .240 hitter in 1999) donned Kaline's number 6; slugging first sacker Tony Clark (31 homers) wore Hank Greenberg's number 5; while center fielder Gabe Kapler wore a uniform without a number in a tribute to Ty Cobb, who played during an era when numbers were not used.

Tigers skipper Larry Parrish gave the starting assignment to 27-year-old Brian Moehler, en route to leading the AL in losses (16). The four-year veteran looked shaky early on. He escaped a one-out, bases-loaded jam in the first inning.

Wasting no time getting on the board, the Tigers' leadoff hitter, Luis Polonia, launched Jeff Suppan's 1-and-2 pitch, according to John Lowe of the *Detroit Free Press*, "an estimated 435 feet into the far section of the lower deck in right center" for the game's first run.[10]

Moehler yielded a leadoff homer to rookie Mike Quinn in the second inning. The Tigers took a 2-1 lead in the bottom of the frame when designated hitter Robert Fick hit a deep sacrifice fly to the right-field power alley to drive in second baseman Damion Easley, who had led off the frame with a double and taken third on a groundout.

In the third Moehler surrendered three singles and a walk, but only one run on Joe Randa's infield hit to drive in rookie Carlos Beltran and tie the game, 2-2. "Moehler had nothing" early in the game, said Parrish, but the righty settled down to yield just two hits in the next three innings before giving way to the first of three relievers.[11]

The game remained tied, 2-2, until the bottom of the sixth inning. Third baseman Dean Palmer, who had departed Kansas City via free agency in the previous offseason, led off with a single. Two batters later, Garcia launched a go-ahead two-run homer off Suppan.

The highlight of the game occurred in the eighth inning. Kansas City reliever Jeff Montgomery loaded the bases on a double to Palmer, single to Easley, and an intentional walk to Garcia. After Palmer was forced at home on Kapler's grounder to the mound, Parrish intended Frank Catalanotto to pinch-hit for Fick, suffering through a miserable season following shoulder surgery in March. But the 25-year-old rookie persuaded his skipper to let him bat and the result was memorable. Fick blasted a towering grand slam, the last homer (indeed, the final hit) in the history of Tiger Stadium, for a convincing 8-2 lead. According to Gene Guidi of the *Detroit Free Press*, the clout hit "the roof above the third deck in right field before bouncing back on the field."[12] "This is definitely the most exciting thing that's ever happened to me," said Fick after the game.[13]

After Fick's round-tripper, the partisan crowd remained standing and screaming for the rest of the game. The noise reached a crescendo when closer Todd Jones registered two quick outs in the ninth. With cameras flashing on every pitch, Jones delivered the fateful last pitch in Tiger Stadium to Beltran on a 2-and-2 count. "Here's a swing, and a MISS—The GAME'S OVER!" exclaimed Harwell in his soothing Southern accent. "And Tiger Stadium is no more. The final score, the Tigers 8, and the Royals 2."[14] Jones fooled Beltran with a curveball in the dirt; catcher Brad Ausmus scooped up the ball and tagged Beltran for the final out. "I guess the flashes got him," said Jones exuberantly after the game.[15] Matching their season high with their third consecutive victory, the Tigers moved to 65-91; the Royals fell to 62-95. Moehler picked up his 10th victory to reach double figures for the third of four consecutive seasons while Suppan fell to 10-11.

The game ended shortly after 7:00 and almost immediately, reported Nicholas J. Cotsonika of the *Detroit Free Press*, the grounds crew dug up home plate which was transported that night to the Tigers' new stadium, Comerica Park, located about a mile away. The smiles and laughter of victory soon gave way to the tears and quivering lips of the final ceremony emceed by Harwell. With "feeling of a wake" and music from the film *Field of Dreams* in the background, Harwell read a short history of baseball played at the intersection of Michigan and Trumbull and then introduced a short film.[16] Suddenly, the center-field door opened and one by one, 65 former players from the 1930s to the 1990s strode in and went to their former position. According to sportswriter Mitch Albom, the "crowd fell into a church-like reverence."[17] "It was like watching a rewind film," wrote Albom. The first to appear was Mark "The Bird" Fidrych; he was followed by the great and not-so-great, from Kaline, Kirk Gibson, Alan Trammell, Lou Whitaker (the latter two, befitting history, came out together), and Cecil Fielder to Dick McAuliffe and Dave Bergman. The oldest was Elden Auker, who pitched for Detroit from 1933 to 1938. The crowd was in no mood to be disturbed. "Every mention of the new ballyard," reported David A. Markiewicz, "drew a round of boos."[18]

But all games, and even nostalgic ceremonies, have an end. The scoreboard was turned off at 8:19 and the stands were empty by 9:00. After 6,873 regular-season games, 35 postseason contests, and three All-Star Games, Tiger Stadium was, in Ernie Harwell's words, "no more."

NOTES

1   "Grand Finale Slam, Smiles, and Tears … A Fond Farewell For The Corner Tigers," *Detroit Free Press*, September 28, 1999.

2   The entire game, including portions of the pregame and postgame ceremonies, is available via Classic MLB on You Tube at youtube.com/watch?v=QwjZG249iNo.

3   Nicholas J. Cotsonika, "Final Visit Much Like The first For No. 6," *Detroit Free Press*, September 28, 1999.

4   Ibid.

5   Steve Crowe, "Bringing Down the House Again. Kaline Performs Fitting Four-Minute Farewell to Stadium," *Detroit Free Press*, September 28, 1999.

6   Bill McGraw, "Plot to Abandon Park Stretches Back to 40s. For Decades, Fans Fought Replacement," *Detroit Free Press*, September 28, 1999.

7   Ibid.

8   From video of game. youtube.com/watch?v=QwjZG249iNo.

9   Cotsonika, "Final Visit Much Like The first For No. 6."

10   Ibid.

11   John Lowe, "Out Of The Park. Fick's Slam Caps Tigers' 3-HR Finale At Stadium," *Detroit Free Press*, September 28, 1999.

12   Gene Guidi, "First, Fick Had To Change LP's Mind," *Detroit Free Press*, September 28, 1999.

13   Ibid.

14   Crowe.

15   David Markiewicz, "Jones Ends An Era On A Blazing Note. Cameras' Flashes Might Have Aided Final Strikeout," *Detroit Free Press*, September 28, 1999.

16   Nicholas J. Cotsonika, "Past, Present Come Together One Last Time," *Detroit Free Press*, September 29, 1999.

17   Mitch Albom, "Look There, And There: Faces Of The Past Are Here," *Detroit Free Press*, September 28, 1999.

18   Markiewicz.

CONTRIBUTORS

DAVID W. ANDERSON is author of *More than Merkle: A History of the Best and Most Exciting Baseball Season in Human History* and *You Can't Beat the Hours: Umpires in the Deadball Era 1901-1909*. He has made presentations at various Seymour conferences and SABR conventions.

WILLIAM M. ANDERSON is the author/editor of several books dealing with the history of the Detroit Tigers. His first history is entitled *The Detroit Tigers: The Greatest Players and Moments in Tigers history*. He is now finishing the fifth edition of this book. He edited *The View From the Dugout: The Journals of Red Rolfe*, Tiger manager from 1949 until early July 1952. He co-authored *Rick Ferrell, Knuckleball Catcher* with Kerrie Ferrell. After his distinguished playing career, Ferrell coached with Detroit and later became a senior executive. In 2012, Bill wrote *The Glory Years of the Detroit Tigers: 1920-1950* which won the Independent Publishers award as the best sports book of the year.

WILL BENNETT, musician and frontman of Will Bennett & the Tells, is a 2013 graduate of Grinnell College, where he studied English and played baseball. His chapter in *Tigers by the Tale: Great Games at Michigan & Trumbull* is his first contribution to a SABR publication. He lives in Columbus, Ohio.

RICH BOGOVICH is the author of *Kid Nichols: A Biography of the Hall of Fame Pitcher*, a very good friend of Detroit legend Charlie Bennett. Most recently Rich wrote the chapter on Jorge Comellas of the Cubs for *Who's on First: Replacement Players in World War II*. In between those two profiles Rich contributed to *Inventing Baseball: The 100 Greatest Games of the Nineteenth Century*. His only visits to Detroit's legendary ballpark were during its final homestand ever. He resides in Rochester, Minnesota.

RAYMOND BUZENSKI is a lifelong Detroit area resident and Tiger fan. He has been hooked on baseball since hearing about his father's first game as a child—the 1941 All-Star Game in Detroit. He is a pediatrician known for wearing Tigers jerseys in the office throughout the baseball season. He lives in a northeastern suburb of Detroit with his lovely and tolerant wife Jessica and four wonderful kids. He has been a SABR member since 2009. He was a contributing writer to the book, *Detroit the Unconquerable: The 1935 World Champion Tigers*.

MARCUS W. DICKSON is a Professor of Organizational Psychology at Wayne State University in Detroit, Michigan. He plays base ball by the rules of 1867 for the Greenfield Village Lah-de-dahs, and is a member of SABR's 19th Century Committee, and of the Rules and Customs committee of the Vintage Base Ball Association. Writing about the only 19th century game in this collection was thus a natural for him. He is currently writing a chapter about the base ball winter meetings of 1866. His favorite teams are the Tigers, Pirates, Crawfords, and Unions of Morrisania (the champions of 1867). He lives in Farmington, Michigan, with his wife Heather, and son, Michael.

SCOTT DOMINIAK is a retired English/ journalism teacher who taught at Eisenhower High School in Blue Island, Illinois. Growing up, he split time between Inkster and Livonia, Michigan and graduated from Michigan State University in 1976. Scott lives with his wife, Judy, and has three grown stepchildren. He is a lifelong Detroit Tigers fan who has been a member of the Mayo Smith Society since its inception, 1983. Scott wrote the biography of Hugh Shelley for the book *Detroit the Unconquerable: The 1935 World Champion Tigers*.

The baseball writings of **SCOTT FERKOVICH** have appeared in *TheNationalPastimeMuseum.com*, the *Detroit Free Press*, *DetroitAthletic.com*, *HardballTimes.com*, and *Seamheads.com*. He was a judge for the 2014 Casey Award for best new baseball book of the year. Scott was the editor of the classic SABR book, *Detroit the Unconquerable: The 1935 World Champion Tigers*, and is willing to listen to cash offers from some of the major studios for the film rights. If you follow only one person on Twitter, make it him @scottferk.

DAVID FLEITZ is a writer and computer systems analyst from Pleasant Ridge, Michigan. While working in the information technology field, David wrote numerous articles for magazines and newspapers on a freelance basis before turning his attention to writing books. Since 2001, he has written eight books on baseball history, including biographies of Shoeless Joe Jackson, Louis Sockalexis (the first Native American major league player), and 19th-century star Cap Anson. His latest work, *Napoleon Lajoie: King of Ballplayers*, was published by McFarland in 2013. David is a three-time winner of SABR's annual national baseball trivia championship.

BRENT HEUTMAKER has been a member of the Halsey Hall Chapter of SABR for nearly a year. The game bio of the 1934 World Series Game Seven is his first published work. Brent resides in the Minneapolis — St. Paul metro area and works in the litigation support industry. Currently, Brent is working on two games for the upcoming Astrodome book to be published by SABR.

MAXWELL KATES is a chartered accountant who lives and works in midtown Toronto. His essays and abstracts have been included in several SABR publications, including *Sock It To 'Em, Tigers* and *Wire To Wire: Inside The 1984 Detroit Tigers Championship*. His first Tigers game took place on August 30, 1992 - Heroes of Baseball Day at The Corner of Michigan and Trumbull. Between the old timers and the contemporary club, the most talented player in a Detroit uniform he witnessed that day was a first baseman named Tom Selleck.

MATT KEELEAN, a first-time SABR contributor, is a business analyst for Florida State University in Tallahassee, but grew up in Grand Rapids, Michigan, hence his lifelong devotion to the Tigers. He is a founding member of the SABR North Florida/Buck O'Neil Chapter, based in Tallahassee, and currently serves as the Chapter's president. Matt and his wife Diana live in Havana, Florida, and are long-time Florida State baseball season-ticket holders.

JEFFREY KOSLOWSKI is an NSHSS Educator of Distinction award winner who currently teaches World and Advanced U.S. History at Henry Ford Academy in Dearborn, Michigan. He received his M.A. and B.A. in History from Eastern Michigan University in 2015 and 2007, respectively. He is currently working on an article that tells the story of Branch Rickey while he was head coach of the University of Michigan. During the summers, Jeff is a player and historical advisor for the Lah-de-dah historic base ball club of Greenfield Village. He and his wife Stephanie currently live in Westland, Michigan.

A lifelong Tigers fan, **STEVEN KUEHL** was born in Michigan's Upper Peninsula, but now resides in Wisconsin with his wife, Kathleen, and labrador retrievers, Lola and Oliver. An Assistant Professor of Mathematics and Department Chair at Silver Lake College in Manitowoc, Wisconsin, his article "The 20/30 Game Winner: An Endangered/Extinct Species" was published in the *Baseball Research Journal* (Fall 2013). He has also worked on a SABR book project about County Stadium.

MARC LANCASTER has been a sports journalist since 1996, working as a reporter, editor and web producer for several outlets. He spent six seasons as a baseball beat writer, covering the Reds for the *Cincinnati Post* (2004-06) and the Rays for *The Tampa Tribune* (2007-09). Marc contributed bios of former Tigers Chuck Hostetler and Bobby Maier to the SABR book, *Who's On First: Replacement Players in World War II*. A Michigan native, he now lives in Charlotte, North Carolina.

SUSAN A. LANTZ, PH.D., a forensic mechanical, biomechanical, and biomedical engineer and former college professor, attended her first baseball game at the ripe old age of 26 and was immediately and forever hooked on Wrigley Field and the Cubs. She began her professorial career in Detroit, in the days when cable TV was limited to a few channels, and since Cubs games were few and far between, she began following the Detroit Tigers, watching their games every evening while writing lecture notes for Thermodynamics. Much to her husband's dismay, she will watch any baseball game, but she prefers to see her beloved Cubs or Tigers play.

DOUG LEHMAN is the library director at Wittenberg University in Springfield, Ohio. He grew up in northwestern Ohio, listening to Ernie Harwell on the radio at night and dreaming of taking Al Kaline's place in right field.

The Tigers were **LEN LEVIN**'s second favorite team growing up. (He was a Red Sox homey but had a cousin in Detroit.) Len, a retired newspaper editor (*Providence Journal*), has copyedited most of the SABR "team" books. He has experience in SABR governance and is chairman of the Southern New England Chapter.

MITCH LUTZKE is a high school history teacher and track and field coach, who previously worked as a radio news reporter. He is married with three children and resides in Williamston, Michigan. He has published two books and is currently working on a third about the 1890s Negro baseball team, the Page Fence Giants.

MIKE LYNCH was born in Boston in the year of Yastrzemski and has been a diehard Red Sox fan ever since. A member of SABR since 2004, he lives in West Roxbury, Massachusetts. His first book, *Harry Frazee, Ban Johnson and the Feud That Nearly Destroyed the American League*, was published in 2008 and was named a finalist for the 2009 Larry Ritter Award in addition to being nominated for the Seymour Medal. He's also written *It Ain't So: A Might-Have-Been History of the White Sox in 1919 and Beyond* and *Baseball's Untold History: Volume I—The People*, and his work has been featured in SABR books about the 1912 Boston Red Sox and 1914 Boston Braves.

JOHN MILNER has made multiple contributions to SABR books relating to the Detroit Tigers. These include biographies in *Sock It To'em Tigers: The Incredible Story of the 1968 Detroit Tigers* (Don Wert and Bob Christian) and *Detroit Tigers 1984: What a Start! What a Finish!* (Alan Trammell and Lou Whitaker). John also contributed a piece dealing with the Mickey Cochrane trade in *Detroit the Unconquerable: The 1935 World Champion Tigers*. He works as a counselor at Tivy High School in Kerrville, Texas. John enjoys spending time with his family consisting of his wife of 20 years, Yvette, son J.T. (17), and daughter Olivia (14)

Chip Mundy is a lifelong resident of Jackson, Michigan, who spent more than 30 years in the newspaper business, mostly as a sports writer for the *Jackson Citizen Patriot*. Now retired, he was the lead author of a book called *Michigan Sports Trivia*. He continues to write as a free-lancer for the MHSAA.com Second Half, profiling high school athletes and covering state championship events in Michigan, and he has contributed to BioProject.

JERRY NECHAL is a retired administrator at Wayne State University, who resides in Sylvan Lake, Michigan. He has previously written for the Baseball Research Journal and completed several Detroit Tiger biographies for BioProject. In addition to SABR, he is also a member of the Mayo Smith Society. Other interests include architecture, theater, listening to live music, hiking and mountain biking. He continues to long for a bleacher seat in old Tiger Stadium.

BILL NOWLIN rarely gets angry at airlines, but he had a flight booked to Detroit to see the last two games the Red Sox would ever play at Tiger Stadium. Dropped off at the airport in Austin, he got to the counter and found the flight had been canceled. There was no way to get there in time for the first game, so he bagged the whole thing and went to see the last show ever at Austin's legendary Liberty Lunch, where local bands bid the place farewell with a 24-hour "Gloria-thon"—playing the Van Morrison song "Gloria" for 24 hours. But, still, that meant he never got to see a game at Tiger Stadium. A co-founder of Rounder Records, Bill writes and edits a lot of books about the Red Sox and other teams, helping organize many of SABR's books.

DAVE RAGLIN has been the co-editor and an author for two SABR BioProject books, *Sock It To 'Em Tigers: The Incredible Story of the 1968 Detroit Tigers* and *Detroit Tigers 1984: What a Start! What a Finish!* He has contributed to other BioProject books and is the co-author of three other books on the Tigers, including *Detroit Tigers Lists and More* with Mark Pattison. Dave is also the Vice President of the Bob Davids chapter of SABR. He and his wife Barb Mantegani live in McLean, Virginia, where they root for the Tigers (his team), the Red Sox (her team), and the Nationals (their team together).

RICHARD RIIS is a writer, researcher, and professional genealogist. On the subject of baseball he has written for *Vintage and Classic Baseball Collector* and contributed to SABR books *Bridging the Dynasties: The 1947 New York Yankees* by Lyle Spatz and forthcoming titles in the Great Games series on County Stadium in Milwaukee and the Houston Astrodome. He resides in South Setauket, New York.

RUTH SADLER is a former newspaper sports copy editor and reporter and contributed to *Detroit the Unconquerable: The 1935 World Champion Tigers.* Thanks to marriage to a Detroit native, she was able to enjoy many games at The Corner (often peering around an obstruction). Her SABR hometown is the newly formed Babe Ruth chapter in Baltimore and her first baseball game was at Connie Mack Stadium. She remembers watching Mark "The Bird" Fidrych pitch against the Yankees at Tiger Stadium. Years later, she did the wave during the magical season of 1984.

JEFF SAMORAY is a freelance health care writer in suburban Detroit. His claim to fame is that he was born on the day the Tigers clinched the 1968 American League pennant. He has written about baseball for publications such as *Baseball Digest, Michigan History Magazine, DBusiness,* and *The Detroit News.* His essays appear in the SABR publications *Inventing Baseball: The 100 Greatest Games of the Nineteenth Century* and *Sock It To 'Em Tigers: The Incredible Story of the 1968 Detroit Tigers.* Jeff is currently writing a biography of Detroit Tigers founder George A. Vanderbeck.

TERRY SLOOPE served as the chair of SABR's Magnolia Chapter from 1998 until 2012 and was the chairperson of the 2010 SABR Convention held in Atlanta. He authored the biography of Rudy York for the SABR BioProject website and the biographies of Curt Flood and Bob Gibson for *Drama and Pride in the Gateway City: The 1964 St. Louis Cardinals* (University of Nebraska Press: 2013). He was a contributing author to Gary Land's *Growing Up with Baseball* (University of Nebraska Press: 2004) and David Porter's *Latino and African-American Athletes Today: A Biographical Dictionary* (Greenwood Press, 2004). He lives in Cartersville, Georgia.

STEVE J. WEISS is an attorney with Hertz Schram PC in Bloomfield Hills, Michigan, past president of the Bloomfield Hills School Board, and a long-time Macabbi Youth Games basketball coach. He is the author of two published novels, *The Farewell Principle* and *About Face.* The year the Tigers last won the World Series, he was married to his awesome wife, Karen; they were engaged at Tiger Stadium, with Karen's favorite player, Lou Whitaker, at that plate. Steve and Karen have four great sons, and they all longingly await the next Tigers World Series championship.

Upon realizing that he couldn't hit a curveball, **MIKE WHITEMAN** took to reading and researching about the National Pastime. He enjoys nothing more than sitting on his porch in Lancaster, Pennsylvania, listening to ballgames on the radio. His home team includes his wife Nichole and two daughters.

PHIL WILLIAMS is a Philadelphian who has contributed articles to SABR's BioProject on numerous Deadball Era figures, including Detroit mainstays "Kickapoo" Ed Summers and Charley "Boss" Schmidt. He holds no grudges over the Tigers edging the Athletics in the 1907 and 1909 American League pennant races.

JIM WOHLENHAUS is retired and now has more time to devote to baseball history. He doesn't have a specific interest, except for the period prior to 1961. He listens to games still, but does not follow them on television, as the productions are too "Hollywood." In 1961, Jim was a batboy for the Denver Bears, the AAA American Association team of the Detroit Tigers. The best player on that team was probably Dick McAuliffe. He has been a Retrosheet volunteer off and on for several years and was the first MLB data caster covering the Colorado Rockies.

A lifelong Pirates fan, **GREGORY H. WOLF** was born in Pittsburgh, but now resides in the Chicagoland area with his wife, Margaret, and daughter, Gabriela. A Professor of German Studies and holder of the Dennis and Jean Bauman Endowed Chair in the Humanities at North Central College in Naperville, Illinois, he edited the SABR books *"Thar's Joy in Braveland": The 1957 Milwaukee Braves* (2014) and *Winning on the North Side: The 1929 Chicago Cubs* (2015). He is currently working on projects about County Stadium and the Houston Astrodome, and co-editing a book with Bill Nowlin on the 1979 Pittsburgh Pirates.

THE SABR DIGITAL LIBRARY

The Society for American Baseball Research, the top baseball research organization in the world, disseminates some of the best in baseball history, analysis, and biography through our publishing programs. The SABR Digital Library contains a mix of books old and new, and focuses on a tandem program of paperback and ebook publication, making these materials widely available for both on digital devices and as traditional printed books.

GREATEST GAMES BOOKS

BRAVES FIELD:
MEMORABLE MOMENTS AT BOSTON'S LOST DIAMOND
From its opening on August 18, 1915, to the sudden departure of the Boston Braves to Milwaukee before the 1953 baseball season, Braves Field was home to Boston's National League baseball club and also hosted many other events: from NFL football to championship boxing. The most memorable moments to occur in Braves Field history are portrayed here.
Edited by Bill Nowlin and Bob Brady
$19.95 paperback (ISBN 978-1-933599-93-9)
$9.99 ebook (ISBN 978-1-933599-92-2)
8.5"X11", 282 pages, 182 photos

INVENTING BASEBALL: THE 100 GREATEST
GAMES OF THE NINETEENTH CENTURY
SABR's Nineteenth Century Committee brings to life the greatest games from the game's early years. From the "prisoner of war" game that took place among captive Union soldiers during the Civil War (immortalized in a famous lithograph), to the first intercollegiate game (Amherst versus Williams), to the first professional no-hitter, the games in this volume span 1833–1900 and detail the athletic exploits of such players as Cap Anson, Moses "Fleetwood" Walker, Charlie Comiskey, and Mike "King" Kelly.
Edited by Bill Felber
$19.95 paperback (ISBN 978-1-933599-42-7)
$9.99 ebook (ISBN 978-1-933599-43-4)
8"x10", 302 pages, 200 photos

BIOPROJECT BOOKS

WHO'S ON FIRST:
REPLACEMENT PLAYERS IN WORLD WAR II
During World War II, 533 players made the major league debuts. More than 60% of the players in the 1941 Opening Day lineups departed for the service and were replaced by first-times and oldsters. Hod Lisenbee was 46. POW Bert Shepard had an artificial leg, and Pete Gray had only one arm. The 1944 St. Louis Browns had 13 players classified 4-F. These are their stories.
Edited by Marc Z Aaron and Bill Nowlin
$19.95 paperback (ISBN 978-1-933599-91-5)
$9.99 ebook (ISBN 978-1-933599-90-8)
8.5"X11", 422 pages, 67 photos

VAN LINGLE MUNGO:
THE MAN, THE SONG, THE PLAYERS
Although the Red Sox spent most of the 1950s far out of contention, the team was filled with fascinating players who captured the heart of their fans. In *Red Sox Baseball*, members of SABR present 46 biographies on players such as Ted Williams and Pumpsie Green as well as season-by-season recaps.
Edited by Bill Nowlin
$19.95 paperback (ISBN 978-1-933599-76-2)
$9.99 ebook (ISBN 978-1-933599-77-9)
8.5"X11", 278 pages, 46 photos

ORIGINAL SABR RESEARCH

CALLING THE GAME:
BASEBALL BROADCASTING FROM 1920 TO THE PRESENT
An exhaustive, meticulously researched history of bringing the national pastime out of the ballparks and into living rooms via the airwaves. Every play-by-play announcer, color commentator, and ex-ballplayer, every broadcast deal, radio station, and TV network. Plus a foreword by "Voice of the Chicago Cubs" Pat Hughes, and an afterword by Jacques Doucet, the "Voice of the Montreal Expos" 1972-2004.
by Stuart Shea
$24.95 paperback (ISBN 978-1-933599-40-3)
$9.99 ebook (ISBN 978-1-933599-41-0)
7"X10", 712 pages, 40 photos

BASEBALL IN THE SPACE AGE:
HOUSTON SINCE 1961
Here we have a special issue of *The National Pastime* centered almost entirely on the Houston Astros (né Colt .45s) and their two influential and iconic homes, short-lived Colt Stadium and the Astrodome. If you weren't able to attend the SABR convention in Houston, please enjoy this virtual trip tour of baseball in "Space City" through 18 articles.
Edited by Cecilia M. Tan
$14.95 paperback (ISBN 978-1-933599-65-6)
$9.99 ebook (ISBN 978-1-933599-66-3)
8.5"x11", 96 pages, 49 photos

NORTH SIDE, SOUTH SIDE, ALL AROUND
THE TOWN: BASEBALL IN CHICAGO
The National Pastime provides in-depth articles focused on the geographic region where the national SABR convention is taking place annually. The SABR 45 convention took place in Chicago, and here are 45 articles on baseball in and around the bat-and-ball crazed Windy City: 25 that appeared in the souvenir book of the convention plus another 20 articles available in ebook only.
Edited by Stuart Shea
$14.95 paperback (ISBN 978-1-933599-87-8)
$9.99 ebook (ISBN 978-1-933599-86-1)
8.5"X11", 282 pages, 47 photos

THE EMERALD GUIDE TO BASEBALL: 2015
The Emerald Guide to Baseball fills the gap in the historical record created by the demise of *The Sporting News Baseball Guide*. First published in 1942, *The Sporting News* Guide was truly the annual book of record for our National Pastime. The 2015 edition of the *Emerald Guide* runs more than 600 pages and covers the 2014 season; it also includes a 2015 directory of every franchise, rosters, minor league affiliates, and career leaders for all teams.
Edited by Gary Gillette and Pete Palmer
$24.95 paperback (ISBN 978-0-9817929-8-9)
8.5"X11", 610 pages

SABR Members can purchase each book at a significant discount (often 50% off) and receive the ebook edtions free as a member benefit. Each book is available in a trade paperback edition as well as ebooks suitable for reading on a home computer or Nook, Kindle, or iPad/tablet.
To learn more about becoming a member of SABR, visit the website: sabr.org/join

SABR BioProject Books

In 2002, the Society for American Baseball Research launched an effort to write and publish biographies of every player, manager, and individual who has made a contribution to baseball. Over the past decade, the BioProject Committee has produced over 3,400 biographical articles. Many have been part of efforts to create theme- or team-oriented books, spearheaded by chapters or other committees of SABR.

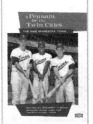

A PENNANT FOR THE TWIN CITIES:
THE 1965 MINNESOTA TWINS
This volume celebrates the 1965 Minnesota Twins, who captured the American League pennant in just their fifth season in the Twin Cities. Led by an All-Star cast, from Harmon Killebrew, Tony Oliva, Zoilo Versalles, and Mudcat Grant to Bob Allison, Jim Kaat, Earl Battey, and Jim Perry, the Twins won 102 games, but bowed to the Los Angeles Dodgers and Sandy Koufax in Game Seven
Edited by Gregory H. Wolf
$19.95 paperback (ISBN 978-1-943816-09-5)
$9.99 ebook (ISBN 978-1-943816-08-8)
8.5"X11", 405 pages, over 80 photos

MUSTACHES AND MAYHEM: CHARLIE O'S THREE TIME CHAMPIONS:
THE OAKLAND ATHLETICS: 1972-74
The Oakland Athletics captured major league baseball's crown each year from 1972 through 1974. Led by future Hall of Famers Reggie Jackson, Catfish Hunter and Rollie Fingers, the Athletics were a largely homegrown group who came of age together. Biographies of every player, coach, manager, and broadcaster (and mascot) from 1972 through 1974 are included, along with season recaps.
Edited by Chip Greene
$29.95 paperback (ISBN 978-1-943816-07-1)
$9.99 ebook (ISBN 978-1-943816-06-4)
8.5"X11", 600 pages, almost 100 photos

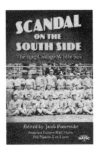

SCANDAL ON THE SOUTH SIDE:
THE 1919 CHICAGO WHITE SOX
The Black Sox Scandal isn't the only story worth telling about the 1919 Chicago White Sox. The team roster included three future Hall of Famers, a 20-year-old spitballer who would win 300 games in the minors, and even a batboy who later became a celebrity with the "Murderers' Row" New York Yankees. All of their stories are included in Scandal on the South Side with a timeline of the 1919 season.
Edited by Jacob Pomrenke
$19.95 paperback (ISBN 978-1-933599-95-3)
$9.99 ebook (ISBN 978-1-933599-94-6)
8.5"x11", 324 pages, 55 historic photos

WINNING ON THE NORTH SIDE
THE 1929 CHICAGO CUBS
Celebrate the 1929 Chicago Cubs, one of the most exciting teams in baseball history. Future Hall of Famers Hack Wilson, '29 NL MVP Rogers Hornsby, and Kiki Cuyler, along with Riggs Stephenson formed one of the most potent quartets in baseball history. The magical season came to an ignominious end in the World Series and helped craft the future "lovable loser" image of the team.
Edited by Gregory H. Wolf
$19.95 paperback (ISBN 978-1-933599-89-2)
$9.99 ebook (ISBN 978-1-933599-88-5)
8.5"x11", 314 pages, 59 photos

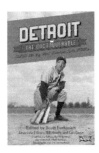

DETROIT THE UNCONQUERABLE:
THE 1935 WORLD CHAMPION TIGERS
Biographies of every player, coach, and broadcaster involved with the 1935 World Champion Detroit Tigers baseball team, written by members of the Society for American Baseball Research. Also includes a season in review and other articles about the 1935 team. Hank Greenberg, Mickey Cochrane, Charlie Gehringer, Schoolboy Rowe, and more.
Edited by Scott Ferkovich
$19.95 paperback (ISBN 9978-1-933599-78-6)
$9.99 ebook (ISBN 978-1-933599-79-3)
8.5"X11", 230 pages, 52 photos

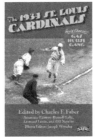

THE 1934 ST. LOUIS CARDINALS:
THE WORLD CHAMPION GAS HOUSE GANG
The 1934 St. Louis Cardinals were one of the most colorful crews ever to play the National Pastime. Some of were aging stars, past their prime, and others were youngsters, on their way up, but together they comprised a championship ball club. Pepper Martin, Dizzy and Paul Dean, Joe Medwick, Frankie Frisch and more are all included here.
Edited by Charles F. Faber
$19.95 paperback (ISBN 978-1-933599-73-1)
$9.99 ebook (ISBN 978-1-933599-74-8)
8.5"X11", 282 pages, 47 photos

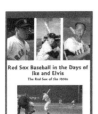

RED SOX BASEBALL IN THE DAYS OF IKE AND ELVIS: THE RED SOX OF THE 1950s
Although the Red Sox spent most of the 1950s far out of contention, the team was filled with fascinating players who captured the heart of their fans. In *Red Sox Baseball*, members of SABR present 46 biographies on players such as Ted Williams and Pumpsie Green as well as season-by-season recaps.
Edited by Mark Armour and Bill Nowlin
$19.95 paperback (ISBN 978-1-933599-24-3)
$9.99 ebook (ISBN 978-1-933599-34-2)
8.5"X11", 372 pages, over 100 photos

THE MIRACLE BRAVES OF 1914
BOSTON'S ORIGINAL WORST-TO-FIRST CHAMPIONS
Long before the Red Sox "Impossible Dream" season, Boston's now nearly forgotten "other" team, the 1914 Boston Braves, performed a baseball "miracle" that resounds to this very day. The "Miracle Braves" were Boston's first "worst-to-first" winners of the World Series. Includes biographies of every player, coach, and owner, a season recap, and other great stories from the 1914 season.
Edited by Bill Nowlin
$19.95 paperback (ISBN 978-1-933599-69-4)
$9.99 ebook (ISBN 978-1-933599-70-0)
8.5"X11", 392 pages, over 100 photos

SABR Members can purchase each book at a significant discount (often 50% off) and receive the ebook edtions free as a member benefit. Each book is available in a trade paperback edition as well as ebooks suitable for reading on a home computer or Nook, Kindle, or iPad/tablet.
To learn more about becoming a member of SABR, visit the website: sabr.org/join

Society for American Baseball Research
Cronkite School at ASU
555 N. Central Ave. #416, Phoenix, AZ 85004
602.496.1460 (phone)
SABR.org

Become a SABR member today!

If you're interested in baseball — writing about it, reading about it, talking about it — there's a place for you in the Society for American Baseball Research. Our members include everyone from academics to professional sportswriters to amateur historians and statisticians to students and casual fans who enjoy reading about baseball and occasionally gathering with other members to talk baseball. What unites all SABR members is an interest in the game and joy in learning more about it.

SABR membership is open to any baseball fan; we offer 1-year and 3-year memberships. Here's a list of some of the key benefits you'll receive as a SABR member:

- Receive two editions (spring and fall) of the *Baseball Research Journal*, our flagship publication
- Receive expanded e-book edition of *The National Pastime*, our annual convention journal
- 8-10 new e-books published by the SABR Digital Library, all FREE to members
- "This Week in SABR" e-newsletter, sent to members every Friday
- Join dozens of research committees, from Statistical Analysis to Women in Baseball.
- Join one of 70 regional chapters in the U.S., Canada, Latin America, and abroad
- Participate in online discussion groups
- Ask and answer baseball research questions on the SABR-L e-mail listserv
- Complete archives of *The Sporting News* dating back to 1886 and other research resources
- Promote your research in "This Week in SABR"
- Diamond Dollars Case Competition
- Yoseloff Scholarships

- Discounts on SABR national conferences, including the SABR National Convention, the SABR Analytics Conference, Jerry Malloy Negro League Conference, Frederick Ivor-Campbell 19th Century Conference
- Publish your research in peer-reviewed SABR journals
- Collaborate with SABR researchers and experts
- Contribute to Baseball Biography Project or the SABR Games Project
- List your new book in the SABR Bookshelf
- Lead a SABR research committee or chapter
- Networking opportunities at SABR Analytics Conference
- Meet baseball authors and historians at SABR events and chapter meetings
- 50% discounts on paperback versions of SABR e-books
- 20% discount on MLB.TV and MiLB.TV subscriptions
- Discounts with other partners in the baseball community
- SABR research awards

We hope you'll join the most passionate international community of baseball fans at SABR! Check us out online at SABR.org/join.

- - - - - - ✂ -

SABR MEMBERSHIP FORM

	Annual	3-year	Senior	3-yr Sr.	Under 30
U.S.:	❏ $65	❏ $175	❏ $45	❏ $129	❏ $45
Canada/Mexico:	❏ $75	❏ $205	❏ $55	❏ $159	❏ $55
Overseas:	❏ $84	❏ $232	❏ $64	❏ $186	❏ $55

Add a Family Member: $15 each family member at same address (list names on back)
Senior: 65 or older before 12/31 of the current year
All dues amounts in U.S. dollars or equivalent

Participate in Our Donor Program!
Support the preservation of baseball research. Designate your gift toward:
❏General Fund   ❏Endowment Fund   ❏Research Resources   ❏_____
❏ I want to maximize the impact of my gift; do not send any donor premiums
❏ I would like this gift to remain anonymous.
Note: Any donation not designated will be placed in the General Fund.
SABR is a 501 (c) (3) not-for-profit organization & donations are tax-deductible to the extent allowed by law.

Name _____

E-mail* _____

Address _____

City _____ ST_____ ZIP_____

Phone _____ Birthday _____

* Your e-mail address on file ensures you will receive the most recent SABR news.

Dues $_____

Donation $_____

Amount Enclosed $_____

Do you work for a matching grant corporation? Call (602) 496-1460 for details.

If you wish to pay by credit card, please contact the SABR office at (602) 496-1460 or visit the SABR Store online at SABR.org/join. We accept Visa, Mastercard & Discover.

Do you wish to receive the *Baseball Research Journal* electronically?: ❏ Yes   ❏ No
Our e-books are available in PDF, Kindle, or EPUB (iBooks, iPad, Nook) formats.

Mail to: SABR, Cronkite School at ASU, 555 N. Central Ave. #416, Phoenix, AZ 85004